The Psychology of Digital Learning

Stephan Schwan • Ulrike Cress
Editors

The Psychology of Digital Learning

Constructing, Exchanging, and Acquiring Knowledge with Digital Media

 Springer

Editors
Stephan Schwan
Realistic Depictions
Leibniz-Institut für Wissensmedien
Tübingen, Germany

Ulrike Cress
Knowledge Construction
Leibniz-Institut für Wissensmedien
Tübingen, Germany

ISBN 978-3-319-49075-5   ISBN 978-3-319-49077-9 (eBook)
DOI 10.1007/978-3-319-49077-9

Library of Congress Control Number: 2017937650

Printed on acid-free paper

This Springer imprint is published by Springer Nature
The registered company is Springer International Publishing AG
The registered company address is: Gewerbestrasse 11, 6330 Cham, Switzerland

It gives us great pleasure to dedicate this book in honor of IWM's founding director Prof. Dr. Dr. Friedrich W. Hesse.

Introduction

Today, hundreds of thousands of students enroll in Internet-based courses (Massively Open Online Courses—MOOCs); digital tablets and multimedia textbooks have found their way into the classroom; people do not only routinely look up information on Wikipedia but also feed their own knowledge into online networks; and learners interact with digital content not only via screen, keyboard, and mouse but have begun to access and actively transform information via immersive displays and bodily activities such as gesture or touch. Putting all these trends together, constructing, exchanging, and acquiring knowledge has undergone a fundamental transformation in the past three decades.

Fifteen years ago, the field of digitally enhanced learning was in the midst of this transformation: Multimedia applications, intelligent tutorial systems, email, and web browsers had already been around for several years. Apple had at this time just introduced the iPod, Marc Prensky coined the term "Digital Natives," Richard Mayer published his influential book on "Multimedia Learning," and eLearning was a trendy buzzword. However, there were neither smartphones, YouTube, Wikipedia, or Facebook, nor a systematic monitoring of these developments for education (the first Horizon report of the New Media Consortium was issued in 2004).

Yet, from 1990 to 2000 the introduction of digital technologies into classrooms, universities, and informal learning settings had gained momentum, and as early as 2001, there was a growing need for both theoretical models and basic empirical research on the implications of digital technologies on processes and outcomes of learning. Thus, many questions arose: Will advanced digital presentation technologies, such as animations or simulations, help learners to better understand the principles of dynamic systems and events? Will self-guided interactive control enable learners to adapt a learning environment to their cognitive needs, or will it introduce an additional cognitive burden that distracts students from the content to be learned? Will nonlinear content allow for more flexible mental representations, or will it confuse users, making them become lost in hyperspace? How do small groups solve knowledge-related tasks, and how can each member be made aware of intragroup differences and commonalities of knowledge? How can large online communities be utilized for knowledge construction and knowledge exchange?

It quickly became clear that the answers to these and related questions could not be given on the basis of purely technological or educational considerations, but also required a psychological stance, firmly grounded in current cognitive models of the underlying structures and mechanisms of human information processing and learning. Thus, it does not come as a surprise that it was an acknowledged expert from the field of basic experimental research in psychology who met the challenge of linking modes and technologies of digital learning to models and paradigms of experimental psychology.

Friedrich W. Hesse had studied psychology in Marburg and Düsseldorf, had received his PhD in Aachen, and completed his habilitation in Göttingen before he was appointed a full professor at the University of Tübingen and became head of a research group at the Deutsches Institut für Fernstudienforschung (DIFF). He was well recognized for his expertise in human problem solving and in the interplay of cognition and emotion. Soon after his move to the DIFF, he realized the necessity of what later would be termed as use-inspired basic research, namely, empirically investigating and explaining phenomena of learning with digital media "in the wild" by applying theories and methods from basic cognitive research. In the course of closing the DIFF in 2000, he envisioned the idea of a research institute exclusively devoted to addressing knowledge processes with digital media by means of a fruitful fusion of basic and applied perspectives. It was exactly the right time for bringing this vision into being, and in the following months, Friedrich Hesse devoted all his energy and expertise to convince the relevant stakeholders of the importance of this endeavor for both the scientific community and society. Armed with strong arguments brought forward by his passionate personality, he succeeded to receive the necessary institutional and financial support, and finally in 2001, the Leibniz Institut für Wissensmedien (IWM) was inaugurated with Friedrich Hesse as its founding director.

Luckily, from its beginning the IWM was part of the Leibniz Gemeinschaft, a network of 91 scientific institutes that all pursue the philosophy of "theoria cum praxis," thus bridging basic and applied perspectives by doing research that is both excellent in scientific terms and at the same time of high relevance for important issues currently being dealt with in our society. The IWM fits perfectly well into this program, and in the last fifteen years, Friedrich Hesse has continued his pioneering work both within the IWM and also on the level of the Leibniz Gemeinschaft as a whole. One prominent example of his innovative impulses was the first virtual Ph.D. program of the German Research Foundation (DFG), where insights from the IWM's research were applied to the scientific community itself by making heavy use of the opportunities provided by modern digital media for scientific research and exchange. Another tremendously influential initiative by Friedrich Hesse was the first German science campus, a close collaboration between the IWM and the University of Tübingen, again bringing forward the idea that scientific research at its best will be an interdisciplinary combination of basic and applied perspectives.

Against this background, the aim of this book is to provide an overview of the state of the art of psychological research on learning and knowledge exchange with digital media, based on the comprehensive research program that was realized at the

IWM during the past decade. At the same time, it honors the enormous impact that Friedrich W. Hesse, the founder and current director of the institute, has had on this field. These two goals go together well because, since its foundation in 2001, the IWM has become one of leading institutes for research on processes of knowledge acquisition, knowledge exchange, and knowledge communication using innovative technologies.

Research at the IWM has covered a dramatic rise of new tools and technologies that have fundamentally reshaped teaching, learning, and knowledge exchange from the perspective of human information processing. Eight different labs cover a broad spectrum of topics, ranging from questions of appropriate strategies for searching the internet, optimal conditions for mental integration of multimedia presentations, the neural correlates of learning, determinants of active contribution of pieces of knowledge to online forums, facilitating conditions and tools for knowledge management to the motivations for knowledge sharing in organizational contexts, the role of social networks, and tie strength in receiving informational benefits. Hence, the book provides an easily accessible overview of the main theoretical approaches and empirical results that have been accumulated at the IWM over the past years.

In essence, learning, knowledge construction, and knowledge exchange with digital media are conceptualized as an interplay between the information processing structures of the users and the enabling and enhancing capabilities of a certain digital technology, with the goal of comprehending or exchanging a particular content or piece of knowledge. Human information processing is used in a broad sense, comprising not only perception and attention, working memory and long-term memory together with processes of metacognition, information selection, activation of prior knowledge, elaboration, and social cognition, but also seeing learners as social agents, who actively participate in knowledge construction, communication, exchange, and collaborative problem solving. Also, with reference to digital technology, emphasis is put on its generic attributes such as nonlinearity, multimedia, visibility, persistence, editability, or association, instead of narrowly focusing on specific, quickly outdated implementations.

In accordance with the institute's lab structure, the present book charts the field of learning with digital media in ten chapters. The first four chapters deal with the role of different presentation formats of digital content—texts, numbers, visualizations—and their interplay for knowledge processes. In Chap. 1, Katharina Scheiter, Anne Schüler, and Alexander Eitel review the empirical findings from studies that have been conducted in Katharina Scheiter's lab regarding knowledge acquisition via combinations of verbal and pictorial representations. In particular, both the cognitive underpinnings of learning with multiple types of representation formats and effectiveness of instructional interventions fostering cognitive integration of text and pictures are discussed. Based on Korbinian Moeller's research program and his lab, Chap. 2, written by Ursula Fischer, Elise Klein, Tanja Dackermann, and Korbinian Moeller, focuses on the acquisition of numerical skills by use of computer-supported embodied numerical trainings and their underlying neuro-cognitive mechanisms. In Chap. 3, the main focus is on the role of realistic pictures in digital learning environments. Based on findings of Stephan Schwan's lab, differences and commonalities between perception and mental processing of realistic pictures in comparison to real-world information are described. In Chap. 4, the first block of chapters closes with an overview of research results from Peter Gerjets' lab about new developments in learning with hypermedia environments that are structured in a nonlinear manner. Here, learners are required to evaluate and integrate multiple sources of information, often accessed via novel interaction formats, including gesture or touch.

The second block of chapters is devoted to processes of knowledge production, knowledge exchange, and knowledge processing within networked groups. Chapter 5, written by Annika Scholl, Florian Landkammer, and Kai Sassenberg, summarizes a research program in Kai Sassenberg's lab about the impact of a great variety of characteristics of social relations on information exchange in context of computer-mediated communication. Information exchange is conceptualized as a socially motivated process in which certain social constellations elicit group- or self-serving motives that influence how information is shared and received. In Chap. 6, Jürgen Buder outlines a conceptual framework of knowledge exchange in small groups of learners, integrating dimensions of context, input, process, and output on the basis of the lab's empirical research on group awareness tools. Based on a large set of empirical studies in their lab, Ulrike Cress and Joachim Kimmerle have developed a complementary cognitive-systemic framework of the interplay of individual learning and collective knowledge construction, described in detail in Chap. 7. In Chap. 8, Carmen Zahn discusses the notion of "design-based learning" as a powerful approach for fostering a learner's comprehension of a given topic. She reports on the findings of five experimental studies on how dyads make use of advanced video tools for collaboratively solving design problems. In Chap. 9, Sonja Utz and Ana Levordashka show how social media users derive professional informational benefits from online networks such as Facebook, LinkedIn, or Twitter, depending on platform usage, networking behavior, and network composition. They report on a large-scale longitudinal study currently underway in Sonja Utz's lab.

Finally, in his afterword, the long-standing chairman of the institute's scientific board, Hans Spada, closes the book giving a knowledgeable view from outside and thoughtfully reflecting on the IWM's scientific and institutional history of the past 15 years.

Stephan Schwan
Ulrike Cress

Contents

Chapter 1
Learning from Multimedia: Cognitive Processes and Instructional Support

Katharina Scheiter, Anne Schüler, and Alexander Eitel

Abstract Multimedia materials have become ubiquitously available as educational resources in the digital age. In multimedia learning environments, verbal and pictorial representations are presented jointly for explaining and illustrating a subject matter. In order to benefit from multimedia instruction, learners need to construct a coherent mental model from text and pictures by mentally integrating information from both external sources. In the present chapter, we will first review findings that aim at providing a more thorough description of the cognitive underpinnings of learning from multimedia and of the integration process in particular. Second, we will introduce empirical evidence illustrating the effectiveness of instructional interventions aimed at supporting the integration process in multimedia learning. The interlinking of these two lines of research is seen as an example for contributing to use-inspired basic research.

Keywords Multimedia learning • Integration of text and pictures • Dual coding • Instructional guidance

Introduction

Multimedia materials have become ubiquitously available as resources for learning and instruction, especially due to the increasing use of technology in education. Even though many people associate the term "multimedia" with the use of flashy technology such as interactive dynamic visualizations, in research on learning with multimedia the term refers to any combination of explanatory spoken or written text and illustrations such as static pictures, diagrams, or animations (Mayer,

K. Scheiter (✉) • A. Schüler
Leibniz-Institut für Wissensmedien, Schleichstraße 6, 72076 Tübingen, Germany
e-mail: k.scheiter@iwm-tuebingen.de; a.schueler@iwm-tuebingen.de

A. Eitel
Albert-Ludwigs-Universität Freiburg, Institut für Psychologie,
Engelbergerstraße 41, 79085 Freiburg, Germany
e-mail: alexander.eitel@psychologie.uni-freiburg.de

© Springer International Publishing AG 2017
S. Schwan, U. Cress (eds.), *The Psychology of Digital Learning*,
DOI 10.1007/978-3-319-49077-9_1

2009)—some of which can, however, only be implemented by using technology. In general, the combination of text and pictures has been shown to yield better learning compared with text alone, a finding that is often referred to as multimedia effect (Mayer, 2009; cf. Anglin, Vaez, & Cunningham, 2004; Butcher, 2006; Levin, Anglin, & Carney, 1987). In science learning, in particular, students show better comprehension of the content if it is illustrated by a picture, for instance, when learning about cell reproduction (Schüler, Scheiter, & Gerjets, 2013), the working principle of a pulley system (Eitel, Scheiter, & Schüler, 2013), or the development of a thunderstorm (Schmidt-Weigand & Scheiter, 2011).

Even though there is strong evidence supporting the multimedia effect, the latter is subject to some preconditions. First, the pictures should be relevant to what is being conveyed; that is, they should not only serve decorative purposes (cf. Levin et al., 1987; Rey, 2012). Second, the picture should convey information that is complementary to the text rather than being redundant (Schmidt-Weigand & Scheiter, 2011). Third, students often face difficulties when learning from text and pictures, which may limit the effectiveness of multimedia materials. As discussed in more detail by Renkl and Scheiter (in press), students may be biased when learning from text and pictures in that they overly focus their attention on the text at the expense of the picture (e.g., Hegarty & Just, 1993; Schmidt-Weigand, Kohnert, & Glowalla, 2010) and suffer from illusions of understanding regarding their comprehension of multimedia materials (Eitel, 2016; Serra & Dunlosky, 2010). Moreover, learners may lack prerequisite skills and knowledge such as spatial abilities that will help them to fully comprehend a multimedia instruction. Finally, learners may fail to conduct certain cognitive processes that are, however, required to successfully learn from multimedia. For instance, they may refrain from integrating information from the text with that from the picture, which in turn will lead to an incomprehensive mental model. As a consequence of these difficulties, the multimedia effect is more likely to occur when students show unbiased information processing, possess the necessary prerequisites for learning, and adequately process text and pictures. These preconditions can be established by accordingly designing multimedia materials and by nudging students to use relevant strategies (cf. Renkl & Scheiter, in press).

Whereas there is ample evidence that pictures aid learning under certain conditions, the underlying cognitive processes when learning with multimedia are less clear. However, knowing about the underlying mechanisms is relevant not only for the sake of theory building, but it also advances our ability to design more effective multimedia learning materials.

Cognitive Theories of Multimedia Learning

Comprehensive theories of multimedia learning aim at specifying how learners process multimedia messages as well as how multimedia messages should be designed to foster learning. These theories claim to derive their scientific value from the fact that they are grounded in basic cognitive psychology research. In particular, well-established models of human information processing are used as a backbone to justify the theories' assumptions concerning learning with multimedia.

At present, the most prominent theory for learning with multimedia is the Cognitive Theory of Multimedia Learning (CTML; e.g., Mayer, 2009). CTML applies the multi-store memory model of Atkinson and Shiffrin (1968) to multimedia learning. According to Atkinson and Shiffrin, human information processing can be characterized as taking place in three distinct memory stores, where information is passed on from one store to another: sensory memory, short-term (or working) memory, and long-term memory. In line with this reasoning, CTML proposes that information extracted from text and pictures needs to pass through all three memory stores to yield meaningful learning, with the working memory playing a pivotal role. To account for differences in representational formats, Mayer superimposes two information-processing channels onto the multi-store model, a visual-pictorial channel and an auditory-verbal channel (*dual channel assumption*). According to Mayer, the distinction between the two channels according to the sensory mode of representations (i.e., visual vs. auditory) is based on Baddeley's (1999) working memory model although this interpretation of the Baddeley model is controversial (cf. Rummer, Schweppe, Scheiter, & Gerjets, 2008). According to Baddeley (1999), the working memory consists of multiple systems, namely, the phonological loop, the visuospatial sketchpad as well as the central executive which controls and coordinates the operation of the two subsystems. While the phonological loop deals with either written or spoken verbal information, the visuospatial sketchpad enables processing of visual and spatial information. Thus, differently from what is being suggested in CTML, Baddeley's distinction of the subsystems is not based on the sensory mode of information (see also Schüler, Scheiter, & van Genuchten, 2011, for a review on multimedia learning and working memory involvement). The distinction between the two channels according to the presentation code of information (i.e., pictorial vs. verbal) is based on Paivio's (1991) dual coding theory. Dual coding theory suggests that processing of verbal and nonverbal information will yield different types of memory representations of that information, namely, a linguistic presentation (i.e., a logogen) and an analogical, picture-like representation (i.e., an imagen), respectively. Accordingly, CTML proposes that text and pictures are processed to yield a verbal and a pictorial mental model, respectively. Importantly, information that is coded in both ways is more likely to be retrieved from memory (Paivio, 1991). Hence, if text and pictures are presented together, information will be dual coded and better accessible in memory compared with when only text is presented, which points towards one possible explanation of the multimedia effect. In line with the theory's cognitive foundations, the two channels are both limited in the amount of information that can be processed in parallel (*limited capacity assumption*), which causes the pivotal bottleneck when learning with multimedia.

CTML assumes that to benefit from multimedia, learners need to engage in active processing (*active processing assumption*). That is, learners have to select relevant information from the multimedia materials and then build thereof a coherent pictorial and verbal mental representation, respectively. Most importantly, they need to integrate these mental representations with each other and with prior knowledge into a coherent mental model that can be consolidated in the long-term memory (cf. Johnson-Laird, 1983). This mental model is assumed to reflect deeper understanding of the materials and is required for performing tasks that differ from the learning tasks (i.e., transfer tasks). As a consequence, integration of text and pictures is the process considered as most relevant to successfully learning with multimedia.

As an alternative to CTML, Schnotz (2005) has proposed the Integrated Model of Text and Picture Comprehension (ITPC). Similar to CTML, ITPC proposes that the cognitive system consists of two channels, an auditory-verbal channel and a visual-pictorial channel. Both channels are limited in capacity. The theory assumes that learners initially construct a text surface representation of the text, which results in a propositional model and a visual image of the picture, which results in a mental model. The propositional representation and the mental model interact with each other; that is, the propositional representation may trigger the construction of the mental model and the mental model can be used to read off information in a propositional format. Furthermore, Schnotz (2002) suggests that there may also be an interaction between the text surface representation and the mental model as well as between the visual image of the picture and the propositional representation even though no detailed assumptions are provided as to how these processes may look like. Nevertheless, ITPC refers from the very beginning more explicitly to the interaction of text and picture processing, whereas CTML proposes that text and pictures are proposed simultaneously, but to a large extent independently from each other prior to being integrated.

The Special Role of Integration for Multimedia Learning

CTML and ITPC both assume that linking text and pictures to each other is the most crucial step in multimedia learning, because this will not only support remembering of the information presented, but also foster deeper understanding of the contents of the multimedia lesson.

What Is Integration?

According to Mayer (1997), this linking process is related to the process of building referential connections proposed within the dual coding theory (Paivio, 1991). In the dual coding theory, it is assumed that connections are made between representations that are constructed within the verbal and pictorial processing system, respectively, and that stand for the same concept (e.g., the word "house" and a picture of a house). Analogously, Mayer (1997) assumes that learning from multimedia involves building one-to-one correspondences or mappings between the verbal and the pictorial mental model, that is, between their elements, actions, and causal relations. For example, to map the verbal description of how a pump works to a picture depicting this process, learners must first identify the corresponding elements in the text and the picture (e.g., they have to realize that the word "handle" refers to the image of the handle at the top of the pump, cf. Mayer, 1997). Second, they must map actions described in the text to actions depicted in the picture (e.g., they have to note that the phrase "the handle is pulled up" corresponds to the handle moving from the lower to the upper position depicted in the picture, cf. Mayer, 1997). Third, they must map causal relations between actions mentioned in the text and actions depicted in the picture (e.g., they have to realize that the causal relation described in the text between "the handle is pulled up" and the "piston moves up" is the same as the causal relation between the two actions depicted in the picture, cf. Mayer, 1997).

Schnotz et al. (2014; see also Ullrich et al., 2015; Seufert, 2003) further differentiate between different types and scopes of mapping. They distinguish between mapping at a surface structure level and mapping at a semantic deep structure level. Surface structure mapping occurs when verbal and pictorial elements are linked to each other based on external surface cues, for example, when similar colors, numbers, or labels are used to code corresponding verbal and pictorial elements. Semantic deep structure mapping, on the other hand, comprises mapping of single elements as well as mapping of relations at different levels of complexity depending on the number of to-be-mapped elements.

To conclude, there exist rather differentiated theoretical accounts of what is meant by integrating text and pictures which are, however, not backed up by an equally sophisticated empirical state of affairs. In fact, despite the alleged importance of the integration process for multimedia learning, there are only very few empirical studies trying to investigate this process in a direct manner.

Early Evidence for Text–Picture Integration

Some of the earliest evidence of text–picture integration comes from two studies on text comprehension. Glenberg and Langston (1992) presented subjects with texts describing four-step procedures, where the two middle steps of these procedures were always described as occurring simultaneously. Importantly, although both middle steps occurred at the same time, the texts described them sequentially, that is, step 2 was described before step 3, but it was noted explicitly that both steps occurred simultaneously. Half of the subjects were additionally presented with pictures depicting both middle steps as occurring simultaneously (i.e., next to each other; Experiment 1). Interestingly, subjects receiving only texts represented the relationships between the four steps sequentially, that is, they did not relate the middle steps equally strongly to the first and the last step in the procedure despite their simultaneous occurrence. On the other hand, subjects receiving pictures related the middle steps equally strongly to the first and the last step, which indicates that they did not represent only the sequential text structure, but integrated the temporal structure of the picture with the facts provided by the text. McNamara, Halpin, and Hardy (1992) conducted a series of experiments in which they examined whether subjects integrated spatial information about locations with nonspatial facts about these locations. Subjects first had to memorize a spatial layout containing different locations, for example, a road map. After they had studied the spatial layout, subjects were asked to learn nonspatial facts about the locations depicted in the map (e.g., that one town had a theater). In the next step, subjects performed a task that required them to decide whether a specific location had been in one region of the learned map or in another. Integration of picture (i.e., the map) and text (i.e., the facts) was assessed with this task by comparing performance under two different conditions: In the "near" condition the location was primed (i.e., pre-activated) with a nonspatial fact of a location in its near vicinity in the road map, whereas in the "far" condition the location was primed with a nonspatial fact of a location far away from it in the road map. The authors demonstrated a distance effect, that is, responses to the locations were more accurate when primed with a nonspatial fact about a near location than when primed with a nonspatial fact about a far location (Experiments 1 & 3). This distance effect was replicated with spatial materials the subjects were already familiar with; namely, they had to learn nonspatial facts about buildings on the university campus well-known to them. Overall, these findings speak in favor of the assumption that verbal information about nonspatial facts was integrated with pictorial information about locations, leading to the observed priming effects of facts as a function of distance.

The two studies suggest that when being asked to recall information, students are able to relate information from text to pictorial information; however, they leave open the question whether integration occurs already during learning and if so, how.

Does Integration Occur During Learning?

As with many cognitive processes related to learning, an important question is whether integration occurs online while learners are studying text and pictures or whether it occurs only offline, for instance, when a test question requires learners to use information from both text and picture. To answer this question, eye tracking has been deployed in multimedia learning research. With this method, a person's eye movements are recorded while he/she is processing an external stimulus such as a written text or text–picture combination. Eye tracking parameters such as fixations and saccades can be used not only to make statements about students' distribution of visual attention; rather, they are seen as evidence of when, how long, and in which order externally presented information is processed at the cognitive level (cf. eye-mind assumption, Just & Carpenter, 1980). To study the process of integrating text and pictures, look-froms and the number of saccades between text and pictures (i.e., text–picture transitions) have been determined as indicators. According to Mason, Tornatora, and Pluchino (2013, 2015), look-froms describe the duration (fixation times) for rereading text while reinspecting the picture (i.e., look-froms picture to text) and vice versa (i.e., look-froms text to picture: reinspection of the picture during rereading of the text). Text–picture transitions refer to the number of times a person moves his/her eyes from a verbal to a pictorial element and vice versa.

Hegarty and Just (1993) were the first to use eye tracking to study text–picture integration. Their students read an explanation of how a pulley system works, accompanied by a corresponding picture of a pulley system while their eye movements were recorded. The results showed that learners proceeded in an incremental fashion and alternated between text and pictures when constructing a mental model in a highly interleaved fashion. That is, they read the text, upon reaching the end of a semantic unit (typically composed of 1–2 sentences) they moved their eyes to the picture to investigate the part of the picture corresponding to that unit, and then continued reading the text. Since the seminal study of Hegarty and Just, a number of eye tracking studies have confirmed that integrative processing of text and pictures occurs during learning and predicts performance in subsequent memory and transfer tests (e.g., Hannus & Hyönä, 1999; Mason, Tornatora, et al., 2013, 2015; O'Keefe, Letourneau, Homer, Schwartz, & Plass, 2014), which confirms one of the major assumptions of theories of multimedia learning, namely, that integration is pivotal to mental model construction. For instance, O'Keefe et al. (2014) assessed eye movements while students learned about the Ideal Gas Laws with a multimedia simulation composed of multiple representations (i.e., a container filled with gas particles; sliders to control temperature, pressure, and the container's volume; a graph showing the relationship between two variables). Students who switched their eyes more often between the control sliders and the graph and between the gas container and the graph scored better in a comprehension and a transfer test. Mason, Tornatora, et al. (2015) assessed the eye movements of Seventh graders in a multimedia lesson on the food chain. Analyses of the data showed that students differed in the number of transitions between text and picture elements corresponding to one another as well as in the duration of look-froms from text to pictures. These differences in integrative processing predicted better verbal and pictorial recall, as well as transfer performance. Taken together, these studies show that text–picture integration occurs during learning in that (good) learners switch several times between text and picture processing in the attempt to incrementally construct a coherent mental representation.

How Early Does Integration Occur?

This leads to the question of how much information from each representation needs to be processed before integration takes place. Especially CTML suggests that at least to some extent text and pictures are first processed independently from each other and only after modality-specific mental models have been constructed, text and pictures are being integrated. However, findings from our lab suggest that integration of text and pictures may occur already at an early stage of multimedia learning. To substantiate this, it was first investigated how quickly information is extracted from instructional pictures, followed by studying whether this information is integrated with text to support comprehension. Against the backdrop of theoretical models from scene and object perception (e.g., Oliva & Torralba, 2001), the gist or global theme of a scene picture is abstracted very early during perception, and along with it the global spatial structure of the scene (Greene & Oliva, 2009). Eitel, Scheiter, and Schüler (2012) found that also for instructional pictures used to study multimedia learning (i.e., causal system pictures) the gist with its global spatial structure was extracted early, that is, already when presented for as short as 50 ms. Whether the global spatial structure (extracted from such brief presentation times) is reactivated and integrated with text to support comprehension was then studied in a follow-up experiment (Eitel, Scheiter, Schüler, Nyström, & Holmqvist, 2013). Some students were only asked to listen to a spoken text, whereas others were for a short time (600 ms, 2 s) exposed to a picture of the pulley system before listening to the text. The text described the spatial structure of the pulley system; however, it did not mention that the three pulleys were oriented diagonally from bottom-left to top-right (i.e., global spatial structure). This information could be extracted only from the picture. While listening to the text, students from all conditions sat in front of a blank screen and their eye movements were recorded. Results revealed that the eye movements resembled the global spatial structure of the initially presented pulley system picture, even when the picture was presented for a brief time only. Moreover, comprehension was fostered by brief initial picture inspection. Hence, results suggest that the global spatial structure from a quick glance at the picture was reactivated and integrated with text to facilitate mental model construction, supporting the idea of early integration. This idea was further reinforced by another study of Eitel, Scheiter, and Schüler (2013) who showed that when presenting written text, a brief initial presentation of the pulley system picture before reading fostered comprehension and also facilitated processing of spatial information in the text, as became evident by shorter reading times of the section in the text describing the system's spatial structure. Taken together, these findings suggest that a quick glance at a picture will already allow extracting its global spatial structure, which in turn serves as a mental scaffold for further processing. This mental scaffold is reactivated during text processing and facilitates mental model construction from the text, thereby yielding a coherent mental model from both information sources.

Does Integration Yield a Single Mental Model or Two Interconnected Models?

According to CTML, multimedia learning leads to a single mental model which comprises information from picture and text. On the other hand, the process of integration per se does not necessarily imply that a single mental model results from integration: If integration means that learners map contents from the picture and the

general picture / general sentence	specific picture / specific sentence	general picture / specific sentence	specific picture / general sentence
Auf der kleinen Insel steht nur ein Turm (On the small island is only a tower)	Auf der kleinen Insel steht nur ein Leuchtturm (On the small island is only a lighthouse)	Auf der kleinen Insel steht nur ein Leuchtturm (On the small island is only a lighthouse)	Auf der kleinen Insel steht nur ein Turm (On the small island is only a tower)
Neben dem Haus sind Parkplätze (Next to the house are parking places)	Neben dem Reihenhaus sind Parkplätze (Next to the row house are parking places)	Neben dem Reihenhaus sind Parkplätze (Next to the row house are parking places)	Neben dem Haus sind Parkplätze (Next to the house are parking places)

Fig. 1.1 Examples of stimulus material used in Schüler et al. (2015). Note: English translations were not given in the original experiment

text to each other, it might also be possible that learning with multimedia results in two separate mental models which are connected to each other as alluded to in the ITPC model.

Schüler, Arndt, and Scheiter (2015) used a modified paradigm from Gentner and Loftus (1979) to investigate whether learning with multimedia results in two separate representations (a pictorial model and a verbal model) or whether learning with multimedia results in one representation integrating information from text and pictures. They presented sentences and pictures that differed with respect to their degree of specificity (general vs. specific). The specific sentences and pictures always contained additional information compared to the general sentences and pictures. Therefore, specific pictures and sentences provided information that general sentences and pictures did not contain. For example, a general picture showed a tower on a small island while a specific picture showed a lighthouse on a small island (Fig. 1.1). The corresponding general/specific sentence was "There is only a tower/lighthouse on the small island." So the additional information in this example was the information that the tower is a lighthouse. After the learning phase, participants answered a forced-choice recognition test of sentences and pictures. In this test, subjects were instructed to decide whether they had seen earlier a general or specific version of the sentences or pictures. Dependent variable was the frequency of choosing a specific version of the sentences and pictures in the recognition tests. In the general picture/general sentence and the specific picture/specific sentence conditions, sentences and pictures provided the same information (e.g., about a tower or a lighthouse) resulting in a general or specific integrated representation. Therefore, it was expected that participants should have no problems in correctly rejecting or accepting the specific version.

Of special interest for the research question were the remaining two conditions, namely the conditions where sentences and pictures provided information at different levels of specificity (i.e., general pictures/specific sentences or specific pictures/ general sentences). If learning with multimedia results in two separate mental models, learners should have problems in recognizing the specific sentence (in the sentence forced-choice test) when seeing specific sentences paired with general pictures in the learning phase, because the specific information is not dual coded (i.e., the pictorial model did not contain specific information). Accordingly, learners should have problems in recognizing the specific picture (in the picture forced-choice test) when seeing specific pictures paired with general sentences in the learning phase, because again the specific information was not dual coded (i.e., the verbal model did not contain specific information). On the other hand, if learning with multimedia results in one mental model containing information from both texts and pictures, another data pattern is expected: Here, learners should have no problem in recognizing the specific sentence when seeing specific sentences paired with general pictures in the learning phase, because the specific information is included in the mental model. However, they should more often falsely recognize the specific sentences when seeing in the learning phase general sentence information paired with specific picture information, which is due to the fact that the mental model contains the specific information of the picture. When learners draw on the mental model to decide which sentence to read during learning, they will falsely decide in favor of the specific sentence. The same rationale holds true for the picture forced-choice test: Here, learners should more often falsely recognize the specific picture if seeing general pictures paired with specific sentences during learning. They should have no problem, however, to recognize the specific picture if seeing specific pictures paired with general sentences.

The observed data patterns in the sentence forced-choice tests (Arndt, Schüler, & Scheiter, 2015; Schüler et al., 2015) speak in favor of the assumption that learners construct a single mental model which integrates information from text and pictures. For picture recognition, the expected data pattern was only observed after a delay of one week, probably because when testing immediately, surface representations of the pictures were available which masked the integration effect (see Arndt et al., 2015).

To summarize, current research suggests that the process of integration occurs online (i.e., while learning), does not require extensive processing of either text or pictures and likely yields a single mental model of information from both sources. Moreover, using methodologies from basic cognitive psychology research the studies corroborate the assumption that integration is pivotal to multimedia learning. Accordingly, in the final section we will turn our attention towards the question of how to facilitate integration and thus foster multimedia learning.

How to Support Learning from Multimedia

Pictures have the potential to aid learning; however, their positive effects should not be taken for granted. If multimedia materials are not designed to support effective cognitive learning processes or if learners lack the necessary prerequisites to apply those processes, learning will be hampered. As a consequence, a lot of research in the field of multimedia learning has focused on how to improve the design of text–picture combinations as well as on how to ensure adequate processing of the materials. It is beyond the scope of this chapter to review the corresponding literature in a comprehensive fashion; rather, we will focus on those instructional measures that particularly aim at supporting integration of text and pictures, given the centrality of this process.

How to Design Multimedia Materials in Order to Foster Integration

As outlined in the previous section, integration of text and pictures heavily relies on students' ability to identify correspondences between verbal and pictorial elements and relations. The most straightforward way of supporting learners in doing so is to highlight these correspondences in the materials rather than having learners identify them by themselves. Highlighting of important information without altering the content of the instructional message is referred to in the literature on multimedia learning as signaling or cueing (van Gog, 2014). In multimedia learning, signals such as color coding, where corresponding elements are printed in the same color, or labels are used to highlight correspondences between text and pictures, which helps students map and integrate information from text and picture into a coherent mental representation (Mayer, 2009). In a recent comprehensive meta-analysis by Richter, Scheiter, and Eitel (2016), effects of multimedia integration signals were analyzed across 45 pair-wise comparisons, and a small-to-medium overall effect of signaling on comprehension outcomes was found ($r = 0.17$). Moreover, the meta-analysis revealed that only students with low prior knowledge profited more from multimedia integration signals, whereas students with high prior knowledge did not, which suggests that with less prior knowledge students are more at risk of failing to integrate corresponding information from text and picture.

The cueing or signaling effect is typically traced back by referring to two nonexclusive explanations: First, signals reduce visual search for corresponding text–picture elements, thereby rendering processing of multimedia materials more efficient. Second, signals provide visual guidance towards relevant information so that learners will spend more time on processing of this information. There are several eye tracking studies that have investigated the effects of signaling in closer detail by providing evidence for either of these explanations (Jamet, 2014; Mason, Pluchino, & Tornatora, 2013; Ozcelik, Arslan-Ari, & Cagiltay, 2010; Ozcelik, Karakus, Kursun, & Cagiltay, 2009). These studies consistently show that signaling improves learning and changes visual attention processes, with the two aspects being correlated with each other.

However, even though these two effects co-occur, it does still not become clear from these studies whether changes in visual attention can explain the positive effect signaling has on learning outcomes. To address this limitation, Scheiter and

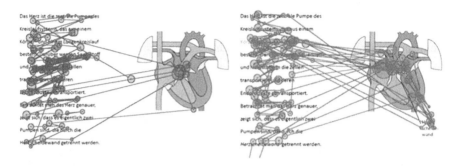

Fig. 1.2 Students' processing of unsignaled (*left panel*) and signaled (*right panel*) multimedia materials from Scheiter and Eitel (2015)

Eitel (2015) deployed mediation analyses to test whether the relationship among signaling, visual attention, and learning outcomes can be interpreted this way. In their study, students learned either with unsignaled multimedia materials explaining how the heart works or with a signaled version using a variety of signals (e.g., labels, color coding) to highlight text–picture correspondences (Fig. 1.2). Across two experiments, mediation analyses revealed that attending earlier and more frequently to relevant (highlighted) pictorial information fully explained the positive effects signals had on comprehension. Taken together, there is conclusive evidence suggesting that signaling can support integration of text and pictures and, as a consequence, aid learning.

Another way to support integration rests on the assumption that in order to construct a coherent mental model, the to-be-integrated information should be co-activated in working memory. Co-activation of text and picture elements corresponding to one another is more likely the larger the temporal proximity between their processing is and the fewer (unnecessary) cognitive processes intersperse processing of these elements. Accordingly, the *temporal contiguity principle* suggests that the mental integration of verbal and pictorial information is facilitated when text and picture can be perceived and processed simultaneously, which is the case for simultaneous but not for sequential presentation of text and pictures (Mayer, 2009). If spoken text accompanies a picture, learners can listen to the verbal information while looking at the corresponding picture. Hence, information from both sources is processed at the same time and can be held active in working memory, which should support its integration into a coherent mental representation. Accordingly, there is empirical evidence that the simultaneous presentation of spoken text and pictures leads to a better performance than their sequential presentation (Ginns, 2006; Mayer, 2009). It should be noted that according to Mayer (2009) the temporal contiguity principle applies especially to the presentation of spoken text and pictures. For written text there is anyway a time lag between processing of the verbal and the pictorial information, which is due to the fact that only one source of information can be perceived at a time. Hence, in order to integrate verbal and pictorial information into a single mental representation, one of the information sources needs to be constantly rehearsed and possibly even reconstructed from long-term memory in order to be active in working memory at the same time as its corresponding counterpart.

For multimedia presentations using written text, the need to constantly rehearse and potentially reconstruct information from memory can be reduced by presenting text and pictures in close spatial proximity. Thus, according to the *spatial contiguity principle*, written text and picture corresponding to one another should be presented near in space rather than far away in space (Mayer, 2009). This principle is based on the assumption that if written text is presented far away from the picture, visual attention has to be split between the text and the picture and visual search processes have to be conducted in order to identify which part of the text corresponds to which part of the picture, thereby interfering with mapping processes in working memory. According to the spatial contiguity principle, split spatial attention can be reduced by presenting written text near to the picture, thereby improving learning outcomes (Cierniak, Scheiter, & Gerjets, 2009; Ginns, 2006; Mayer, 2009). Johnson and Mayer (2012) studied the effects of physically integrating text into the picture. They used eye tracking to test three alternative explanations for the spatial contiguity effect: First, when text is physically integrated into the picture, learners might be more inclined to attempt to integrate both representations, which should be visible through a higher number of transitions from text to picture, irrespective of whether the verbal and pictorial elements fixated with the eyes correspond to each other (integrative transitions). Second, physical integration might provide guidance for successfully identifying text–picture correspondences as reflected by a higher number of transitions between *corresponding* text and picture elements (corresponding transitions). Finally, it might more generally guide learners' attention towards the picture, thereby increasing the proportion of time spent on processing it. In two out of three experiments students showed better transfer after having learned with an integrated illustrated text; moreover, across all three experiments students did more integrative and/or more corresponding transitions, but did not show increased attention towards the diagram. It was concluded from the occurrence of differences between transfer performance and integrative processing that integrative processing caused better transfer, but no mediation analyses were conducted.

Taken together, signaling text–picture correspondences as well as presenting text and pictures in close temporal and spatial proximity serve all to foster integration of verbal and pictorial information into a coherent mental model, thereby yielding better learning. However, in real-life educational situations students often face multimedia materials that are not designed after the aforementioned principles, but which they have nevertheless to use for learning. Especially in those situations, it seems important to teach and instruct learners so that they attempt to establish text–picture correspondences even if the material does not lend itself to it. Thus, rather than being externally guided by the materials, learners are required to self-regulate the use of effective processing strategies such as integration.

Nudging Students to Integrate Text and Pictures

One way of stimulating integration processes in learners is to give them verbal instructions such as prompts (e.g., "please search the picture for information corresponding to the text") prior to or during learning. Prompts are assumed to activate already available strategies that learners are basically able to apply, but they will not do it or if at all, they will apply them to an only insufficient degree (Renkl & Scheiter, in press). As reviewed by Renkl and Scheiter, prompts that ask students to integrate text and pictures yield equivocal effects, their effectiveness depending on a number of boundary conditions. Whereas in some studies no benefits of prompting (Bartholomé & Bromme, 2009) or even negative effects were obtained (e.g., Berthold & Renkl, 2009; Bodemer & Faust, 2006), others have found integration prompts to be helpful for learning (e.g., Berthold, Eysink, & Renkl, 2009; Kombartzky, Plötzner, Schlag, & Metz, 2010).

The alleged effectiveness of prompts can be conceptualized against the background of self-regulated learning. As to Veenman, Hout-Wolters, and Afflerbach (2006), in order to be effective self-regulated learners need to know what to do, when to do it, and how. In many cases prompts might not be specific enough so that students might actually fail in knowing about the what, when, and how of learning, even after having received a prompt. In our lab, we thus make use of an alternative to prompts, namely, implementation intentions which have features that alleviate some of these problems. According to Gollwitzer (1999), implementation intentions are "if-then" plans that strongly link an opportunity to act (e.g., "IF I have finished reading a paragraph") with an action that will help attain a learning goal (e.g., "THEN I will search for corresponding information in the picture"). Once properly internalized, the plan is assumed to work automatically, that is, without the need to monitor when, where, and how to execute the specified action. Rather, the action will be triggered once the situation that was specified in the if-part is encountered (cf. Gollwitzer & Sheeran, 2006). Importantly, the differences between prompts and implementation intentions are very subtle. Both nudge learners into performing specific cognitive processes, that is, they tell learners what to do. However, implementation intentions are more specific in that they additionally tell students when to act, thereby reducing the need to self-regulate one's learning.

Stalbovs, Scheiter, and Gerjets (2015) studied the effectiveness of implementation intentions for supporting multimedia learning by varying the number of implementation intentions (1 vs. 3) as well as the type of cognitive process supported by them (text processing, picture processing, text–picture integration, or a combination thereof). Additionally, a control group received no implementation intentions prior to learning. Across two studies, implementation intentions improved learning outcomes compared to the control group, especially if they supported a combination of all types of cognitive processes. Moreover, the combined implementation intention condition led to a higher number of transitions between text and pictures, which in turn was linked to better learning outcomes, suggesting that it improved learning via supporting text–picture integration.

Prompts and implementation intentions can be both considered as rather direct ways of instructing learners what to do. Another successful way of fostering learners' integration behavior is more strongly based on perceptual guidance by demonstrating learners how to adequately process text and pictures. The approach rests on the assumption that if certain learner actions traceable via eye tracking are related to a better understanding of what they learned, it might be helpful to let students observe this behavior prior to learning and use it as a model for their own processing of the multimedia materials. This is the basic idea implemented in Eye Movement Modeling Examples (EMME). EMME consist of videos showing the gaze behavior of a skilled learner who carefully studies text and pictures (Jarodzka, van Gog, Dorr, Scheiter, & Gerjets, 2013; Jarodzka et al., 2012; Mason, Pluchino, & Tornatora, 2015). EMME that are designed to support multimedia learning show how a skilled (instructed) learner reads the text, inspects the picture, and moves back and forth between these two activities. These eye movements are superimposed onto the multimedia materials, resulting in a video of the model's learning behavior. This video is shown to learners before they study multimedia materials and for which they do not get any further instructional guidance. Recent research has shown that EMME improve students' processing of text and pictures in that they show more integrative processing and devote more attention towards the pictorial information. Moreover, EMME lead to better learning outcomes in both, children (Mason, Pluchino, & Tornatora, 2015, in press) and adults (Schubert, Scheiter, & Schüler, 2014), which can be explained by the effects that EMME have on students' processing behavior.

Conclusions

In the present chapter, we have reviewed the literature on learning from text and pictures by discussing its foundations in cognitive psychology, introducing studies that have tried to get a better understanding of the underlying processes, and showing how findings from these studies can inspire the design of interventions that aim at improving learning outcomes. Thus, the research reviewed constitutes a nice example of what Stokes (1997) has called use-inspired basic research, that is, research that uses basic methodological paradigms and theories and contributes to the refinement and extension of these theories, while being of high practical relevance.

Theories of multimedia learning are assumed to hold true, no matter whether multimedia is implemented without technology (e.g., in printed textbooks) or whether educational technology is used, which among other things allows for a larger variety of different representational formats including dynamic visualizations such as animations or videos. While this may be true for the basic underlying processes of learning with multimedia such as integration, the state of affairs is less clear for the effective design of multimedia materials. For instance, designing effective signals for dynamic visualizations appears to be far more challenging than it is for static visualizations (cf. De Koning, Tabbers, Rikers, & Paas, 2009).

Moreover, theories of multimedia learning ignore the representational differences that exist between highly realistic and schematic visualizations, which may, however, have profound effects on how we learn from these representations (Schwan, this volume). Likewise, theories of multimedia learning only slowly come to acknowledge that learning does not result only from processing of predefined representations; rather, students can use technology to create their own representations and learn from designing digital artifacts (Zahn, this volume). Finally, current research ignores that there may be differences in terms of processing demands and effectiveness between those instructional interventions that rely on technology for their implementation (such as EMME) and those that are technology-poor (such as implementation intentions). Accordingly, future research on multimedia learning needs to address how respective theories need to be extended to accommodate the specific features and requirements technology adds to the equation of what aids learning and how.

References

Anglin, G. J., Vaez, H., & Cunningham, K. L. (2004). Visual representations and learning: The role of static and animated graphics. In D. Jonassen (Ed.), *Handbook of research on educational communications and technology* (Vol. 2, pp. 865–916). Mahwah, NJ: Erlbaum.

Arndt, J., Schüler, A., & Scheiter, K. (2015). Text-picture integration: How delayed testing moderates recognition of pictorial information in multimedia learning. *Applied Cognitive Psychology, 29*, 702–712.

Atkinson, R. C., & Shiffrin, R. M. (1968). Human memory: A proposed system and its control processes. In K. W. Spence & J. T. Spence (Eds.), *The psychology of learning and motivation* (Vol. 2, pp. 89–195). London: Academic Press.

Baddeley, A. D. (1999). *Essentials of human memory*. Hove, UK: Psychology Press.

Bartholomé, T., & Bromme, R. (2009). Coherence formation when learning from text and pictures: What kind of support for whom? *Journal of Educational Psychology, 101*, 282–293.

Berthold, K., Eysink, T. H., & Renkl, A. (2009). Assisting self-explanation prompts are more effective than open prompts when learning with multiple representations. *Instructional Science, 37*, 345–363.

Berthold, K., & Renkl, A. (2009). Instructional aids to support a conceptual understanding of multiple representations. *Journal of Educational Psychology, 101*, 70–87.

Bodemer, D., & Faust, U. (2006). External and mental referencing of multiple representations. *Computers in Human Behavior, 22*, 27–42.

Butcher, K. R. (2006). Learning from text with diagrams: Promoting mental model development and inference generation. *Journal of Educational Psychology, 98*, 182–197.

Cierniak, G., Scheiter, K., & Gerjets, P. (2009). Explaining the split-attention effect: Is the reduction of extraneous cognitive load accompanied by an increase in germane cognitive load? *Computers in Human Behavior, 25*, 315–324.

De Koning, B. B., Tabbers, H. K., Rikers, R. M. J. P., & Paas, F. (2009). Towards a framework for attention cueing in instructional animations: Guidelines for research and design. *Educational Psychology Review, 21*, 113–140.

Eitel, A. (2016). How repeated studying and testing affects multimedia learning: Evidence for adaptation to task demands. *Learning and Instruction, 41*, 70–84.

Eitel, A., Scheiter, K., & Schüler, A. (2012). The time course of information extraction from instructional diagrams. *Perceptual and Motor Skills, 115*, 677–701.

Eitel, A., Scheiter, K., & Schüler, A. (2013). How inspecting a picture affects processing of text in multimedia learning. *Applied Cognitive Psychology, 27*, 451–461.

Eitel, A., Scheiter, K., Schüler, A., Nyström, M., & Holmqvist, K. (2013). How a picture facilitates the process of learning from text: Evidence for scaffolding. *Learning and Instruction, 28*, 48–63.

Gentner, D., & Loftus, E. F. (1979). Integration of verbal and visual information as evidenced by distortions in picture memory. *The American Journal of Psychology, 92*, 363–375.

Ginns, P. (2006). Integrating information: A meta-analysis of the spatial contiguity and temporal contiguity effects. *Learning and Instruction, 16*, 511–525.

Glenberg, A., & Langston, W. E. (1992). Comprehension of illustrated text: Pictures help to build mental models. *Journal of Memory and Language, 31*, 129–151.

Gollwitzer, P. M. (1999). Implementation intentions: Strong effects of simple plans. *American Psychologist, 54*, 493–503.

Gollwitzer, P. M., & Sheeran, P. (2006). Implementation intentions and goal achievement: A meta-analysis of effects and processes. In M. P. Zanna (Ed.), *Advances in experimental social psychology* (Vol. 38, pp. 69–119). San Diego, CA: Elsevier Academic Press.

Greene, M. R., & Oliva, A. (2009). The briefest of glances: The time course of natural scene understanding. *Psychological Science, 20*, 464–472.

Hannus, M., & Hyönä, J. (1999). Utilization of illustrations during learning of science textbook passages among low- and high-ability children. *Contemporary Educational Psychology, 24*, 95–123.

Hegarty, M., & Just, M. A. (1993). Constructing mental models of machines from text and diagrams. *Journal of Memory and Language, 32*, 717–742.

Jamet, E. (2014). An eye-tracking study of cueing effects in multimedia learning. *Computers in Human Behavior, 32*, 47–53.

Jarodzka, H., Balslev, T., Holmqvist, K., Nyström, M., Scheiter, K., Gerjets, P., & Eika, B. (2012). Conveying clinical reasoning based on visual observation via eye-movement modelling examples. *Instructional Science, 40*, 813–827.

Jarodzka, H., van Gog, T., Dorr, M., Scheiter, K., & Gerjets, P. (2013). Learning to see: Guiding students' attention via a model's eye movements fosters learning. *Learning and Instruction, 25*, 62–70.

Johnson, C. I., & Mayer, R. E. (2012). An eye movement analysis of the spatial contiguity effect in multimedia learning. *Journal of Experimental Psychology: Applied, 18*, 178–191.

Johnson-Laird, P. N. (1983). *Mental models: Towards a cognitive science of language, inference, and consciousness*. Cambridge: Cambridge University Press.

Just, M. A., & Carpenter, P. A. (1980). A theory of reading: From eye fixations to comprehension. *Psychological Review, 87*, 329–354.

Kombartzky, U., Plötzner, R., Schlag, S., & Metz, B. (2010). Developing and evaluating a strategy for learning from animations. *Learning and Instruction, 20*, 424–433.

Levin, J. R., Anglin, G. J., & Carney, R. N. (1987). On empirically validating functions of pictures in prose. In D. M. Willows & H. A. Houghton (Eds.), *The psychology of illustration* (Vol. 1, pp. 51–85). New York: Springer.

Mason, L., Pluchino, P., & Tornatora, M. C. (in press). Using eye-tracking technology as an indirect instruction tool to improve text and picture processing and learning. *British Journal of Educational Technology*. doi:10.1111/bjet.12271.

Mason, L., Pluchino, P., & Tornatora, M. C. (2015). Eye-movement modeling of integrative reading of an illustrated text: Effects on processing and learning. *Contemporary Educational Psychology, 41*, 172–187.

Mason, L., Pluchino, P., & Tornatora, M. C. (2013). Effects of picture labeling on science text processing and learning: Evidence from eye movements. *Reading Research Quarterly, 48*, 199–214.

Mason, L., Tornatora, M. C., & Pluchino, P. (2013). Do fourth graders integrate text and picture in processing and learning from an illustrated science text? Evidence from eye-movement patterns. *Computers & Education, 60*, 95–109.

Mason, L., Tornatora, M. C., & Pluchino, P. (2015). Integrative processing of verbal and graphical information during re-reading predicts learning from illustrated text: An eye-movement study. *Reading and Writing, 28*, 851–872.

Mayer, R. E. (1997). Multimedia learning: Are we asking the right questions? *Educational Psychologist, 32*, 1–19.

Mayer, R. E. (2009). *Multimedia learning* (2nd ed.). New York, NY: Cambridge University Press.

McNamara, T. P., Halpin, J. A., & Hardy, J. K. (1992). The representation and integration in memory of spatial and nonspatial information. *Memory & Cognition, 20*, 519–532.

O'Keefe, P. A., Letourneau, S. M., Homer, B. D., Schwartz, R. N., & Plass, J. L. (2014). Learning from multiple representations: An examination of fixation patterns in a science simulation. *Computers in Human Behavior, 35*, 234–242.

Oliva, A., & Torralba, A. (2001). Modeling the shape of the scene: A holistic representation of the spatial envelope. *International Journal of Computer Vision, 42*, 145–175.

Ozcelik, E., Arslan-Ari, I., & Cagiltay, K. (2010). Why does signaling enhance multimedia learning? Evidence from eye movements. *Computers in Human Behavior, 26*, 110–117.

Ozcelik, E., Karakus, T., Kursun, E., & Cagiltay, K. (2009). An eye-tracking study of how color coding affects multimedia learning. *Computers & Education, 53*, 445–453.

Paivio, A. (1991). Dual coding theory: Retrospect and current status. *Canadian Journal of Psychology, 45*, 255–287.

Renkl, A., & Scheiter, K. (in press). Studying visual displays: How to instructionally support learning. *Educational Psychology Review*. doi:10.1007/s10648-015-9340-4.

Rey, G. D. (2012). How seductive are decorative elements in learning material? *Journal of Educational Multimedia and Hypermedia, 21*, 257–283.

Richter, J., Scheiter, K., & Eitel, A. (2016). Signaling text-picture relations in multimedia learning: A comprehensive meta-analysis. *Educational Research Review, 17*, 19–36.

Rummer, R., Schweppe, J., Scheiter, K., & Gerjets, P. (2008). Lernen mit Multimedia: Die kognitiven Grundlagen des Modalitätseffekts. *Psychologische Rundschau, 59*, 98–107.

Scheiter, K., & Eitel, A. (2015). Signals foster multimedia learning by supporting integration of highlighted text and diagram elements. *Learning and Instruction, 36*, 11–26.

Schmidt-Weigand, F., Kohnert, A., & Glowalla, U. (2010). A closer look at split visual attention in system-and self-paced instruction in multimedia learning. *Learning and Instruction, 20*, 100–110.

Schmidt-Weigand, F., & Scheiter, K. (2011). The role of spatial descriptions in learning from multimedia. *Computers in Human Behavior, 27*, 22–28.

Schnotz, W. (2002). Commentary: Towards an integrated view of learning from text and visual displays. *Educational Psychology Review, 14*, 101–120.

Schnotz, W. (2005). An integrated model of text and picture comprehension. In R. E. Mayer (Ed.), *The Cambridge handbook of multimedia learning* (pp. 49–69). New York, NY: Cambridge University Press.

Schnotz, W., Ludewig, U., Ullrich, M., Horz, H., McElvany, N., & Baumert, J. (2014). Strategy shifts during learning from texts and pictures. *Journal of Educational Psychology, 106*, 974–989.

Schubert, C., Scheiter, K., & Schüler, A. (2014). Modeling eye movements to support multimedia learning. Poster presented at the Meeting of the EARLI SIG2 Text and Graphics Comprehension. Rotterdam, The Netherlands.

Schüler, A., Arndt, J., & Scheiter, K. (2015). Processing multimedia material: Does integration of text and pictures result in a single or two interconnected mental representations? *Learning and Instruction, 35*, 62–72.

Schüler, A., Scheiter, K., & Gerjets, P. (2013). Is spoken text always better? Investigating the modality and redundancy effect with longer text presentation. *Computers in Human Behavior, 29*, 1590–1601.

Schüler, A., Scheiter, K., & van Genuchten, E. (2011). The role of working memory in multimedia instruction: Is working memory working during learning from text and pictures? *Educational Psychology Review, 23*, 389–411.

Schwan, S. (this volume). Digital pictures, videos, and beyond: Knowledge acquisition with realistic images.

Serra, M. J., & Dunlosky, J. (2010). Metacomprehension judgements reflect the belief that diagrams improve learning from text. *Memory, 18,* 698–711.

Seufert, T. (2003). Supporting coherence formation in learning from multiple representations. *Learning and Instruction, 13,* 227–237.

Stalbovs, K., Scheiter, K., & Gerjets, P. (2015). Implementation intentions during multimedia learning: Using if-then plans to facilitate cognitive processing. *Learning and Instruction, 35,* 1–15.

Stokes, D. E. (1997). *Pasteur's quadrant—Basic science and technological innovation.* Washington, DC: Brookings Institution Press.

Ullrich, M., Schnotz, W., Horz, H., McElvany, N., Schroeder, S., & Baumert, J. (2015). Kognitionspsychologische Aspekte eines Kompetenzmodells zur Bild-Text-Integration. *Psychologische Rundschau, 63,* 11–17.

Van Gog, T. (2014). The signaling (or cueing) principle in multimedia learning. In R. E. Mayer (Ed.), *The Cambridge handbook of multimedia learning* (2nd ed., pp. 263–278). New York: Cambridge University Press.

Veenman, M. V. J., Hout-Wolters, B. H. A. M., & Afflerbach, P. (2006). Metacognition and learning: Conceptual and methodological considerations. *Metacognition and Learning, 1,* 3–14.

Zahn, C. (this volume). Digital design and learning.

Chapter 2
The Physiology of Numerical Learning: From Neural Correlates to Embodied Trainings

Ursula Fischer, Elise Klein, Tanja Dackermann, and Korbinian Moeller

Abstract Numbers are an important part of everyday life in our modern knowledge societies. Accordingly, numerical deficits are associated with severe consequences for life prospects of affected individuals and society as a whole. Therefore, increasing research interest is devoted to broaden our understanding of the neurocognitive underpinnings of numerical learning and the development of new training approaches using new digital media. In this chapter, we will first evaluate the neural correlates of numerical cognition with a specific focus on structural and functional connectivity and how numerical learning is reflected in the human brain. In the second part of the chapter, we will elaborate on how numerical learning can be corroborated by computer-supported embodied spatial-numerical trainings. In these trainings, participants engage physically in a task using interactive input devices such as a digital dance mat or the Kinect sensor to corroborate spatial-numerical associations as reflected by the conceptual metaphor of a mental number line. Integrating these two lines of argument we discuss the possible origins of numerical cognition as redeployed neural correlates from physical experiences.

Keywords Mental number line • Embodied numerical training • Neural correlates • Magnitude manipulation • Fact retrieval

U. Fischer (✉)
Leibniz-Institut für Wissensmedien (IWM), Schleichstraße 6, 72076 Tübingen, Germany

Department of Educational Sciences, University of Regensburg,
Universitätsstraße 31, 93053 Regensburg, Germany
e-mail: ursula.fischer@ur.de

E. Klein • T. Dackermann
Leibniz-Institut für Wissensmedien (IWM), Schleichstraße 6, 72076 Tübingen, Germany
e-mail: e.klein@iwm-tuebingen.de; t.dackermann@iwm-tuebingen.de

K. Moeller
Leibniz-Institut für Wissensmedien (IWM), Schleichstraße 6, 72076 Tübingen, Germany

Department of Psychology, Eberhard Karls University, Tübingen, Germany

LEAD Graduate School, Eberhard Karls University, Tübingen, Germany
e-mail: k.moeller@iwm-tuebingen.de

© Springer International Publishing AG 2017   21
S. Schwan, U. Cress (eds.), *The Psychology of Digital Learning*,
DOI 10.1007/978-3-319-49077-9_2

Introduction

Numbers are more or less omnipresent in everyday life. On a typical day, we may be confronted with numbers as soon as the alarm clock rings at 06.00 o'clock. One may then pick it up to read the time and estimate whether there is still enough time to put the alarm on snooze for another 8 min when one has to catch tube number 4 leaving from platform 2 which one usually takes to get to the office. On the way, one may evaluate whether there is still enough money in one's wallet to pay for the expensive coffee at the train station. These scenes nicely illustrate the prevalence of numerical information in our everyday life.

Accordingly, there is accumulating empirical evidence indicating that success in managing modern life at the beginning of the twenty-first century is associated substantially with the ability to appropriately deal with and handle numbers (e.g. Parsons & Bynner, 2005). Deficits in numerical competencies can entail both considerable personal handicaps (e.g. Dowker, 2005) and socio-economic costs (e.g. Gross, Hudson, & Price, 2009). Generally, there is now evidence that the ability to reason with numbers seems even more important than literacy for individual life and career prospects (see Butterworth, Varma, & Laurillard, 2011 for a review).

Therefore, it is of particular importance to investigate the processes underlying numerical cognition from its neuronal correlates to its developmental trajectories and how it can be acquired best. This chapter aims at providing a brief overview of these aspects. In the first part, we will summarize current research on the neural correlates of numerical cognition with a specific focus on the neural fibre pathways connecting the involved brain areas, as well as the neural correlates of numerical learning. In part two we will then describe related approaches for numerical learning using embodied and interactive training methods for numerical competencies drawing on the metaphor of a mental number line (henceforth: MNL) representation. Finally, by integrating these two lines of research, we open up a new perspective on the possible origins of numerical cognition as redeployed neural correlates from physical experiences.

Neural Correlates of Numerical Cognition

Considering the scenes from daily life described above, it is obvious that they require an adequate understanding of numbers. However, there seem to be different aspects of numbers that are meaningful in different situations. For example, reading the time requires knowledge of Arabic number symbols. Estimating the money left in our wallet as well as time needed requires understanding the meaning of number magnitude and computational processes. Finally, for the mere naming of number words, but also for the use of numerical labels (i.e. tube number 4), verbal processes are involved. From a scientific point of view, these processes are specified by the currently most influential model of numerical cognition, the *Triple-Code Model* (Dehaene, 1992; Dehaene, Piazza, Pinel, & Cohen, 2003).

The Triple-Code Model

As already reflected in its name, this model assumes three numerical codes or representations underlying our numerical and mathematical competencies. The codes comprise (1) a *visual Arabic number form* necessary for identifying number symbols, (2) a *verbal representation* for processing spoken number words and storing arithmetic facts such as multiplication tables, and (3) an *analogue representation of number magnitude* (Dehaene & Cohen, 1995). This analogue magnitude representation is assumed to be essential for our understanding of (numerical) magnitudes. Interestingly, the analogue magnitude code was also hypothesized to contain a spatial component reflected in a left-to-right ordering of numbers along the MNL (e.g. Dehaene, Bossini, & Giraux, 1993; Fischer & Shaki, 2014 for a review; see below for a more elaborate discussion on the MNL).

Importantly, however, the TCM not only provides a theoretical differentiation of representations involved in numerical cognition but gained its high influence on the field because of its unique integration of behavioural and neuro-functional aspects— making it an anatomo-functional model. This means that the three representational codes introduced above can be associated with specific brain regions: (1) The visual number form representation was attributed to the fusiform gyrus (e.g. Klein et al., 2014). (2) The verbal representation of numbers and with it the representation of arithmetic facts seems to be associated with left-lateralized perisylvian language areas and the angular gyrus in particular (e.g. Klein, Willmes, et al., 2010). Finally, (3) the analogue magnitude representation is supposed to be situated in the bilateral intraparietal sulci (IPS, Arsalidou & Taylor, 2011 for a meta-analysis) as well as additional posterior parietal areas associated with navigating upon the MNL (e.g. Dehaene et al., 2003)—reflecting a spatial representation of number magnitude.

The most important content-wise postulate of the triple-code model is the general distinction between a mental representation of number magnitude on the one side and rather verbally mediated retrieval processes for arithmetic facts on the other side. It is important to note that these two representational codes (e.g. number magnitude vs. verbal code for arithmetic facts) can dissociate. For instance, patients suffering from a stroke in the left hemisphere can present with a selective deficit of rote verbal knowledge (including multiplication facts) with preserved semantic knowledge of numerical quantities. On the other hand, patients with intraparietal lesions can show specific impairments of quantitative numerical knowledge (e.g. in subtraction), whereas knowledge of rote arithmetic facts is preserved (Dehaene & Cohen, 1997). Such double dissociations corroborate that numerical information is processed in different formats within distinct cerebral areas (for reviews, see Nuerk, Klein, & Willmes, 2012; Willmes & Klein, 2014). These two dissociable systems have also been substantiated by recent neuroimaging studies (i.e. left-hemispheric perisylvian areas and angular gyrus for arithmetic facts: e.g. Delazer et al., 2003, Klein, Willmes et al., 2010, bilateral IPS for number magnitude information: e.g. Klein, Nuerk, Wood, Knops, & Willmes, 2009; Klein, Moeller, Nuerk, & Willmes, 2010; Klein, Mann, et al., 2013).

In this context, it is important to note, however, that the vast majority of existing studies investigating the neural correlates of numerical cognition in general and numerical learning in particular focused on grey matter activation patterns and their changes. In contrast, knowledge on how these observed brain areas work together considering their connectivity is still rather patchy.

Adding Neural Connectivity to the Triple-Code Model

Already in its initial form, the TCM assumed that mental arithmetic requires the close interplay of parietal as well as additional (pre)frontal processes (Dehaene & Cohen, 1995). Therefore, numerical cognition and mental arithmetic are a clear case of multi-modular and distributed processing within the human brain (i.e. involving different number-specific representations as well as number-unspecific processes associated with different brain regions). However, even though numerous neuroimaging studies localized grey matter cortical structures recruited during number processing (see Arsalidou & Taylor, 2011; Dehaene et al., 2003 for reviews), the white matter pathways connecting these areas have largely been neglected so far. Thus, the TCM so far does not take into account the connecting fibre pathways underlying its multi-modular organization of numerical cognition. Accordingly, this approach has been criticized as "corticocentric myopia" (Parvizi, 2009) because it does not take into account that any given brain function depends on the integrity of a widespread network integrating cortical areas across the entire brain. Therefore, attempts to explain typical and atypical cognitive functioning in general and numerical cognition in particular should combine (1) localized neural correlates of cognitive functions in circumscribed grey matter areas *and* (2) the connectivity of these cortical areas via white matter pathways to other cortical and subcortical areas.

However, hodology, the science of connectional anatomy (Catani & ffytche, 2005), has only recently become accessible to evaluation in the living brain by using DTI (diffusion tensor imaging). While functional magnetic resonance imaging (fMRI) identifies functionally defined cortical areas, DTI tractography also indicates the white matter tracts connecting these areas. This provides a powerful non-invasive tool to study brain connectivity patterns underlying cognitive functions. Employing diffusion tensor tractography, perisylvian language networks (e.g. Saur et al., 2008) but also networks underlying attentional processes (e.g. Umarova et al., 2010) have already been specified. In contrast, research interest into brain connectivity underlying numerical cognition has increased only recently (see Matejko & Ansari, 2015; Moeller, Willmes, & Klein, 2015 for reviews).

Importantly, there are currently only two studies worldwide which systematically investigated white matter connections of the representational codes suggested by the TCM (Klein, Moeller, Glauche et al., 2013, Klein et al., 2014, see Fig. 2.1). In these studies, we showed that the representations of arithmetic facts and number magnitude were subserved by two largely distinct neural networks, which do not share common neural pathways. This is of particular interest because the TCM

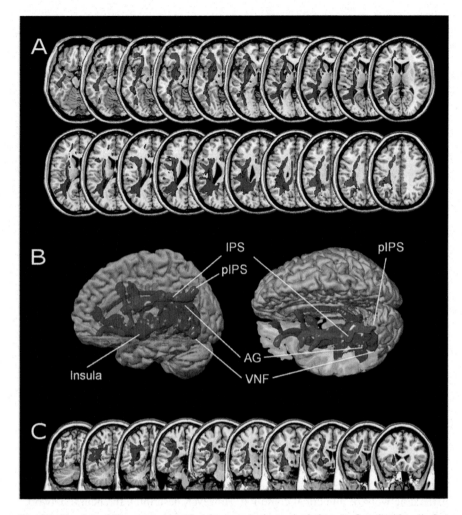

Fig. 2.1 Overlay of fibre tracts identified for magnitude manipulations (*red*) and arithmetic fact retrieval (*blue*). Panel A gives a detailed view on the course of the fibre tracts in axial orientation. Two anatomically largely distinct dorsal vs. ventral fibre pathway profiles for magnitude manipulations (*red*) and arithmetic fact retrieval (*blue*) can be observed. Importantly, the two networks differ not only in localization of activation but also in the connections between associated cortex areas. Additionally, the connection between the visual number form area (VNF) and the number magnitude representation (IPS/pIPS) is displayed in red. Panel B again reflects the identified pathways in a 3D volume rendering. Finally, Panel C depicts a detailed view on the course of the fibre tracts in coronal orientation

proposes a contribution of both magnitude manipulations and arithmetic fact retrieval to complex arithmetic. However, our recent results further add to answering the question how magnitude manipulations and arithmetic fact retrieval actually interact. In the latter study by Klein et al. (2014) we suggested the idea that it might not be a question of either magnitude manipulation or fact retrieval. Instead, both networks will contribute to numerical cognition in a 'more or less' manner. Thus, it seems reasonable to assume that single digit multiplications or additions with summands up to five are primarily solved by processes of fact retrieval. However, there is also evidence for magnitude-related influences on these very easy tasks (e.g. Thevenot et al., 2007). The other way around, multiplying two three-digit numbers requires calculation and thus the manipulation of number magnitudes. Nevertheless, column-wise processing (i.e. unit digit * unit digit, tens digit * tens digit, etc.) involves single digit multiplications so that intermediate steps can be solved using arithmetic fact retrieval. Even though this idea seems to work for what is going on cognitively, we still can only speculate on the neural structures at which the two networks might interact. From an anatomical point of view, this might most probably be at the junction of the left angular gyrus and the IPS. These structures are not only anatomically close but are also well connected via association fibres and most probably via U-fibres as well (Caspers et al., 2011). However, future studies will have to evaluate this claim.

Furthermore, there is also evidence extending the TCM by means of identifying new structures and their connectivity involved in numerical cognition. Only recently, studies on functional/effective connectivity also indicated a specific role of the hippocampus in numerical development (Qin et al., 2014; Supekar et al., 2013). In children, hippocampal-prefrontal as well as hippocampal-parietal connectivity was found to be associated with the acquisition of retrieval-based solution strategies, while in adults hippocampal-parietal connectivity was associated with the retrieval of arithmetic facts. This latter finding was corroborated by our structural connectivity analyses (Klein et al., 2014) but also by a recent intervention study evaluating the neural correlates of multiplication fact learning in adults (Bloechle et al., 2016).

In summary, it can be said that our structural connectivity results not only updated the TCM by considering fibre pathways for the representations of magnitude (manipulations) and verbally driven arithmetic fact retrieval (Klein et al., 2014). Additionally, we were able to specify how brain structures associated with long-term memory processes (such as the hippocampus) are involved in the fronto-parietal network of numerical cognition. However, describing the neural networks subserving numerical cognition is only the first step. In a next step, it is important to evaluate the changes within these networks through numerical development and learning.

Neural Correlates of Numerical Learning

After initial scepticism, the majority of researchers are now confident that neuro-scientific research offers new approaches to investigate brain plasticity—a necessary prerequisite for both numerical instruction/education and rehabilitation—because it is able to specify the functional relationship between brain and behaviour (e.g. Ansari, De Smedt, & Grabner, 2012; Goswami, 2008). Recent research indicates that this can not only be achieved on the theoretical but also on the empirical level.

Importantly, there are now first studies investigating the neural correlates of numerical learning by means of evaluating changes in activation patterns within the above described neural networks. On an ontogenetic level, the meta-analyses of Kaufmann et al. (2011) indicated that numerical development in children is reflected by a frontal-to-parietal shift of activation associated with the processing of numerical information. This shift of activation within the fronto-parietal network of number processing is usually argued to indicate that the processing of numerical activation gets more specific and automated with increasing age and experience. Accordingly, neural activation in frontal brain areas associated with domain-general processes such as working memory and executive control (e.g. Nee et al., 2013) decreases while activation in parietal areas primarily associated with the processing of numerical content increases.

A more specific and controlled evaluation of the neural correlates of numerical learning was pursued by intervention studies. As regards the processing of arithmetic facts, Zaunmüeller et al. (2009) evaluated the effects of a training of arithmetic facts for a stroke patient. Following a left-hemispheric lesion, he showed a severe multiplication deficit (see also Klein, Moeller, & Willmes, 2013). An intensive training of multiplication tables restored the patient's ability to directly retrieve results from memory instead of having to calculate results. On the neural level, the authors observed a specific increase in activation of right-hemispheric areas (e.g. the angular gyrus) homologue to those of the lesioned left hemisphere which are usually associated with the processing of arithmetic facts. This indicated that the intact right hemisphere seemed to have taken over arithmetic fact retrieval—at least to some degree. Moreover, Bloechle et al. (2016) measured brain activation in healthy participants before and after an extensive multiplication training to evaluate the neural correlates of arithmetic fact acquisition more specifically. When comparing activation patterns for trained and untrained problems in the post-training fMRI session, the authors replicated a higher activation of the left AG for trained problems as observed previously (Delazer et al., 2003; Ischebeck et al., 2007). However, in a pre-post comparison of activation for trained problems and the same problems in the pretraining fMRI session, no signal change in the AG was observed. Instead, we observed changes in neural activation through the training in hippocampal, parahippocampal, and retrosplenial structures suggesting the involvement of these areas associated with long-term memory in arithmetic fact retrieval.

With respect to the representation of number magnitude and its spatial dimension, Kucian et al. (2011) evaluated the effects of a number line estimation training for children at both the behavioural and the neural level. The authors found that the training not only improved children's performance in number line estimation, but also led to functionally related remediation of neural activation in number-related parietal brain areas. For children with mathematics learning difficulties in particular, the training led to a specific change in the brain activation pattern: differences between the activation of children with and without mathematics learning difficulties in number-specific parietal cortex areas were reduced after the training.

Thereby, these studies demonstrated that it is possible to directly associate effects of numerical learning with changes in brain activation patterns (see also Delazer et al., 2003; Ischebeck et al., 2006). The effects of the spatial-numerical training of number line estimation in children as found by Kucian et al. (2011) seem of particular importance. These fit nicely with the suggestion of Dehaene et al. (2003) that apart from the content-wise differentiation between magnitude manipulations and arithmetic fact retrieval, spatial processes associated with the internal navigation on the MNL have a specific neural correlate in the posterior superior parietal lobules. Following this rationale and considering the results of Kucian et al. (2011), an association of numbers with physical space should be observable at the neural level.

Spatial-Numerical Associations at the Neural Level

First evidence for spatial-numerical associations to be represented at the neural level comes from observations of patients with hemi-spatial neglect (see Umiltà, Priftis, & Zorzi, 2009 for a review). These patients treat any objects, people, etc. in the neglected hemi-field (most often the left one following a right-hemispheric stroke) as if they did not exist at all (Bisiach, Capitani, Luzzatti, & Perani, 1981; Guariglia, Palermo, Piccardi, Iaria, & Incoccia, 2013). Accordingly, in case there is a spatial representation of number magnitude (in terms of a left-to-right oriented MNL), it should be affected in patients suffering from neglect. And indeed, the characteristic rightward bias observed in neglect patients for spatial tasks such as line bisection (see Jewell & McCourt, 2000 for a review) was found to generalize to numerical tasks. Accordingly, neglect patients not only misplaced the midpoint of a physical line towards the right, but also the middle of a numerical interval (e.g. indicating 7 as the middle between 1 and 9; Zorzi, Priftis, & Umiltà, 2002, see also Hoeckner et al., 2008 for two-digit numbers). These results demonstrated that spatial neglect influences the representation of number magnitude and its mapping onto physical space (see also Mihulowicz, Klein, Nuerk, Willmes, & Karnath, 2015).

Further corroboration for the claim of spatial-numerical associations on the neural level is provided by the results of Knops, Thirion, Hubbard, Michel, and Dehaene (2009). These authors investigated the interrelation between addition and subtraction and saccadic eye movements. In particular, the authors used the brain activation associated with either left- or rightward saccades to predict whether participants were performing either addition or subtraction problems. The authors observed that participants' completion of addition problems was predicted reliably by the neural activity observed for rightward saccades, whereas the completion of subtraction problems was predicted by neural activation associated with leftward saccades. Interestingly, this nicely fits with the idea of the operational momentum effect (McCrink, Dehaene, & Dehaene-Lambertz, 2007), which assumes that addition reflects a rightward movement on the MNL, whereas subtraction reflects a leftward movement. Knops et al. (2009) argue that the association of leftward saccades with subtraction and of rightward saccades with addition indicates systematic navigation upon the MNL during subtraction and addition.

Taken together, these findings indicate a reliable association of the neural representation of number magnitude and physical space as reflected by the conceptual metaphor of the MNL. Importantly, the idea of a spatial representation of number magnitude is not restricted to basic research on the neural underpinnings of numerical cognition but generalizes to research on children's numerical development and has already been applied in intervention studies.

Development and Applications of Spatial-Numerical Associations

The metaphor of a MNL is a well-established theoretical concept (1) investigated in research on children's numerical development in general but also (2) used successfully as an instructional tool to corroborate numerical development in primary school years. In the following part of this chapter we will elaborate on these points in more detail.

Spatial-Numerical Associations in Children's Numerical Development

Research on the development of numerical abilities in infants suggests that an innate sensitivity to magnitudes exists (e.g. Xu, Spelke, & Goddard, 2005). This means that only a few months old infants already seem to recognize differences in number—an interpretation that is supported by an increasing number of studies (e.g. De Hevia, Izard, Coubart, Spelke, & Streri, 2014; McCrink & Wynn, 2004). Moreover, infants have even been reported to be able to perform simple arithmetic (e.g. McCrink & Wynn, 2004, 2009). For instance, in one of the first studies on the topic, Wynn (1992) used a habituation paradigm considering infants' looking times as an indicator of their number-related cognitive processing. The author placed one object behind a screen and then added a second object while the infant was watching the scene. The screen was then removed to reveal either one or two objects. Infants looked longer at the display when there was only one instead of two objects. Wynn (1992) interpreted this to indicate that infants were surprised about the outcome because it violated their expectation to see two objects. This was observed not only for addition but also subtraction problems and thus indicates infants' innate sensitivity to numerical magnitude. Likewise, there is also first evidence on systematic spatial-numerical associations early in numerical development.

First systematic evidence for a left-to-right oriented association of number and physical space came from the *Spatial Numerical Association of Response Codes* (SNARC) effect (Dehaene et al., 1993; see also Wood et al., 2008, for a meta-analysis). This effect describes the phenomenon that in Western cultures, participants tend to react faster to smaller numbers with their left hand and to larger numbers with their right hand (Dehaene et al., 1993). Initially, the fact that the effect was not observed before primary school was interpreted to indicate that it is driven by culture (e.g. Cohen-Kadosh, Lammertyn, & Izard, 2008; Zebian, 2005). This hypothesis, however, seems outdated as spatial-numerical associations other than the SNARC effect have already been observed for kindergartners (e.g. Ebersbach, 2015; Patro & Haman, 2012) and even infants (de Hevia et al., 2014, see Patro, Nuerk, Cress, & Haman, 2014 for a review). In the study by de Hevia et al. (2014), 7-months-old infants were found to associate the dimensions of physical space and number, as indicated by infants preference in looking times for left-to-right oriented increasing numerical sequences. This indicates that the analogue magnitude representation described in the TCM (Dehaene & Cohen, 1995) might be innately associated with physical space (de Hevia & Spelke, 2010).

Although this indicates a very early association of physical space and number, which is preserved through life (de Hevia & Spelke, 2009), a precise mapping of number magnitude onto space (reflecting a number line) nevertheless takes time to develop, as indicated by children's number line estimation performance (e.g. Siegler & Booth, 2004). For instance, when asked to estimate the position of a target number on a given number line, young children tend to systematically overestimate the spatial positions of small numbers (i.e. placing 10 where 40 should be on an number line ranging from 0 to 100, e.g. Moeller, Pixner, Kaufmann, & Nuerk, 2009).

However, an accurate number-to-space mapping was argued to be an important building block for the development of later arithmetic skills. In line with this notion, there is convincing evidence showing that children's number line estimation accuracy is correlated reliably with their arithmetic performance (e.g. Link et al., 2014; Schneider, Grabner, & Paetsch, 2009; Siegler & Booth, 2004). Even more so, children with mathematics learning difficulties were observed to present with particularly worse number line estimation performance (e.g. Geary, Hoard, Nugent, & Byrd-Craven, 2008; Landerl, 2013). Accordingly, there have even been attempts to identify subtypes of mathematics learning difficulties that suggest the existence of a specific *weak MNL* subtype (e.g. Wilson & Dehaene, 2007; see also Bartelet, Ansari, Vaessen, & Blomert, 2014 for a data-driven approach).

However, the argument on the importance of a MNL representation also works the other way around. Not only is the MNL influential in numerical development, it can also be trained successfully by approaches specifically strengthening children's spatial-numerical associations.

Towards an Embodied Training of the Mental Number Line

In recent years, an increasing number of trainings have been developed to train number magnitude understanding in general (e.g. *The Number Race*, Wilson, Revkin, Cohen, Cohen, & Dehaene, 2006) and spatial-numerical associations in particular (e.g. Ramani & Siegler, 2008). Some approaches even address the MNL metaphor explicitly and directly train the association between numbers and physical space. For example, a preliminary version of the now commercially available Dybuster® Calcularis program (for an evaluation see Käser et al., 2013) specifically trained children in the number line estimation task. In this study, Kucian et al. (2011) found their number line estimation training to be effective. Children with and without mathematics learning difficulties improved significantly not only in number line estimation but also arithmetic problem solving. Considering recent theoretical developments on embodied cognition in general (e.g. Barsalou, 2008; Wilson, 2002) and embodied representations of numbers in particular (e.g. Fischer & Brugger, 2011; Myachikov et al., 2013 for theoretical considerations), we aimed to increase the effects of number line trainings by allowing for an embodied interaction and experience of the trained spatial-numerical association through movement-based elements.

In a new training approach building on the concept of *embodied numerosity* (Domahs, Moeller, Huber, Willmes, & Nuerk, 2010), we evaluated the benefits of incorporating whole-body movement into the training of spatial-numerical associations. The rationale behind this idea were findings of other types of number-related physical movement such as finger counting that influenced spatial-numerical associations (Fischer, 2008). However, not just finger counting has been associated with numerical processing. In recent years, accumulating evidence suggested a link between whole-body movement and numerical processing (Hartmann, Farkas, & Mast, 2012; Hartmann, Grabherr, & Mast, 2012; Shaki & Fischer, 2014). For example, Shaki and Fischer (2014) showed that the magnitude of numbers that participants should generate randomly while walking influenced their decision whether to turn left or right after some steps. When the last generated number was relatively small, this led to a significant increase of left turns, whereas relatively large numbers were associated with reliably more right turns.

In line with the results of this and other previous studies, we developed an embodied spatial-numerical training on a digital dance mat (Fischer, Moeller, Bientzle, Cress, & Nuerk, 2011). In this training, kindergarteners had to perform number magnitude comparisons in a set-up in which one number was presented on a number line, and another number had to be classified as either larger or smaller than the first one. Children's responses had to be made by jumping from the central field of the dance mat to the left for a *smaller* decision and to the right for a *larger* decision (see Fig. 2.2). This training was compared to a similar training performed on a tablet PC. In a randomized crossover design, each child received both trainings in a balanced order, and improvements over the two training phases were compared against each other. Importantly, we observed that children not only improved their number line estimation performance more through the experimental than the control training, but also showed more pronounced improvements in their understanding of counting principles.

Follow-up studies were conducted using different digital media and training different numerical concepts (Fischer et al., 2015; Link et al., 2014; Link et al., 2013; see Fischer et al., 2014; Dackermann et al., 2016 for overviews). For instance, in another study (Link et al., 2013), we trained first-graders to perform the number line

Fig. 2.2 Schematic illustrations of embodied trainings: Panel A depicts a training set-up with the digital dance mat as in Fischer et al. (2011). Panel B shows a simplified version of the training set-up used by Link, Moeller, Huber, Fischer, and Nuerk (2013), with the green screen indicating from which end of the number line the child should start walking

estimation task with their entire body. On an up to 3 m long number line taped on the floor, children marked their estimates by walking to the estimated location of the target numbers on the number line (see Fig. 2.2). We used a Kinect™ sensor to record children's estimates. Results following a randomized crossover design revealed that the embodied training was equally effective compared to a PC training of the very same content. However, the embodied training led to more pronounced improvements of children's performance on simple addition problems and addition problems involving a carry operation. What is more, we observed that children with lower general cognitive abilities and visual working memory capacity specifically benefitted from the embodied training.

In a recent study (Fischer et al., 2015), we used an interactive whiteboard to train the number line estimation task. Due to the width of the whiteboard (about 1.5 m), second-graders had to move left or right to mark their estimates on the presented number line. Compared to a number line training on a PC and a non-numerical training on the interactive whiteboard (controlling for the motivational appeal of this medium), the experimental training again led to more pronounced improvement in children's number line estimation but also their addition performance.

In another innovative approach, promising results were obtained when training children's understanding of the equidistant spacing of numbers upon the number line in an embodied fashion (Dackermann, Fischer, Cress, Nuerk, & Moeller, 2016). In this study, the embodied training condition required children to walk a certain distance in a given number of equally spaced steps. In the control training children had to subdivide a given line—presented on a tablet PC—into equally spaced segments without any embodied experience of the equidistance principle. Importantly, results indicated that children not only improved more strongly through the embodied training condition in their ability to divide distances into equally spaced segments. Additionally, their performance on an unbounded number line estimation task also increased more strongly after the embodied compared to a control training.

Taken together, these promising results indicate that embodied numerical trainings are effective in corroborating children's basic numerical concepts. In light of current numbers of about 6 % of children who suffer from mathematics learning difficulties (e.g. Fischbach et al., 2013; see Moeller, Fischer, Cress, & Nuerk, 2012 for an overview), our next step will be a training specifically addressing these children. Since our trainings are designed to promote basic numerical competencies, and children with mathematics learning difficulties are facing problems already at this level of competencies, this seems a reasonable and promising starting point for applying embodied intervention methods.

Overlapping Brain Activation for Numbers and Space

An additional benefit of such embodied trainings addressing basic numerical competencies is that these basic competencies have been associated with specific brain areas (see above, e.g. Arsalidou & Taylor, 2011; Dehaene et al., 2003). Thus, it should be possible to evaluate changes of the way in which numerical information is processed in the brain through training as previously attempted by Kucian et al. (2011). Therefore, neuro-scientific methods such as fMRI may not only be used to evaluate specificities of brain activation associated with number processing but also changes in brain activation due to numerical training and instruction in particular.

As described above, there is now accumulating evidence corroborating the idea that the underpinnings of numerical cognition but also the effects of specific (embodied) spatial-numerical trainings can be evaluated on the neural level. Interestingly however, when it comes to spatial-numerical associations, the evidence also suggests a major involvement of brain areas not primarily associated with the processing of number magnitude. For example, an involvement of areas associated with attentional shifts in physical space reflected by saccades (Knops et al., 2009, see above) or mental navigation (Dehaene et al., 2003) was observed. Moreover, there are empirical findings suggesting an involvement of further brain areas in numerical cognition more broadly such as areas associated with specific motoric functioning and finger movements in particular (e.g. Kaufmann et al., 2008; Tschentscher, Hauk, Fischer, & Pulvermüller, 2012). Furthermore, there is even more specific empirical evidence indicating overlapping neural activation in (intra) parietal cortex areas for the processing of numbers, the execution of saccades, but also grasping and pointing movements (Simon, Mangin, Cohen, Le Bihan, & Dehaene, 2002; Simon et al., 2004). Importantly, these prominent co- and overlapping activations of brain areas associated with the mental representation of physical space and the representation of the body (as required for saccades and grasping/pointing movements) raise the question how and why these areas are specifically related to the processing of numerical information. In the following, we will discuss a neuro-functional account on this question.

Numerical Cognition: Reused Neural Circuits for Physical Experiences

The question how and why specific brain areas are co-activated for or show overlapping activation with the processing of numerical information addresses the issue of how specific observed neural correlates reflect specific cognitive functions such as motor abilities, spatial cognition, attention, and also numerical cognition. However, while it is reasonable to assume that neural circuits for motor abilities and also the processing of spatial information are necessary phylogenetic developments to allow interactions with the environment, this does not hold for the human ability to use symbol systems such as Arabic numbers for numerical cognition. In fact, such cultural acquisitions are far too recent to evolve their specific brain mechanisms (with Arabic numbers being used for about 1000 years, cf. Menninger, 1957, see also Chrisomalis, 2004). Instead, it was suggested that the capacity of numerical cognition (and also other cultural competencies such as reading) may have evolved through a specific form of cortical plasticity unique to humans termed *neural recycling* (Dehaene, 2005). Following the neural recycling hypothesis, "the human ability to acquire new cultural objects relies on a process [...] whereby those novel objects invade cortical territories initially devoted to similar or sufficiently close functions. According to this view, our evolutionary history, and therefore our genetic organization, has created a cerebral architecture that is both constrained and partially plastic, and that delimits a space of learnable cultural objects. New cultural acquisitions are therefore possible only inasmuch as they are able to fit within the pre-existing" (Dehaene, 2005, p. 126).

For the case of numerical cognition, it was suggested that even for tasks with symbolic Arabic numbers humans rely on an analogue magnitude code, also described as a MNL (Dehaene et al., 2003). Importantly, this analogue magnitude code does not seem to be specific to the processing of number magnitude but may generalize to the processing of physical and temporal magnitudes (i.e. spatial distances and time durations, e.g. Bueti & Walsh, 2009; Santiago & Lakens, 2015; Walsh, 2003). This indicates that the cultural acquisition of processing number magnitude may have invaded the phylogenetically older circuits for processing physical space and time. This seems reasonable as all three domains share and build upon a generalized representation of magnitude. Accordingly, this might not only account for spatial-numerical associations on the behavioural level such as the SNARC effect but also explain co-activation and overlapping activation of brain areas associated with grasping and saccades (which require the integration of spatial and temporal information) and numerical processing (e.g. Simon et al., 2002, 2004).

Related to the neural recycling hypothesis and providing a more specific account on the involvement of brain areas associated with finger movements in numerical cognition (e.g. Kaufmann et al., 2008; Tschentscher et al., 2012), Penner-Wilger and Anderson (2008, 2011; see also Anderson & Penner-Wilger, 2013) suggested what they termed the *massive redeployment hypothesis*. This hypothesis suggests that at least parts of the neural circuitry originally subserving finger use may have been redeployed to support the representation of number. Because this part serves both functions now, this neural circuit should be commonly activated in tasks requiring finger use or number processing. Thereby, the massive redeployment hypothesis also accounts for the finding that finger gnosis (i.e. the ability to recognize one's fingers without visual control) is a reliable predictor of children's numerical development with those children presenting with better finger gnosis also showing better numerical performance (e.g. Noël, 2005; Wyschkon, Poltz, Höse, von Aster, & Esser, 2015).

Although very similar at first glance, there is an important difference between this hypothesis and the neural recycling hypothesis. The massive redeployment hypothesis proposes that existing components are reused and thus lower level circuits are combined to evolve more complex cognitive functions. In contrast, the neuronal recycling hypothesis suggests that novel cultural acquisitions such as number invade and change existing neural circuits that show sufficient proximity (cf. the idea of a generalized magnitude representation, e.g. Walsh, 2003).

Coming back to the idea of our embodied numerical training, both of these hypotheses on the neuro-functional organisation and integration of the neural circuits underlying numerical cognition may actually account for (parts of) the beneficial effects of the embodied training approach. As these trainings require participants to move their whole body in physical space to perform a numerical task, the respective correlated or even overlapping brain areas should be activated jointly. Thereby, the systematic association of physical space and number magnitude (following the neural recycling hypothesis) and/or the systematic involvement of bodily movements (following the massive redeployment hypothesis) should provide an additional access to the relevant representation of numerical magnitude.

Taken together, we have come full circle from embodied interaction beneficial for numerical learning to the neural correlates of numerical cognition and its integration into brain circuits originally subserving spatial and motor-related processes, which substantiate the idea of systematically training spatial-numerical associations in an embodied way.

References

Anderson, M. L., & Penner-Wilger, M. (2013). Neural reuse in the evolution and development of the brain: Evidence for developmental homology? *Developmental Psychobiology, 55*, 42–51.

Ansari, D., De Smedt, B., & Grabner, R. H. (2012). Neuroeducation—A critical overview of an emerging field. *Neuroethics, 5*, 105–117.

Arsalidou, M., & Taylor, M. J. (2011). Is 2+2=4? Meta-analyses of brain areas needed for numbers and calculations. *NeuroImage, 54*, 2382–2393.

Barsalou, L. W. (2008). Grounded Cognition. *Annual Review of Psychology, 59*, 617–645.

Bartelet, D., Ansari, D., Vaessen, A., & Blomert, L. (2014). Cognitive subtypes of mathematics learning difficulties in primary education. *Research in Developmental Disabilities, 35*, 657–670.

Bisiach, E., Capitani, E., Luzzatti, C., & Perani, D. (1981). Brain and conscious representation of outside reality. *Neuropsychologia, 19*, 543–551.

Bloechle, J., Huber, S., Bahnmueller, J., Rennig, J., Willmes, K., Cavdaroglu, S., et al. (2016). Fact learning in complex arithmetic—The role of the angular gyrus revisited. *Human Brain Mapping.* doi:10.1002/hbm.23226.

Bueti, D., & Walsh, V. (2009). The parietal cortex and the representation of time, space, number and other magnitudes. *Philosophical Transactions of the Royal Society B, 364,* 1831–1840.

Butterworth, B., Varma, S., & Laurillard, D. (2011). Dyscalculia: From brain to education. *Science, 332,* 1049–1053.

Caspers, S., Eickhoff, S. B., Rick, T., von Kapri, A., Kuhlen, T., Huang, R., et al. (2011). Probabilistic fibre tract analysis of cytoarchitectonically defined human inferior parietal lobule areas reveals similarities to macaques. *Neuroimage, 58,* 362–380.

Catani, M., & ffytche, D. H. (2005). The rise and fall of disconnection syndromes. *Brain, 128,* 2224–2239.

Chrisomalis, S. (2004). A cognitive typology for numerical notation. *Cambridge Archaeological Journal, 14,* 37–52.

Cohen-Kadosh, R., Lammertyn, J., & Izard, V. (2008). Are numbers special? An overview of chronometric, neuroimaging, developmental and comparative studies of magnitude representation. *Progress in Neurobiology, 84,* 132–147.

Dackermann, T., Fischer, U., Cress, U., Nuerk, H.-C., & Moeller, K. (2016). Bewegtes Lernen numerischer Kompetenzen. *Psychologische Rundschau, 67,* 102–109.

Dackermann, T., Fischer, U., Huber, S., Nuerk, H.-C., & Moeller, K. (2016). Training the equidistant principle of number line spacing. *Cognitive Processing, 17,* 243–258. doi:10.1007/s10339-016-0763-8.

De Hevia, M. D., & Spelke, E. S. (2009). Spontaneous mapping of number and space in adults and young children. *Cognition, 110,* 198–207.

De Hevia, M. D., & Spelke, E. S. (2010). Number-space mapping in human infants. *Psychological Science, 21,* 653–660.

De Hevia, M. D., Izard, V., Coubart, A., Spelke, E. S., & Streri, A. (2014). Representations of space, time, and number in neonates. *Proceedings of the National Academy of Sciences of the United States of America, 111,* 4809–4813.

Dehaene, S. (1992). Varieties of numerical abilities. *Cognition, 44,* 1–42.

Dehaene, S. (2005). Evolution of human cortical circuits for reading and arithmetic: The "neuronal recycling" hypothesis. In S. Dehaene, J.-R. Duhamel, M. D. Hauser, & G. Rizolatti (Eds.), *From monkey brain to human brain* (pp. 133–157). Cambridge, MA: MIT Press.

Dehaene, S., & Cohen, L. (1995). Towards an anatomical and functional model of number processing. *Mathematical Cognition, 1,* 83–120.

Dehaene, S., & Cohen, L. (1997). Cerebral pathways for calculation: Double dissociation between rote verbal and quantitative knowledge of arithmetic. *Cortex, 33,* 219–250.

Dehaene, S., Bossini, S., & Giraux, P. (1993). The mental representation of parity and number magnitude. *Journal of Experimental Psychology: General, 122,* 371–396.

Dehaene, S., Piazza, M., Pinel, P., & Cohen, L. (2003). Three parietal circuits for number processing. *Cognitive Neuropsychology, 20,* 487–506.

Delazer, M., Domahs, F., Bartha, L., Brenneis, C., Lochy, A., Trieb, T., & Benke, T. (2003). Learning complex arithmetic—A fMRI study. *Cognitive Brain Research, 18,* 76–88.

Domahs, F., Moeller, K., Huber, S., Willmes, K., & Nuerk, H.-C. (2010). Embodied numerosity: Implicit hand-based representations influence symbolic number processing across cultures. *Cognition, 116,* 251–266.

Dowker, A. (2005). *Individual differences in arithmetic: Implications for psychology, neuroscience and education.* Hove, UK: Psychology Press.

Ebersbach, M. (2015). Evidence for a Spatial–Numerical Association in Kindergartners Using a Number Line Task. *Journal of Cognition and Development, 16,* 118–128.

Fischbach, A., Schuchardt, K., Brandenburg, J., Klesczewski, J., Balke-Melcher, C., Schmidt, C., et al. (2013). Prävalenz von Lernschwächen und Lernstörungen: Zur Bedeutung der Diagnosekriterien. *Lernen und Lernstörungen, 2,* 65–76.

Fischer, M. H. (2008). Finger counting habits modulate spatial-numerical associations. *Cortex, 44,* 386–392.

Fischer, M. H., & Brugger, P. (2011). When digits help digits: Spatial-numerical associations point to finger counting as prime example of embodied cognition. *Frontiers in Psychology, 2,* 260.

Fischer, M. H., & Shaki, S. (2014). Spatial associations in numerical cognition - From single digits to arithmetic. *The Quarterly Journal of Experimental Psychology, 67,* 1461–1483.

Fischer, U., Link, T., Cress, U., Nuerk, H.-C., & Moeller, K. (2014). Math with the dance mat: On the benefits of embodied numerical training approaches. In V. Lee (Ed.), *Learning technologies and the body: Integration and implementation in formal and informal learning environments* (pp. 149–163). New York, NY: Routledge.

Fischer, U., Moeller, K., Bientzle, M., Cress, U., & Nuerk, H.-C. (2011). Sensori-motor spatial training of number magnitude representation. *Psychonomic Bulletin & Review, 18,* 177–183.

Fischer, U., Moeller, K., Huber, S., Cress, U., & Nuerk, H.-C. (2015). Full-body movement in numerical trainings: A pilot study with an interactive whiteboard. *International Journal of Serious Games, 4,* 23–35.

Geary, D. C., Hoard, M. K., Nugent, L., & Byrd-Craven, J. (2008). Development of number line representations in children with mathematical learning disability. *Developmental Neuropsychology, 33,* 277–299.

Goswami, U. (2008). Neuroscience and education: From research to practice? *Nature Reviews Neuroscience, 7,* 406–413.

Gross, J., Hudson, C., & Price, D. (2009). *The long term costs of numeracy difficulties.* London: Every Child a Chance Trust and KPMG.

Guariglia, C., Palermo, L., Piccardi, L., Iaria, G., & Incoccia, C. (2013). Neglecting the left side of a city square but not the left side of its clock: Prevalence and characteristics of representational neglect. *PloS One, 8,* e67390.

Hartmann, M., Farkas, R., & Mast, F. W. (2012). Self-motion perception influences number processing: Evidence from a parity task. *Cognitive Processing, 13,* 189–192.

Hartmann, M., Grabherr, L., & Mast, F. W. (2012). Moving along the mental number line: Interactions between whole-body motion and numerical cognition. *Journal of Experimental Psychology: Human Perception and Performance, 38,* 1416–1427.

Hoeckner, S. H., Moeller, K., Zauner, H., Wood, G., Haider, C., Gassner, A., & Nuerk, H.-C. (2008). Impairments of the mental number line for two-digit numbers in neglect. *Cortex, 44,* 429–438.

Ischebeck, A., Zamarian, L., Egger, K., Schocke, M., & Delazer, M. (2007). Imaging early practice effects in arithmetic. *NeuroImage, 36,* 993–1003.

Ischebeck, A., Zamarian, L., Siedentopf, C., Koppelstätter, F., Benke, T., Felber, S., & Delazer, M. (2006). How specifically do we learn? Imaging the learning of multiplication and subtraction. *Neuroimage, 30,* 1365–1375.

Jewell, G., & McCourt, M. E. (2000). Pseudoneglect: a review and meta-analysis of performance factors in line bisection tasks. *Neuropsychologia, 38,* 93–110.

Käser, T., Baschera, G., Kohn, J., Kucian, K., Richtmann, V., Grond, U., et al. (2013). Design and evaluation of the computer-based training program Calcularis for enhancing numerical cognition. *Frontiers in Psychology, 4,* 489.

Kaufmann, L., Vogel, S. E., Wood, G., Kremser, C., Schocke, M., Zimmerhackl, L. B., & Koten, J. W. (2008). A developmental fMRI study of nonsymbolic numerical and spatial processing. *Cortex, 44,* 376–385.

Kaufmann, L., Wood, G., Rubinsten, O., & Henik, A. (2011). Meta-Analyses of Developmental fMRI Studies Investigating Typical and Atypical Trajectories of Number Processing and Calculation. *Developmental Neuropsychology, 36,* 763–787.

Klein, E., Mann, A., Huber, S., Bloechle, J., Willmes, K., Karim, A. A., Nuerk, H.-C., & Moeller, K. (2013). Bilateral bi-cephalic tDCS with two active electrodes of the same polarity modulates bilateral cognitive processes differentially. *PlosONE, 8,* e71607.

Klein, E., Moeller, K., & Willmes, K. (2013). A neural disconnection hypothesis on impaired numerical processing. *Frontiers in Human Neuroscience, 7*:663.

Klein, E., Moeller, K., Glauche, V., Weiller, C., & Willmes, K. (2013). Processing pathways in mental arithmetic—Evidence from probabilistic fiber tracking. *PLoS ONE, 8*, e55455.

Klein, E., Moeller, K., Nuerk, H.-C., & Willmes, K. (2010). On the cognitive foundations of basic auditory number processing. *Behavioral and Brain Functions, 6*:42.

Klein, E., Nuerk, H.-C., Wood, G., Knops, A., & Willmes, K. (2009). The exact vs. approximate distinction in numerical cognition may not be exact, but only approximate: How different processes work together in multi-digit addition. *Brain and Cognition, 69*, 369–381.

Klein, E., Suchan, J., Moeller, K., Karnath, H.-O., Knops, A., Wood, G., et al. (2014). Considering structural connectivity in the triple code model of numerical cognition—Differential connectivity for magnitude processing and arithmetic facts. *Brain Structure & Function, 221*, 979–995.

Klein, E., Willmes, K., Dressel, K., Domahs, F., Wood, G., Nuerk, H.-C., & Moeller, K. (2010). Categorical and continuous—Disentangling the neural correlates of the carry effect in multi-digit addition. *Behavioral and Brain Functions, 6*, 70.

Knops, A., Thirion, B., Hubbard, E. M., Michel, V., & Dehaene, S. (2009). Recruitment of an area involved in eye movements during mental arithmetic. *Science, 324*, 1583–1585.

Kucian, K., Grond, U., Rotzer, S., Henzi, B., Schönmann, C., Plangger, F., et al. (2011). Mental number line training in children with developmental dyscalculia. *NeuroImage, 57*, 782–795.

Landerl, K. (2013). Development of numerical processing in children with typical and dyscalculic arithmetic skills—A longitudinal study. *Frontiers in Psychology, 4*, 459.

Link, T., Moeller, K., Huber, S., Fischer, U., & Nuerk, H.-C. (2013). Walk the number line—An embodied training of numerical concepts. *Trends in Neuroscience and Education, 2*, 74–84.

Link, T., Schwarz, E. J., Huber, S., Fischer, U., Nuerk, H.-C., Cress, U., & Moeller, K. (2014). Mathe mit der Matte—Verkörperlichtes Training basisnumerischer Kompetenzen [Math with the mat—embodied training of basic numerical competencies]. *Zeitschrift für Erziehungswissenschaft, 17*, 257–277.

Matejko, A. A., & Ansari, D. (2015). Drawing connections between white matter and numerical and mathematical cognition: A literature review. *Neuroscience & Biobehavioral Reviews, 48*, 35–52.

McCrink, K., & Wynn, K. (2004). Large-number addition and subtraction by 9-month-old infants. *Psychological Science, 15*, 776–781.

McCrink, K., & Wynn, K. (2009). Operational momentum in large-number addition and subtraction by 9-month-olds. *Journal of Experimental Child Psychology, 103*, 400–408.

McCrink, K., Dehaene, S., & Dehaene-Lambertz, G. (2007). Moving along the number line: Operational momentum in nonsymbolic arithmetic. *Perception & Psychophysics, 69*, 1324–1333.

Menninger, K. (1957). *Zahlwort und Ziffer: Eine Kulturgeshichte der Zahlen*. Göttingen: Vandehoeck & Ryprecht.

Mihulowicz, U., Klein, E., Nuerk, H.-C., Willmes, K., & Karnath, H. O. (2015). Spatial displacement of numbers on a vertical number line in spatial neglect. *Frontiers in Human Neuroscience, 9*, 240.

Moeller, K., Fischer, U., Cress, U., & Nuerk, H.-C. (2012). Diagnostics and intervention in developmental dyscalculia: Current issues and novel perspectives. In Z. Breznitz, O. Rubinsten, V. Molfese, & D. L. Molfese (Eds.), *Reading, writing, mathematics and the developing brain: Listening to many voices* (pp. 233–276). Heidelberg: Springer.

Moeller, K., Pixner, S., Kaufmann, L., & Nuerk, H.-C. (2009). Children's early mental number line: Logarithmic or decomposed linear? *Journal of Experimental Child Psychology, 103*, 503–515.

Moeller, K., Willmes, K., & Klein, E. (2015). A review on functional and structural brain connectivity in numerical cognition. *Frontiers in Human Neuroscience, 9*, 227.

Myachikov, A., Scheepers, C., Fischer, M. H., & Kessler, K. (2014). TEST: A Tropic, Embodied, and Situated Theory of Cognition. *Topics in Cognitive Science, 6*, 442–460.

Nee, D. E., Brown, J. W., Askren, M. K., Berman, M. G., Demiralp, E., Krawitz, A., & Jonides, J. (2013). A meta-analysis of executive components of working memory. *Cerebral Cortex, 23*, 264–282.

Noël, M. P. (2005). Finger gnosia: A predictor of numerical abilities in children? *Child Neuropsychology, 11*, 413–430.

Nuerk, H.-C., Klein, E., & Willmes, K. (2012). Zahlenverarbeitung und Rechnen [Number processing and calculation]. In F. Schneider & G. Fink (Eds.), *Funktionelle MRT in Psychiatrie und Neurologie* (2nd ed., pp. 443–455). Heidelberg: Springer.

Parsons, S., & Bynner, J. (2005). *Does numeracy matter more?* London: National Research and Development Centre for Adult Literacy and Numeracy.

Parvizi, J. (2009). Corticocentric myopia: Old bias in new cognitive sciences. *Trends in Cognitive Sciences, 13*, 354–359.

Patro, K., & Haman, M. (2012). The spatial–numerical congruity effect in preschoolers. *Journal of Experimental Child Psychology, 111*, 534–542.

Patro, K., Nuerk, H.-C., Cress, U., & Haman, M. (2014). How number-space relationships are assessed before formal schooling: A taxonomy proposal. *Frontiers in Psychology, 5*, 419.

Penner-Wilger, M., & Anderson, M. L. (2008). An alternative view of the relation between finger gnosis and math ability: Redeployment of finger representations for the representation of number. In*Proceedings of the 30th Annual Meeting of the Cognitive Science Society* (pp. 1647–1652). Austin, TX: Gognitive Science Society.

Penner-Wilger, M., & Anderson, M. L. (2011). The relation between finger gnosis and mathematical ability: Can we attribute function to cortical structure with cross-domain modeling? In*Proceedings of the 33rd Annual Cognitive Science Society* (pp. 2445–2450). Austin, TX: Cognitive Science Society.

Qin, S., Cho, S., Chen, T., Rosenberg-Lee, M., Geary, D. C., & Menon, V. (2014). Hippocampal-neocortical functional reorganization underlies children's cognitive development. *Nature Neuroscience, 17*, 1263–1269.

Ramani, G. B., & Siegler, R. S. (2008). Promoting broad and stable improvements in low-income children's numerical knowledge through playing number board games. *Child Development, 79*, 375–394.

Santiago, J., & Lakens, D. (2015). Can conceptual congruency effects between number, time, and space be accounted for by polarity correspondence? *Acta Psychologica, 156*, 179–191.

Saur, D., Kreher, B. W., Schnell, S., Kuemmerer, D., Kellermeyer, P., Vry, M.-S., et al. (2008). Ventral and dorsal pathways for language. *Proceedings of the National Academy of Sciences of the United States of America, 105*, 18035–18040.

Schneider, M., Grabner, R. H., & Paetsch, J. (2009). Mental number line, number line estimation, and mathematical achievement: Their interrelations in grades 5 and 6. *Journal of Educational Psychology, 101*, 359.

Shaki, S., & Fischer, M. H. (2014). Random walks on the mental number line. *Experimental Brain Research, 232*, 43–49.

Siegler, R. S., & Booth, J. L. (2004). Development of numerical estimation in young children. *Child Development, 75*(2), 428–444.

Simon, O., Kherif, F., Flandin, G., Poline, J. B., Rivière, D., Mangin, J. F., et al. (2004). Automatized clustering and functional geometry of human parietofrontal networks for language, space, and number. *Neuroimage, 23*, 1192–1202.

Simon, O., Mangin, J. F., Cohen, L., Le Bihan, D., & Dehaene, S. (2002). Topographical layout of hand, eye, calculation, and language-related areas in the human parietal lobe. *Neuron, 33*, 475–487.

Supekar, K., Swigart, A. G., Tenison, C., Jolles, D. D., Rosenberg-Lee, M., Fuchs, L., & Menon, V. (2013). Neural predictors of individual differences in response to math tutoring in primary-grade school children. *Proceedings of the National Academy of Sciences, 110*, 8230–8235.

Thevenot, C., Fanget, M., & Fayol, M. (2007). Retrieval or nonretrieval strategies in mental arithmetic? An operand recognition paradigm. *Memory & Cognition, 35*, 1344–1352.

Tschentscher, N., Hauk, O., Fischer, M. H., & Pulvermüller, F. (2012). You can count on the motor cortex: Finger counting habits modulate motor cortex activation evoked by numbers. *Neuroimage, 59*, 3139–3148.

Umarova, R. M., Saur, D., Schnell, S., Kaller, C. P., Vry, M. S., Glauche, V., et al. (2010). Structural connectivity for visuospatial attention: Significance of ventral pathways. *Cerebral Cortex, 20*, 121–129.

Umiltà, C., Priftis, K., & Zorzi, M. (2009). The spatial representation of numbers: Evidence from neglect and pseudoneglect. *Experimental Brain Research, 192*, 561–569.

Walsh, V. (2003). A theory of magnitude: Common cortical metrics of time, space and quantity. *Trends in Cognitive Sciences, 7*, 483–488.

Willmes, K., & Klein, E. (2014). Akalkulie [Acalculia]. In H.-O. Karnath, W. Ziegler, & G. Goldenberg (Eds.), *Klinische neuropsychologie—Kognitive neurologie* (pp. 133–146). Stuttgart: Thieme.

Wilson, A. J., & Dehaene, S. (2007). Number sense and developmental dyscalculia. In D. Coch, G. Dawson, & K. Fischer (Eds.), *Human behavior, learning, and the developing brain: Atypical development* (pp. 212–237). New York: Guilford Press.

Wilson, A. J., Revkin, S. K., Cohen, D., Cohen, L., & Dehaene, S. (2006). An open trial assessment of "The Number Race", an adaptive computer game for remediation of dyscalculia. *Behavioral and Brain Functions, 2*, 1.

Wilson, M. (2002). Six views of embodied cognition. *Psychonomic Bulletin & Review, 9*, 625–636.

Wood, G., Willmes, K., Nuerk, H.-C., & Fischer, M. H. (2008). On the cognitive link between space and number: A meta-analysis of the SNARC effect. *Psychology Science Quarterly, 50*, 489–525.

Wynn, K. (1992). Addition and subtraction by human infants. *Nature, 358*, 749–750.

Wyschkon, A., Poltz, N., Höse, A., von Aster, M., & Esser, G. (2015). Schwache Fingergnosie als Risikofaktor für zukünftiges Rechnen? *Lernen und Lernstörungen, 4*, 159–175.

Xu, F., Spelke, E. S., & Goddard, S. (2005). Number sense in human infants. *Developmental Science, 8*, 88–101.

Zaunmüeller, L., Domahs, F., Dressel, K., Lonnemann, J., Klein, E., Ischebeck, A., & Willmes, K. (2009). Rehabilitation of arithmetic fact retrieval via extensive practice. A combined fMRI and behavioural case-study. *Neuropsychological Rehabilitation, 19*, 422–443.

Zebian, S. (2005). Linkages between number concepts, spatial thinking, and directionality of writing: The SNARC effect and the reverse SNARC effect in English and Arabic monoliterates, biliterates, and illiterate Arabic speakers. *Journal of Cognition and Culture, 5*, 165–190.

Zorzi, M., Priftis, K., & Umiltà, C. (2002). Neglect disrupts the mental number line. *Nature, 417*, 138–139.

Chapter 3
Digital Pictures, Videos, and Beyond: Knowledge Acquisition with Realistic Images

Stephan Schwan

Abstract While the distinction between pictures and texts is well established on theoretical grounds and has attracted much research, the differences and common-alities between realistic depictions and its real-world counterparts have received much less attention. This chapter aims to contribute to closing this gap by systemati-cally comparing life-like images to real-world events in terms of commonalities and differences in visual appeal as well as in perception and mental processing. Based on the notion of a "dual character" of digital images, both closely resembling reality but simultaneously being systematically different, several issues regarding pro-cesses of knowledge acquisition will be discussed, including: Are viewers aware of differences between real-world information and mediated information—and do they take them into account? Do realistic images require specific competencies for comprehension? Should the realism of visual representations be maximized for learning? How do viewers deal with the informational complexity and ambiguity of realistic images?

Keywords Realistic pictures • Authenticity • Event cognition • Video

Introduction

Take a brief look at a current school textbook for biology, physics, geography, or history, and you will find that nearly 50 % of the page space is occupied by visual depictions the majority being realistic images (i.e., drawings or photographs that resemble real-world referents; Lee, 2010; Yasar & Seremet, 2007). Also, use of real-istic depictions in education is not restricted to static pictures in textbooks. Instead, according to a recent survey, moving images such as films and videos are the most frequent types of media used in German classrooms (Institut für Demoskopie Allensbach, 2013). This abundance of realistic depictions is not a new development. From the beginning, modern science and education has been coupled with usage of

S. Schwan (✉)
Leibniz-Institut für Wissensmedien, Schleichstraße 6, Tübingen 72076, Germany
e-mail: s.schwan@iwm-tuebingen.de

© Springer International Publishing AG 2017   41
S. Schwan, U. Cress (eds.), *The Psychology of Digital Learning*,
DOI 10.1007/978-3-319-49077-9_3

visual depictions as a means of storing and distributing knowledge—be it prints and engravings of plants and animals from distant countries, like Sybilla Merian's famous depictions of exotic insects or the portrayals of technological inventions and machinery in Diderot's Encyclopedia (Stafford, 1994). Ever since the nineteenth century, these early forms of illustrations have been increasingly complemented by advancements in technologies for recording and for mass distribution of images, such as lithography, photography, and filming.

Today, digitization has led to an even broader scope of realistic depictions. From satellites to CCTV, Google Street View and camera traps to webcams, dashcams, or action cams—almost all aspects of reality are portrayed and made available via large Internet repositories such as YouTube or Flickr. Also, scientific research routinely uses digital photographing and filming for documentation and explanation, again building large digital databases (e.g., the Europeana platform in the humanities) or channels for scholarly communication, like the Journal of Visualized Experiments (JoVE) in the science domain. Also, advancements in computer graphics today allow creation of life-like renderings and simulations of objects, scenes, processes, or events with unprecedented fidelity. Accordingly, all these types of digitized images have made their way into formal and informal education, as exemplified by advanced digital textbooks (e.g., Wilson's digital biology textbook *Life on Earth*), game-based learning scenarios, or current museum exhibitions on science or natural history (e.g., the Welcome Wing of the Science Museum in London).

Why do images (in the sense of realistic or iconic depictions of real-world phenomena) play such an important role in science and education? From the perspective of educational psychology, realistic images have usually been treated as one particular class of representational media, and accordingly, the main focus both of theorizing and of empirical research has been on comparing them with other types of representational media. In particular, the most influential models in the field have contrasted visual depictions (with realistic images as an important type) with texts, assuming a difference between depictional and descriptional modes of information presentation (Schnotz, 2002), which is reflected in different subsystems of cognitive processing (Mayer, 2001), in different working memory compartments (Baddeley, 2012), and in different mental representations in long-term memory (Paivio, 1986). Contrasting pictures with text is not only motivated by the fact that both are the dominant modes of disseminating information in our culture, but also by its fundamental differences in terms of representational characteristics (Schnotz, 2002). Texts are based on arbitrary signs, conform to a grammar specifying rules of combining words to larger meaningful chunks, and easily allow for abstractions, generalizations, negations, changes of tempus, or counterfactual arguments. In contrast, pictures are organized in a two- or even three-dimensional manner, do not possess definite basic components (like words), do not conform to syntactical rules but, on the other hand, typically provide the viewer with a denser and detailed array of information which does not follow a single explicit argument and instead allows for inspection regarding various different purposes and questions. Pictures as a certain class of representational media may be further decomposed into logical pictures, such as graphs and diagrams, and images, with the latter having a relationship of resemblance to real-world phenomena. According to Peirce (1940), this relationship can be described as iconic because some visual regularities (like shape or color) of real-world phenomena are mapped onto corresponding visual regularities of the image. Depending on the amount of mapped regularities, the resulting images may range from simple black and white line drawings to film clips with a high visual fidelity.

Scholarly discussion of the role of images in education has often focused on their illustrative, "decorative" purposes. It is assumed that while realistic visualizations may make learning material more attractive, thereby possibly heightening students' motivation and interest, simultaneously they may hinder acquisition of relevant knowledge, eventually distracting students from processing and elaborating the relevant learning matter (which is thought to be primarily provided by texts, graphs, and diagrams; Magner, Schwonke, Aleven, Popescu, & Renkl, 2014; Rey, 2012). Still, realistic visualizations should not be reduced to mere decoration. Instead, the role of images in knowledge acquisition is far more diverse: They may present visual details that are difficult to describe verbally, may make spatial relations be easily picked up perceptually, or may specify the minute changes of biological movement patterns.

While the distinction between pictures and texts is well established on theoretical grounds and has attracted a considerable amount of research, another relevant distinction has received much less attention, namely, the differences and commonalities between realistic depictions and their real-world counterparts; that is, as an alternative, the content of most images can not only be described in words, but can also be perceived and experienced in a direct, unmediated way (at least in principle). A chemical experiment may be shown as a video or it may be verbally described in a textbook; however, it may also be directly demonstrated in the classroom. Similarly, famous architectures, important historical sites, or geomorphologic interesting landscapes can be portrayed as images, described in words, but can also be inspected directly on location. Starting from the distinction between image and real world, both the theoretical perspective and the corresponding research questions change fundamentally. Now we may ask: How does our perceptual and cognitive apparatus deal with life-like pictorial representations? Are they processed in a similar way to real, unmediated percepts or do they require certain kinds of specific visual literacy? Is knowledge acquisition by means of realistic images comparable to real, unmediated visual experiences? How can the differences between both modes of experience be systematically exploited for designing appropriate learning material? Accordingly, possible theoretical underpinnings of this approach can be found in models of everyday perception (Gibson, 1979) and event cognition (Zacks & Tversky, 2001) instead of in theories of text comprehension or models of multimedia learning.

Current developments in digital technologies will make these issues even more relevant. Not only has the realistic appeal of many digital images become nearly perfect—from CGX (i.e., digital effects) in movies to immersive consumer technologies like Oculus Rift. Also, digital technology has left the standard computer cases and has started to inhabit many different devices and objects, from smart watches to home heating, blurring more and more the borderline between reality and digital virtuality. Part of next generation educational tools will not be based on didactically motivated decisions between images and words or combinations of them, but on decisions between life-like visualizations and real-life experiences or, again, combinations of them. Therefore, in the following, I will try to sketch this alternative view of processing digital images for knowledge acquisition in more detail. In particular, I will explore certain questions about the implications of inspecting (static or dynamic) pictorial representations for learning, which look life-like but nevertheless systematically differ from real life in a number of relevant ways.

Real-Life Presentations and Life-Like Representations: Commonalities and Differences

One obvious purpose of realistic depictions is to reproduce a view of a certain real-world phenomenon in a permanent way, thus serving as a materialized, external kind of visual memory. Observing or scrutinizing this phenomenon is thereby no longer bound to its existence at a certain place and time, but instead becomes independent of it. In many circumstances, this is important, for example, if the phenomenon is singular and short-lived or if it cannot be inspected in real life due to its geographical distance—think of the pictures that NASA's "New Horizon" sent from the outer parts of our solar system as the most extreme case. In other words, realistic images allow for cultural transmission of visual information across space and time.

Of course, images do not keep record of a relevant event, object, or any other real-world phenomenon in its entirety but are mostly restricted to its visual appearance, lacking information about its nonoptical aspects, for instance, its acoustics, its odor, or its tactile qualities. On the other hand, images may also result from transforming information that exceeds the scope of the human visual system, as is the case for X-ray, fMRI, or infrared images, as well as microscopic or telescopic depictions. Additionally, with regard to their visual appearance, images may greatly vary in the visual details that they preserve, ranging from high-solution photographs to simple line drawings, from black and white renderings to nuanced color reproductions, or from single view static depictions to dynamic portrayals that capture a phenomenon's changes across time and from different viewpoints. But no matter how restricted the visual fidelity of an image may be, usually it will still keep an iconic relationship to its referent scene.

Although, strictly speaking, iconicity implies a resemblance to real-world referents, the origin of a given image need not necessarily stem from a direct optical source. While in photographs and films a visual array is retained through optical and chemical processes, other types of images are constructed in a more indirect way by drawing, painting, or use of digital tools. As a consequence, such processes of construction may even portray scenes that have no current real-world counterpart in a realistic manner, as in the case of archaeological reconstructions or imagined future scenarios.

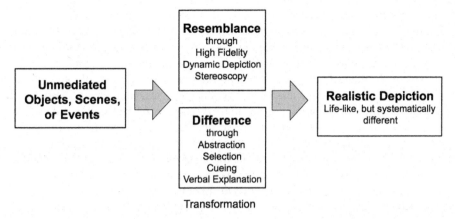

Fig. 3.1 Transforming unmediated objects, scenes, or events into realistic depictions

Due to the mentioned differences, digital images may, on the one hand, be legitimately considered as impoverished surrogates of real-world entities. But, on the other hand, by transforming a given phenomenon into a realistic pictorial representation, the status of the phenomenon is changed as well. From its pure existence, it is transformed into a document that may serve various epistemic purposes, including scientific reasoning and teaching. In particular, because of their loose coupling with reality, images may be tailored according to educational purposes. This is something that could not be accomplished under real-life conditions, for example, by selecting and simplifying content, by adding further layers of information, or by cueing learners' attention. From this "dual character" of digital images (see Fig. 3.1), both closely resembling reality but simultaneously being systematically different, several questions arise regarding processes of knowledge acquisition that will now be discussed in turn.

Are Viewers Aware of the Differences Between Real-World Information and Mediated Information—And Do They Take Them Into Account?

First of all, do viewers readily notice the difference between a real, unmediated object, scene, or event and its pictorial representation—and do they take this difference into account for their information processing behavior? Like in Magritte's famous painting of a pipe, entitled "Ceci n'est pas une pipe," viewers should be aware that an image of an object has a visual resemblance to the real object, but lacks its functionality; that is, the picture may be looked at and inspected visually, but the depicted object cannot be used according to its real-world purposes. We addressed the cognitive implications of this difference in a number of studies in a museum setting (Hampp & Schwan, 2014, 2015; Schwan, Bauer, Kampschulte, & Hampp, in press). We designed several display cabinets at the Deutsches Museum in Munich in which we either placed real objects or corresponding life-size photographs, together with additional material (texts, graphs) informing about nanotechnology and health technology. Although highly similar in their optical information, photographs were inspected less intensively than their real counterparts. Also, after a delay of about 1 h, visitors remembered fewer details of the exhibits if they had seen them as photographs and not as real objects. In line with these findings, a recent study by Sareen, Ehinger, and Wolfe (2015) showed that viewers differentiate ontologically even when inspecting photographs. Sareen et al. presented photos showing scenes of rooms filled with objects that also contained large mirrors reflecting these objects. They found that within the photographs, viewers paid more attention to the objects than to the objects' reflections in the mirror. Taken together, these results indicate that the perceived ontological status of a presentation (real object vs. photography) serves as a metacognitive cue that may modulate the amount of cognitive resources devoted to its processing. Surely, this presupposes that the ontological status of a given presentation can be easily perceived. While this is normally the case even for stereoscopic, three-dimensional representations such as virtual realities (because they rely on salient technical equipment), the ontological status may be blurred for three-dimensional, material reproductions of objects. Here, a new research field for the role of perceived authenticity for information processing and learning opens up.

Do Realistic Images Require Specific Competencies for Comprehension?

As discussed above, images should not be conceived as simple reflections of the real world, but differ from it in a more fundamental way with the introduction of new forms of depiction that have no real-world counterparts. This is particularly true for moving images because for them a repertoire of stylistic means have been developed, including film cuts, zooms, or slow motion, among other things, that provides perceptual experiences substantially deviating from conditions of natural vision. Hence, the question arises whether (static or moving) images require some additional visual literacy beyond the competencies used for natural real-world perception and cognition. Early studies by Hochberg and Brooks with children (1962) and Hudson (1967) with members of cultures that lack images have demonstrated that photographs or even line drawings of familiar objects normally are correctly perceived and identified. In contrast, other drawing conventions such as the inclusion of a horizontal line or placing distant objects in the upper part of a picture and showing them at smaller scale are often misinterpreted by viewers who are unfamiliar with pictures (Hudson, 1967). This indicates that, for appropriate interpretation of drawings, principles of natural perception are not sufficient and have to be complemented by some initial experience with pictorial representations.

Similar arguments also apply to perception of moving images. On the one hand, films are more realistic than static pictures because they additionally preserve temporal characteristics of scenes and events. But this is complemented by a set of cinematic techniques which introduce some substantial differences to conditions of real-world perception. Thus, as for static images, the issue of film-specific competencies is of relevance. We addressed this topic in two studies that we conducted with adults unfamiliar with film, living in a difficult-to-access mountain region in southern Turkey (Schwan & Ildirar, 2010; Ildirar & Schwan, 2015). In individual sessions at their homes, they were shown a set of short video clips, each containing a different type of common cinematic techniques such as a shot-reverse-shot, a temporal gap, an eye line match, or an establishing shot. The cinematic techniques were classified according to the relation between adjacent shots. Shots were linked either by visual, causal, or conceptual overlap. In the case of visual overlap, substantial parts of the scene (e.g., a salient object or person) were shown in both shots. In the case of causal overlap, shots were linked by sequences of activities (not necessarily implying visual overlap), while in the case of conceptual overlap, shots were linked on the basis of semantic relations (e.g., the front of a mosque followed by a prayer inside the mosque). By asking the viewers to describe each video immediately after presentation, we found that the viewers unfamiliar with film had no problem describing the individual shots, indicating that they had understood the objects and activities shown in the videos, but they were often unable to link the shots appropriately. Thus, only a small subset of filmic devices was intelligible to them, whereas a control group of viewers familiar with film and having a similar cultural background gave appropriate descriptions for the whole set of videos. Surprisingly, it was not visual overlap between shots that primarily contributed to immediate comprehension. Instead, shots linked by a sequence of familiar activities were most intelligible to those unfamiliar with film, suggesting that in moving images, the existence of a kind of familiar "story line" helps film novices to comprehend filmic techniques that are at odds with conditions of natural perception.

While filmic means constitute comprehension obstacles for film novices, experienced viewers typically do not show comprehension problems regarding cinematic techniques. In contrast, due to the high amount of time that viewers spend watching films or TV, viewers become so familiar with filmic means that they tend to go unnoticed. Therefore, another facet of visual literacy is to become aware of and critically reflect on filmic means in persuasive contexts like TV ads or propaganda films. This issue was addressed by Merkt and Sochatzy (2015) in two experiments. They found that ninth graders had problems to spontaneously identify persuasive visual film techniques such as the use of low or high camera angles that let persons appear to be powerful or powerless, respectively. Both by training and by cueing specific cinematic techniques during film presentation, the identification rate increased and also transferred to new films without such cues. Thus, in terms of knowledge acquisition from static or moving images, visual literacy goes well beyond the basic skills of identifying pictorial elements and events, and it also includes awareness of filmic techniques and their manipulative power.

Should Realism of Visual Representations Be Maximized for Learning?

At first sight, maximizing realism seems to be the natural strategy for design of images because the more life-like a pictorial representation is, the more it can serve as a substitute for real-life entities. But while a maximum of realism may be indicated for purposes of documentation, research has demonstrated that for learning and knowledge acquisition it might not be the best option. In particular, instead of presenting objects, scenes, or events in rich detail, abstraction by highlighting relevant aspects while leaving out irrelevant or accidental ones may make images serve better for learning (Gerjets, 2017). Therefore, in some studies viewers of simple line drawings outperformed viewers of photorealistic depictions in terms of learning and understanding, both for static (Dwyer, 1968) and dynamic visualizations (Scheiter, Gerjets, Huk, Imhof, & Kammerer, 2009).

Similarly, while films or animations preserve the temporal qualities of a procedure, an activity, or an event with high fidelity, this gain in temporal realism may be outweighed by the transience of the presentation, making it difficult to identify and process its individual steps (Tversky, Bauer Morrison, & Betrancourt, 2002). Depending on the specific learning task, this interplay of opposing factors may either favor the use of dynamic visualizations (like films or animations), or static ones (e.g., comic strip-like sequences of pictures). Accordingly, Lowe and Schnotz (2014) emphasize the fit between the requirements of the learning task and the preservation of corresponding dimensions of pictorial realism. For instance, for comprehending a sequence of several clearly distinguishable steps, a display of the temporal transitions is often not necessary. Therefore, for this type of learning task, several studies have shown that sets of static pictures can be at least as effective for learning as dynamic depictions (e.g., Hegarty, Kriz, & Cate, 2003). However, in other cases such as learning to reproduce a certain pattern of continuous movements, the specifics of temporal transitions require a higher temporal fidelity, thus making dynamic visualizations a more appropriate form of learning material.

A further facet of task appropriateness relates to the congruence of format of learning and format of testing. In a recent series of experiments, we asked participants to learn a set of kanji signs (Soemer & Schwan, 2016). We systematically varied presentation mode (static, static sequential, animated), task requirements (identifying the sign, knowing the stroke order, knowing drawing direction of the individual strokes), and testing mode (static, static sequential, animated). In the experiments, congruence of presentation mode and testing mode (i.e., static-static, static sequential—static sequential) was shown to have the strongest impact on learners' testing performance, well above compatibility of presentation mode and task requirements. Besides important practical consequences, the theoretical implication of these findings is to extend the notion of realism beyond the resemblance between real-world situation and visual presentation in the learning phase to also include the resemblance between visual representation and perceptual circumstances during testing.

Taken together, research both from line drawings and from animations demonstrates that in the realm of learning, pictorial realism is not a value in itself but must be considered in the light of specific learning goals and their information requirements. This is also true for recent advancements in realistic depictions such as stereoscopic presentations (Schwan & Papenmeier, in press). Stereoscopic presentations heighten realism by adding binocular disparity as a further depth cue. While this has been shown to be beneficial for training of complex manual tasks requiring eye-hand-coordination (e.g., medical surgery tasks), advantages for other types of learning content are still under debate. In a series of experiments, participants were presented molecule-like objects, either stereoscopically or monoscopically, which they afterwards had to recognize as accurately and as fast as possible, again either stereoscopically or monoscopically (Papenmeier & Schwan, 2016). We found that learners benefited from stereoscopic presentation in the test phase, while in the learning phase, presenting the molecule-like objects as a continuously rotating animation turned out to be as effective as presenting them stereoscopically. Hence, while stereoscopic presentation enhances realism, its contribution beyond more traditional types of presentations (like the animations in the present case) seems to be limited.

Can Systematic Deviations from Realism Help Comprehension?

Above it has been shown that differences between real-world states and realistic depictions should not be regarded as deficiencies that have to be overcome by advanced technologies that provide a more and more perfect illusion of reality. Instead, in terms of comprehension and knowledge acquisition, deviations from reality may even be purposefully exploited for optimizing the content to be learned for perceptual and cognitive processing. In the past years, this topic has been systematically explored in our lab particularly for realistic dynamic visualizations such as animations and films. In particular, we were interested how the range of design options that dynamic visualizations provide for the portrayal of real-world activities and events may be used for fostering comprehension.

In a first set of experiments, we investigated how the structure of unfamiliar events or activities can be made more salient for viewers. Observers tend to spontaneously segment real-world activities like troubleshooting a machine or assembling a device into a series of discrete segments, separated by event boundaries. Identification of event boundaries and structuring an event accordingly has been shown to be an important prerequisite for event comprehension (Hard, Lozano, & Tversky, 2006). This may pose a problem for viewers who are confronted with a new and unfamiliar event. By analyzing several educational movies produced for classroom presentation in Germany, we found that learners preferably placed event boundaries at the occurrence of formal filmic features such as film cuts (Schwan,

Garsoffky, & Hesse, 1998). In a laboratory study (Schwan, Garsoffky, & Hesse, 2000), we found that placing film cuts at natural event boundaries made the boundaries more salient to viewers who were not familiar with the activity. Additionally, use of film cuts at event boundaries increased recall of the event sequences shown in the films. These findings indicate that by informed use of film techniques, comprehension can be fostered by highlighting the structure of unfamiliar events or activities.

Natural event boundaries can also be used to make learning more efficient by producing event summaries instead of presenting an event over its whole course. From basic research on event cognition, it is known that content at event boundaries is processed more deeply and remembered better than content at non-boundary points in time (Zacks, Speer, Swallow, Braver, & Reynolds, 2007). This indicates that observer tend to preferably select and memorize event boundaries as a kind of compact characterization of the corresponding event segment. Accordingly, preselecting these boundaries in event portrayals may serve as an effective event summary that condenses an event to its most important parts while leaving out irrelevant or redundant aspects. This hypothesis was confirmed in an experiment in which viewers were either shown complete records of events, event summaries consisting of film shots around event boundaries, or event summaries consisting of film shots around non-boundaries (Schwan & Garsoffky, 2004). We found that viewers of event-boundary summaries recalled largely the same event parts as the viewers of the complete event, whereas viewers' recall of the non-boundary summaries corresponded to a much lesser extent to the recall found in the complete event condition. These results indicate that by systematic deviation from real-world conditions, video recordings may forestall cognitive selection processes, thereby making learning more efficient.

Event presentations can also be optimized in terms of the visual perspective from which they are shown. It has been demonstrated that not only static spatial layouts, but also dynamically changing object constellations are mentally represented in a viewpoint-dependent manner (Garsoffky, Schwan, & Hesse, 2002). Also, not all viewpoints are equally well suited for recognition and recall. Instead, the so-called canonical viewpoints that maximize visibility of an object's or event's characteristic features have been shown to possess cognitive processing advantages over noncanonical views (Garsoffky, Schwan, & Huff, 2009). Again, this opens up a number of possibilities for designing realistic images for learning. In real-life presentations, viewing conditions on an object or phenomenon are often suboptimal due to a number of restrictions (e.g., distance is too large, object is partly occluded by other viewers, object is seen from an oblique viewing angle). In contrast, by appropriate choice of viewing distance and angle, images can present objects in an optimized manner.

For events, matters are more complicated because appropriate viewing position may frequently change during the course of event. Again, in real life, these changes are often difficult to carry out, while in videos staging, film techniques, and postproduction allow for adapting viewing position through an event's course. Yet, as another set of experiments in our lab has shown, frequently changing viewpoints come also with some cognitive costs. In particular, abrupt changes of viewing position by film cuts is correlated with loss of spatial orientation and comprehension of spatial configurations, compared to static or continuously changing viewpoints (Garsoffky, Huff, & Schwan, 2007; Huff, Jahn, & Schwan, 2009; Meyerhoff, Huff, Papenmeier, Jahn, & Schwan, 2011). However, producers of instructional films or animations can counteract these problems by adhering to certain principles of film design. In particular, since the early times of Hollywood cinema, the so-called continuity editing rules have been established that tend to make the transitions between shots as unnoticeable (and thereby as intelligible) to the viewers as possible. Part of the continuity editing system is the centerline rule that regulates the viewing positions of adjacent shots, stating that changes in viewing perspective are easily processed as long as the camera stays on the same side of the main axis of action across the cut. In a recent study, we could demonstrate that viewers indeed spontaneously rely on this rule, shortcutting elaborate alignment processes in favor of a simple spatial heuristic which helped them keep spatially oriented across cuts at minimal cognitive processing demands (Huff & Schwan, 2012a). Again, the findings of these studies demonstrate how systematic deviations from perceptual conditions of real-life (in this case by use of film cuts introducing "unnatural" abrupt changes of viewing position) may be utilized for making the spatial structure of ongoing events comprehensible to learners.

As a final example, consider the temporal characteristics of events, which sometimes unfold at a speed which is difficult to handle perceptually or cognitively. This is true on both sides of the temporal scale, encompassing events that unfold at a very high or at a very slow speed (think of high speed collisions on the one hand or growth of plants on the other). Again, creating depictions that systematically deviate from a natural time scale may substantially facilitate learners' comprehension of the underlying processes and mechanisms. In one study, we had learners watch for ten minutes a video showing the inner workings of a mechanical pendulum clock, either in real time or in fast motion (Fischer, Lowe, & Schwan, 2008). We found that viewers of the fast motion depiction better understood the basic principles of pendulum clocks in terms of the regulating role of both the clock's weight and its anchor mechanism. This was because by speeding up the presentation, the operation of these elements became more salient to the participants, which in turn helped them to make more correct inferences about the underlying physical forces at play. In a second study, presenting the clockwork at a higher speed proved to be more effective for comprehension than highlighting the relevant elements of the clock's mechanism by color coding (Fischer & Schwan, 2010).

Overall, the results of the described studies indicate that models of perception and cognition may inform design options that foster memory and comprehension by systematically introducing certain deviations from realism. These deviations include, among others, additional formal structures by cuts, optimization of viewing position by abrupt changes of perspective, or use of slow or fast motion to make dynamic changes during events more salient and comprehensible.

How to Deal with the Informational Complexity and Ambiguity of Realistic Images?

In a seminal study, Yarbus (1967) had viewers look at a picture of a family scene with different goals such as forming an impression of the depicted persons or understanding the activities taking place. Depending on the task at hand, the viewing patterns of the participants were quite different, indicating that their course of processing the picture did substantially differ. Put in more general terms, realistic images, both static and dynamic, usually contain an abundance of elements and details and are open for various different interpretations, thus leaving it up to the viewer which information to extract to answer a specific question or to solve a specific task. Yet, while images are inherently "goal-free" at first sight, particularly in educational contexts, they serve as tools for visual communication based on a specific didactic intention. Therefore, producers of learning materials face the task of guiding the viewers' attention to those elements and attributes of an image that they consider relevant for the current learning goal. Also, cueing attention is even more pressing for dynamic images with their transient, rapidly changing visual content.

While multimedia research has focused mainly on overt forms of cueing important pictorial elements, including graphic signs such as arrows, color coding, shadowing or overlay of expert eye movements (see van Gog, 2014 for an overview), a number of design strategies already discussed in the previous section allow for more unobtrusive, covert means of guiding viewers' spatiotemporal distribution of attention, including simplification of content by line drawings instead of photorealistic depictions or summarizing events by leaving out its non-boundary parts. Also, the mentioned principles of continuity editing in films have been interpreted as instruments for attention guidance (Smith, 2012) but have not been systematically related to learning and knowledge acquisition to date. Additionally, strategies of camera movement, like zooming-in or panning, are frequently found in educational movies (for instance, in the form of the so-called Ken Burns effect, where camera movements are used to visually explore static historical documents such as prints or photographs), but with few exceptions (e.g., Salomon & Cohen, 1977), the analysis of their effects on learning and understanding still awaits systematic empirical research.

New technologies also open up innovative strategies for scaffolding viewers' attention. For instance, autostereoscopic displays allow viewers to switch between different pairs of similar images by slight movements of head (similar to a vexing image) without any necessity for recalibrating attention (e.g., by means of a saccade). In one study, we asked participants to solve a structural task with pairs of different visualizations of complex proteins, namely, a stick-and-ball model and a wireframe model of the protein (Huff, Bauhoff, & Schwan, 2012). The pairs of visualizations were either presented side-by-side, overlaid, or via vexing image display. We found that particularly viewers with low spatial abilities benefitted significantly from the vexing image condition, which helped them to identify corresponding parts of the molecules, thereby minimizing detrimental split attention effects.

Finally, adding written or spoken explanations is a further common strategy of shaping viewers' processing and interpretation of (static or moving) images, ranging from audio guides in museums to narrators in educational films and teacher's explanations in classrooms. Regarding the interplay of text and pictures, several models have been proposed, both in cognitive psychology (Schooler, & Engstler-Schooler, 1990; Yee & Sedivy, 2006) and in educational psychology (Mayer, 2001), that build a theoretical basis for addressing issues of verbal guidance. For instance, verbal overshadowing research indicates that giving a verbal explanation after presentation of an image may decrease the accuracy of memory for pictorial details because the more abstract verbal description interferes with the more concrete visual representation (Schooler, & Engstler-Schooler, 1990). We confirmed and extended this effect in several studies, showing that memory for visual details of an event decreased if its observation was followed by a verbal description (verbal overshadowing), but in contrast, giving a verbal description before observing an event facilitated memory for visual event details instead, presumably because the verbal description serves as an abstract scheme in which visual event details can subsequently be integrated (verbal facilitation; Huff & Schwan, 2008, 2012b, see also Eitel & Scheiter, 2015, Scheiter, Schüler, & Eitel, this volume).

Most often, verbal descriptions and explanations are given not prior or after, but concurrently to viewing a picture. Here, models of multimedia learning (Mayer, 2001) provide a well-established framework of analysis. By assuming separate processing channels for visual and audio information, they posit that, in general, presenting both pictorial and verbal information should lead to better learning and understanding than relying on just one type of information (multimedia effect) and that learning also benefits from complementing pictures with spoken instead of written information (modality effect).

While traditional formulations of the multimedia model treat pictures as illustrative text supplements and ask primarily how the addition of pictures may foster text comprehension, we were interested in the complementary issue, treating text as a complement to images and asking how the addition of text may foster processing of realistic images (Glaser & Schwan, 2015). Working with (fictitious) depictions of reconstructed historical buildings accompanied by audio-guide-like explanations, we found that mentioning a pictorial element in the text led viewers immediately to turn their attention to that element, as indicated by a highly synchronous fixation pattern across participants. Also, in a subsequent memory test, these pictorial elements were better recalled than pictorial elements that were not mentioned in the audio explanation. Overall, the results of the Glaser and Schwan (2015) study indicate that the multimedia effect can be extended, now stating that a combination of pictures and texts fosters learning better than either text or picture alone. Additionally, the findings suggest that accompanying pictures with text provide a twofold advantage both by guiding attention to relevant pictorial elements and by linking these pictorial elements with additional text information. Also, a similar extension from text to images was demonstrated for the modality principle (Dutz & Schwan, 2014). In an experimental art exhibition, the artworks were accompanied by explanations either as labels placed beside each work, as digital text on an iPad, or as spoken text in an audio guide. In line with the modality principle, we found that memory for pictorial details of the artworks was best for audio guide, compared to both text on a label or text on an iPad.

Taken together, these results demonstrate that besides covert visual design principles and overt graphical cues, accompanying (spoken) text does play a major for guiding viewers' attention in complex realistic pictures. Yet, while the addition of spoken text to pictures has been shown to be beneficial for learning, casual observation from various audio guides in museums indicates that, depending on its linguistic features, texts may fulfill this purpose to a higher or lesser degree. Future research will have to determine in more detail what kinds of texts (in terms of organization, formulation, etc.) will be suited best for helping viewers to scrutinize and interpret a given complex image.

Realistic Images and the Active Learner

A last question pertains to overt learning activities that realistic images may afford, which is of particularly importance for moving images as in educational movies, TV documentaries, or video-based lectures from the Internet. Typically lasting several minutes to even an hour or more, they each provide a high amount of densely packed and transient content that the learner has to deal with. Whereas voluminous static media such as books or comics allow readers to inspect their content at will, regulating pace and sequence of their information intake by decreasing or increasing reading speed, rereading difficult parts, or skipping back and forth between pages, possibilities for active regulation of information is significantly more restricted for traditional forms of moving images. For example, besides starting and stopping from time to time, educational films are typically screened in classrooms via VCR without many intervening activities by the teacher or students (Hobbs, 2006).

Digital videos offer new possibilities for individualized, active learning. They allow viewers to regulate their information intake in ways similar to reading books, including stopping the presentation, changing presentation speed (analogous to decrease or increase reading speed), or viewing parts of the video several times (analogous to rereading a text passage several times; Merkt, Weigand, Heier, & Schwan, 2011). Thus, viewers of digital videos are offered advanced opportunities for information acquisition that observers of real-life situations typically lack: Most often, a real-life event cannot be easily slowed down, stopped, or repeated at will. This advantage of interactively viewing a realistic event over its noninteractive observation has also been demonstrated experimentally. Using nautical knots as an example, learners of interactive videos demonstrating the tying of various nautical knots spontaneously used the available features (such as stop, rewind, slow, or fast motion) and thereby outperformed learners of respective noninteractive videos in efficiency of learning to tie the respective knot (Schwan & Riempp, 2004).

Matters get more complicated if we turn from simple recordings of real-life events or activities (like tying a nautical knot) to realistic audiovisual presentation that depict more complex matters, as with explaining historical developments by use of authentic news footage or demonstrating principles of physics with filmed experiments while making extensive use of filmic design features (such as changes of perspective, skipping irrelevant event episodes, and so on) discussed in the previous sections. First, it can be argued that such dynamic audiovisual material has already been optimized for learning by its authors, reducing the necessity for interactive control. In line with this notion, we found that for TV documentaries of principles of physics, learners spontaneously built causal bridging inferences during viewing, despite the videos' fast pace and transience of information (Tibus, Heier, & Schwan, 2013).

Second, it can also be argued that complex educational films require interaction opportunities that go beyond local regulation of information intake by control of presentation speed and allow for direct access of information within a given video. In order to address this issue, we implemented additional tools for information access into an educational film about post-war Germany that were analogous to those in textbooks such as the table of content and alphabetical register (Merkt et al., 2011). Both in the laboratory and in a classroom setting, we found that students used these interactive options only to a small degree. Accordingly, while the interactive features did help students to quickly locate certain bits of information in the film, it did not substantially improve the quality of students' essays about the film's topic (Merkt et al., 2011). In a second study, students' lack of appropriate usage strategies could be identified as one important reason for these findings (Merkt & Schwan, 2014). Thus, if interactive features like a table of contents and an alphabetical register were available and students were trained in active use of videos, these features would not only be used to a substantial degree but also would increase the quality of the students' essays about the film's historical content.

Taken together, the reported findings indicate that introducing possibilities for interaction into realistic moving images is not as simple as it seems at first sight. On the one hand, interactivity gives learners new ways of controlling a video's flow of information, thereby adapting it to her individual cognitive needs. On the other hand, control options not only presuppose some knowledge and skills for appropriate use, but also require additional mental resources for planning and execution (Scheiter, 2014). Also, in contrast to real-life events, realistic moving images may already be designed for learning and knowledge acquisition without the necessity of leaving optimizing information presentation up to the learner herself. For example, by extending film shots or by introducing explicit brief pauses, information density can be reduced and effects of transience minimized without requiring viewers to plan and execute pauses themselves. Further research on the interplay of shaping information presentation by film design versus by the learners' individual activity is needed, in particular, against the backdrop of a proliferation of video material on the Internet.

Conclusion

Due to the digitalization of everyday life, today we face a continuous blurring of the distinction between the real and the virtual. As part of this process, digital types of realistic images including photographs, videos, or virtual reality renderings play an increasingly important role in learning scenarios. This is particularly true for informal learning settings such as museums, television, or the Internet, where realistic visualizations offer the opportunity to present content in a vivid, motivating, and comprehensible way (Glaser, Garsoffky, & Schwan, 2009, 2012; Schwan, Grajal, & Lewalter, 2014; Töpper, Glaser, & Schwan, 2014). While research on differences and commonalities between text and pictures has a long-standing tradition in educational psychology, this chapter aimed to outline a complementary perspective of comparing realistic depictions with conditions of real-life experience. Despite all its similarities, digital images (both static and moving) are not simply reflections of reality, but should instead be seen as purposefully designed modes of presenting information in a comprehensible way. This can be achieved by numerous strategies, ranging from carefully staging objects or events to use of cinematographic techniques to addition of guiding cues or supplementary explanations. This blending of realism with didactical design not only leads to unique forms of learning material that stand in-between real-life experiences and symbolic forms of information presentation (like texts or graphs), but opens up a number of fundamental research questions regarding the relationship between vivid life-like experiences and processes of learning and knowledge acquisition.

References

Baddeley, A. (2012). Working memory: Theories, models, and controversies. *Annual Review Psychology, 63*, 1–29.

Dutz, S., & Schwan, S. (2014). *New media use in art exhibitions: Enriching or annoying?* Paper presented at the 27th Annual Visitor Studies Association Conference, Albuquerque, USA.

Dwyer, F. M. (1968). Effect of varying amount of realistic detail in visual illustrations designed to complement programmed instruction. *Perceptual and Motor Skills, 27*, 351–354.

Eitel, A., & Scheiter, K. (2015). Picture or text first? Explaining sequence effects when learning with pictures and text. *Educational Psychology Review, 27*, 153–180.

Fischer, S., Lowe, R. K., & Schwan, S. (2008). Effects of presentation speed of a dynamic visualization on the understanding of a mechanical system. *Applied Cognitive Psychology, 22*, 1126–1141.

Fischer, S., & Schwan, S. (2010). Comprehending animations. Effects of spatial cueing versus temporal scaling. *Learning and Instruction, 20*, 465–475.

Garsoffky, B., Huff, M., & Schwan, S. (2007). Changing viewpoints during dynamic events. *Perception, 36*, 366–374.

Garsoffky, B., Schwan, S., & Hesse, F. W. (2002). Viewpoint dependency in the recognition of dynamic scenes. *Journal of Experimental Psychology: Learning, Memory, and Cognition, 28*, 1035–1050.

Garsoffky, B., Schwan, S., & Huff, M. (2009). Canonical views of dynamic scenes. *Journal of Experimental Psychology: Human Perception and Performance, 35*, 17–27.

Gerjets, P. (2017). Learning and Problem Solving with Hypermedia in the 21st Century: From Hypertext to Multiple Web Sources and Multimodal Adaptivity.

Gibson, J. J. (1979). *The ecological approach to visual perception*. Boston, MA: Houghton Mifflin.

Glaser, M., Garsoffky, B., & Schwan, S. (2009). Narrative-based learning: possible benefits and problems. *The European Journal of Communication Research, 34*, 429–447.

Glaser, M., Garsoffky, B., & Schwan, S. (2012). What do we learn from docutainment? Processing hybrid television documentaries. *Learning and Instruction, 22*, 37–46.

Glaser, M., & Schwan, S. (2015). Explaining pictures: How verbal cues influence processing of pictorial learning material. *Journal of Educational Psychology, 107*, 1006–1018.

Hampp, C., & Schwan, S. (2014). Perception and evaluation of authentic objects: Findings from a visitor study. *Museum Management and Curatorship, 29*, 349–367.

Hampp, C., & Schwan, S. (2015). The role of authentic objects in museums of the history of science and technology: Findings from a visitor study. *International Journal of Science Education Part B: Communication and Public Engagement, 5*, 161–181.

Hard, B. M., Lozano, S. C., & Tversky, B. (2006). Hierarchical encoding of behavior: Translating perception into action. *Journal of Experimental Psychology: General, 135*, 588–608.

Hegarty, M., Kriz, S., & Cate, C. (2003). The roles of mental animations and external animations in understanding mechanical systems. *Cognition and Instruction, 21*, 325–360.

Hobbs, R. (2006). Non-optimal uses of video in the classroom. *Learning, Media and Technology, 31*, 35–50.

Hochberg, J., & Brooks, V. (1962). Pictorial recognition as an unlearned ability: A study of one child's performance. *The American Journal of Psychology, 75*, 624–628.

Hudson, W. (1967). The study of the problem of pictorial perception among unacculturated groups. *International Journal of Psychology, 2*, 89–107.

Huff, M., Bauhoff, V., & Schwan, S. (2012). Effects of split attention revisited: A new display technology for troubleshooting tasks. *Computers in Human Behavior, 28*, 1254–1261.

Huff, M., Jahn, G., & Schwan, S. (2009). Tracking multiple objects across abrupt viewpoint changes. *Visual Cognition, 17*, 297–306.

Huff, M., & Schwan, S. (2008). Verbalizing events: Overshadowing or facilitation? *Memory & Cognition, 36*, 392–402.

Huff, M., & Schwan, S. (2012a). Do not cross the line: Heuristic spatial updating in dynamic scenes. *Psychonomic Bulletin & Review, 19*, 1065–1072.

Huff, M., & Schwan, S. (2012b). The verbal facilitation effect in learning to tie nautical knots. *Learning and Instruction, 22*, 376–385.

Ildirar, S., & Schwan, S. (2015). First-time viewers' comprehension of films: Bridging shot transitions. *British Journal of Psychology, 106*, 133–151.

Institut für Demoskopie Allensbach (2013). Digitale Medien im Unterricht (Digital media in the classroom). Retrieved from http://www.ifd-allensbach.de/uploads/tx_studies/Digitale_Medien_2013.pdf

Lee, V. R. (2010). Adaptations and continuities in the use and design of visual representations in US Middle School science textbooks. *International Journal of Science Education, 32*, 1099–1126.

Lowe, R., & Schnotz, W. (2014). Animation principles in multimedia learning. In R. E. Mayer (Ed.), *The Cambridge handbook of multimedia learning* (2nd ed., pp. 513–546). Cambridge, MA: Cambridge University Press.

Mager, U. I., Schwonke, R., Aleven, V., Popescu, O., & Renkl, A. (2014). Triggering situational interest by decorative illustrations both fosters and hinders learning in computer-based environments. *Learning and Instruction, 29*, 141–152.

Mayer, R. E. (2001). *Multimedia learning*. Cambridge, MA: Cambridge University Press.

Merkt, M., & Schwan, S. (2014). Training the use of interactive videos: Effects on mastering different tasks. *Instructional Science, 42*, 421–441.

Merkt, M., & Sochatzy, F. (2015). Becoming aware of cinematic techniques in propaganda: Instructional support by cueing and training. *Learning and Instruction, 39*, 55–71.

Merkt, M., Weigand, S., Heier, A., & Schwan, S. (2011). Learning with videos vs. learning with print: The role of interactive features. *Learning & Instruction, 21*, 687–704.

Meyerhoff, H. S., Huff, M., Papenmeier, F., Jahn, G., & Schwan, S. (2011). Continuous visual cues trigger automatic spatial target updating in dynamic scenes. *Cognition, 121*, 73–82.

Paivio, A. (1986). *Mental representations: A dual-coding approach*. New York: Oxford University Press.

Papenmeier, F., & Schwan, S. (2016). If you watch it move, you'll recognize it in 3D: Transfer of depth cues between encoding and retrieval. *Acta Psychologica, 164*, 90–95.

Peirce, C. S. (1940). *The philosophy or Peirce: Selected writings.* New York: Harcourt.

Rey, G. D. (2012). A review of research and a meta-analysis of the seductive detail effect. *Educational Research Review, 7*, 216–237.

Salomon, G., & Cohen, A. A. (1977). Television formats, mastery of mental skills, and the acquisition of knowledge. *Journal of Educational Psychology, 69*, 612–619.

Sareen, P., Ehinger, K. A., & Wolfe, J. M. (2015). Through the looking-glass: Objects in the mirror are less real. *Psychonomic Bulletin & Review, 22*, 980–986.

Scheiter, K. (2014). The learner control principle in multimedia learning. In R. E. Mayer (Ed.), *The Cambridge handbook of multimedia learning* (2nd ed., pp. 487–512). Cambridge, MA: Cambridge University Press.

Scheiter, K., Gerjets, P., Huk, T., Imhof, B., & Kammerer, Y. (2009). The effects of realism in learning with dynamic visualizations. *Learning and Instruction, 19*, 481–494.

Scheiter, K., Schüler, A., Eitel, A. (this volume). Learning from Multimedia: Cognitive Processes and Instructional Support.

Schnotz, W. (2002). Commentary: Towards an integrated view of learning from text and visual displays. *Educational Psychology Review, 14*, 101–120.

Schooler, J. W., & Engstler-Schooler, T. Y. (1990). Verbal overshadowing of visual memories: Some things are better left unsaid. *Cognitive Psychology, 22*, 36–71.

Schwan, S., Bauer, D., Kampschulte, J., & Hampp, C. (in press). Presentation equals representation? *Photographs of objects received less attention and are less well remembered than real objects. Journal of Media Psychology.*

Schwan, S., & Garsoffky, B. (2004). The cognitive representation of filmic event summaries. *Applied Cognitive Psychology, 18*, 37–55.

Schwan, S., Garsoffky, B., & Hesse, F. W. (1998). The relationship between formal filmic means and the segmentation behavior of film viewers. *Journal of Broadcasting & Electronic Media, 42*, 237–249.

Schwan, S., Garsoffky, B., & Hesse, F. W. (2000). Do film cuts facilitate the perceptual and cognitive organization of activity sequences? *Memory & Cognition, 28*, 214–223.

Schwan, S., Grajal, A., & Lewalter, D. (2014). Understanding and engagement in places of science experience: Science museums, science centers, zoos, and aquariums. *Educational Psychologist, 49*, 70–85.

Schwan, S., & Ildirar, S. (2010). Watching film for the first time: How adult viewers interpret perceptual discontinuities in film. *Psychological Science, 21*, 970–976.

Schwan, S., & Papenmeier, F. (in press). Learning from animations: From 2D to 3D? In R. Plötzner & R. Lowe (Eds.), *Learning from dynamic visualizations: Innovations in research and application.* New York: Springer.

Schwan, S., & Riempp, R. (2004). The cognitive benefits of interactive videos: Learning to tie nautical knots. *Learning & Instruction, 14*, 293–305.

Smith, T. J. (2012). The attentional theory of cinematic continuity. *Projections, 6*, 1–27.

Soemer, A., & Schwan, S. (2016). Task-appropriate visualizations: Can the very same visualization format either promote or hinder learning depending on the task requirements? *Journal of Educational Psychology.*

Stafford, B. M. (1994). *Artful science. Enlightment entertainment and the eclipse of visual education.* Cambridge, MA: MIT Press.

Tibus, M., Heier, A., & Schwan, S. (2013). Do films make you learn? Inference processes in expository film comprehension. *Journal of Educational Psychology, 105*, 329–340.

Töpper, J., Glaser, M., & Schwan, S. (2014). Extending social cue based principles of multimedia learning beyond their immediate effects. *Learning and Instruction, 29*, 10–20.

Tversky, B., Bauer Morrison, J., & Betrancourt, M. (2002). Animation: Can it facilitate? *International Journal of Human-Computer Studies, 57*, 247–262.

van Gogh, T. (2014). The signaling (or cueing) principle. In R. E. Mayer (Ed.), *The Cambridge handbook of multimedia learning* (2nd ed., pp. 263–278). Cambridge, MA: Cambridge University Press.

Yarbus, A. L. (1967). *Eye movements and vision*. New York: Plenum Press.

Yasar, O., & Seremet, M. (2007). A comparative analysis regarding pictures included in secondary school geography textbooks taught in Turkey. *International Research in Geographical and Environmental Education, 16*, 157–187.

Yee, E., & Sedivy, J. C. (2006). Movements to pictures reveal transient semantic activation during spoken word recognition. *Journal of Experimental Psychology: Learning, Memory, and Cognition, 32*, 1–14.

Zacks, J. M., & Tversky, B. (2001). Event structure in perception and conception. *Psychological Bulletin, 127*, 3–21.

Zacks, J. M., Speer, N. K., Swallow, K. M., Braver, T. S., & Reynolds, J. R. (2007). Event perception: S mind-brain perspective. *Psychological Bulletin, 133*, 273–293.

Chapter 4
Learning and Problem-Solving with Hypermedia in the Twenty-First Century: From Hypertext to Multiple Web Sources and Multimodal Adaptivity

Peter Gerjets

Abstract Most current digital learning materials are hypermedia environments that have been postulated to stimulate active, individualized and multi-perspective learning because they force learners to explore hyperlinks in an interactive and self-directed way. At the same time, however, it was demonstrated repeatedly that learners easily experience cognitive overload and disorientation when navigating hypermedia environments. Additionally, successful hypermedia learning requires strong learning prerequisites in terms of domain-specific prior knowledge and self-regulated learning skills. This chapter reviews the research on learning from hypermedia with a strong focus on research conducted in our own lab. Additionally, two novel developments in hypermedia research are discussed that received increasing attention recently. First, evaluating the quality of multiple sources of information during hypermedia navigation has become an increasingly important aspect of hypermedia learning. For instance, the World Wide Web (WWW) and particularly the Web 2.0 reflect a global network of information nodes of very diverse origin and quality that require novel skills of source evaluation. Second, interactive displays such as those used in smartphones, tablets, or multi-touch tables as well as other sensor-based interaction devices have led to a paradigm shift in how we navigate hypermedia environments, allowing for an intuitive selection and manipulation of information by means of touch and gestures and even for novel forms of implicit interaction. Accordingly, multimodal interaction with hypermedia environments is an important current research topic that focuses on how bodily interaction may be better used to connect cognition and technology.

Keywords Hypermedia • Self-regualted learning • Instructional Design • Web Search • Source Evaluation • Multimodal Interaction • Implicit interaction

P. Gerjets (✉)
Leibniz-Institut für Wissensmedien, Schleichstraße 6, Tübingen 72076, Germany
e-mail: p.gerjets@iwm-tuebingen.de

© Springer International Publishing AG 2017
S. Schwan, U. Cress (eds.), *The Psychology of Digital Learning*,
DOI 10.1007/978-3-319-49077-9_4

Recent decades have seen rapid developments in the use of computer-based learning environments and information retrieval systems. Most of these devices are based on hypermedia structures, that is, network-like information structures where fragments of (multimedia) information are stored in nodes that are interconnected by electronic hyperlinks (Conklin, 1987; Rouet, Levonen, Dillon, & Spiro, 1996). These nodes are not restricted to text only, but can also involve multimedia, that is other representational codes (e.g., static or dynamic visualizations) or different sensory modalities (e.g., visual or auditory). Computer-based hypermedia resources such as the World Wide Web (WWW) have become one of the primary sources of academic information for a majority of pupils and students in recent years. In line with this expansion into the field of education, the scientific study of learning from hypermedia has become an active field of research that will be briefly reviewed in this chapter.

Hypermedia technology has developed enormously since its original invention more than 70 years ago. At all stages of this development, the potentials of this technology for supporting learning and problem-solving have been discussed in a controversial way. As these discussions have convincingly shown, hypermedia environments are characterized by certain benefits and drawbacks for learners at the same time (Scheiter & Gerjets, 2007). Thus, it is not always clear which of both directions will stronger influence users' learning outcomes. As a result, it is of pivotal importance that hypermedia applications are tailored very specifically to certain educational goals and contexts in order to ensure that they support relevant cognitive processes. In the light of this insight it seems not to be very fruitful to ask global questions like whether hypermedia in general is beneficial to support learning or not.

The aim of this chapter is twofold: It will, first, provide a brief overview of the historical development of hypermedia environments. This provides a timeline of technological innovations ranging from the invention of the hypertext concept in 1945 until today. In this timeline, each milestone yields more and more options for users to select, utilize, and manipulate information. However, the chapter argues, second, that these innovations in technology need contributions from psychology to successfully improve learning and instruction. This is mainly because improvements in learning critically depend on learners' abilities to capitalize on the options technology provides them with. Important contributions from psychology provide insights into the question, which technological options together with which kind of support might benefit which type of learner for specific types of learning processes. To illustrate these contributions, findings from hypermedia research will be reported in the subsequent four sections of the chapter that are tied to four important milestones of the technological development, namely research on hypertext, on hypermedia, on the World Wide Web and—as an outlook—on multimodal adaptivity. These milestones will be discussed with regard to their instructional promises and drawbacks and mainly illustrated by research conducted in our own lab over the past 15 years.

From Memex to the Mobile Web: A Brief History of Hypermedia

1945—Memex. In 1945, Vannevar Bush published his seminal paper "How we might think," which is usually considered to be the first manifestation of the technological idea of representing information by means of a collection of individual information units that contain text or multimedia and that can be navigated in a nonlinear way by using mechanistic associations ("links"). What started as a technological vision more than 70 years ago with Bush's invention of the so-called memory extension device (Memex) has today become the most prominent format for digital information in the world.

1965—Hypertext and Hypermedia. In 1965, the terms "hypertext" and "hypermedia," which are now familiar terms to describe nonlinear information structures, had been coined by Ted Nelson, who began implementing hypertext systems in the 1960s (e.g., Project Xanadu). However, it took another 20 years before the idea of hypertext unfolded its innovative potential. For instance, in 1987, Apple Computer released the HyperCard System for the newly invented Macintosh, which was the first commercially successful hypertext system. Even more important, in 1989, Tim Berners-Lee, a scientist at CERN, invented the concept of a World Wide Web as a global hyperlinked information system.

1990—WWW. In 1990, Berners-Lee developed the first Web browser, thereby bringing the World Wide Web into physical existence. The WWW quickly developed into the largest information resource that has ever been available in history. In 2000, 10 years after the first website had been launched by Berners-Lee (info.cern. ch), approximately 25 million websites were part of this hypermedia structure. The massive amount of information on the WWW made new types of search technologies necessary, such as the page rank algorithm used by Google (launched 1998), which allow for a rapid, nonlinear access to information on the Web by means of dynamically constructed search engine result pages containing lists of hyperlinks.

2000—Web 2.0. Shortly after the year 2000, the so-called Web 2.0 began to rise. It was characterized by strong social components and the innovation of user-generated content (Cormode & Krishnamurthy, 2008). Hypermedia platforms such as Wikipedia (launched 2001), Facebook (launched 2004), Youtube (launched 2005), or Twitter (launched 2006) are prototypical Web 2.0 examples. Here, users do not only consume—but also produce and evaluate—hypermedia contents (e.g., by editing Wikipedia articles), which massively increased the amount of information sources available on the WWW. The following illustrates this information explosion in the Web 2.0: In 2000, Google estimated that the WWW holds about one billion pages, but only 8 years later the estimation was a thousand times higher with one trillion pages, many of which presumably contained user-generated contents (https://googleblog.blogspot.de/2008/07/we-knew-web-was-big.html). These contents may, of course, strongly vary with regard to quality and credibility so that users' ability to constantly evaluate information sources on the WWW became an increasingly important component of information literacy.

2010—Mobile Web. Since 2010, the single most notable development with regard to the use of hypermedia environments is probably the establishment of the mobile Web. This development started with the invention of small Web-devices that allowed for new forms of multimodal and context-adaptive interaction with Web contents (starting with Apples iPhone in 2007, the iPad in 2010, and Google's Android Smartphones in 2011). For decades, the standard device for hypermedia exploration had been the stationary desktop PC equipped with keyboard and mouse, that is, a device used in a rather stable context and with a very limited number of interaction channels. Today, however, there are far more Web users in front of a smartphone or tablet than in front of a desktop PC (Oviatt & Cohen, 2015). Mobile Web devices are not only characterized by flexible contexts of use but also by rich multimodal capabilities for interaction and adaptation due to their built-in sensors such as multi-touch screen, GPS, accelerometer, gyroscope, compass, proximity sensor, ambient light sensor, camera, microphone, and so forth. Both factors—context variability and multimodality—might fundamentally change the way hypermedia environments are navigated in the future. Oviatt and Cohen (2015) even claimed that the fact that smartphones with multimodal interfaces have become the dominant computer interface worldwide has led to a paradigm shift towards multimodality in human–computer interaction. Sensor technologies increasingly provide hypermedia systems with rich input possibilities for context-aware adaptations based on inferences about users' physical, social, or psychological contexts, thereby allowing for new forms of implicit interaction that do not necessitate explicit user commands (Schmidt, 2000). Thus, the information made available to users by means of multimodal and context-adaptive interaction can be much more tailored to their personal needs, preferences, and contexts than ever before.

Each of the abovementioned milestones in the technological development of current hypermedia systems gave rise to specific claims and research questions with regard to their potentials for supporting learning and problem-solving. Some of these claims and research questions will be outlined briefly in the following sections. The first section about hypertext will be the most comprehensive because many general issues on learning and problem-solving with hypermedia will be raised that also apply to all later evolution stages of hypermedia environments as well.

Hypertext: Learning from Nonlinear Text

Scientific research on hypermedia as an educational tool started three decades ago in the 1980s when the first hypermedia systems such as Apple's HyperCard (1987) became commercially available. For many years, most hypermedia studies confined themselves to hyperlinked text materials, that is, to hypertext without additional representational formats like images, video, or sound (cf. Dillon & Jobst, 2005). The most important characteristic of hypertext is that it is "capable of being explored in different ways, with the different exploration paths producing what are essentially *multiple texts for the same topic*" (Spiro & Jehng, 1990, p. 166). Thus, learners can select information units as well as choose the point of time, the pacing, and sequence of their presentation in a self-directed way.

In the 1980s, many authors strongly advocated the educational potential of hypertext by pointing out its general advantages, for instance, that it (1) provides nonlinear access to huge amounts of information (Nielsen, 1990), (2) allows exploring information in depth on demand (Collier, 1987), (3) is engaging to use (Jonassen, 1989), (4) has a cognitively plausible network-like information structure (Jonassen, 1986; Landow, 1992), (5) enables situated learning in specific contexts (Duffy & Knuth, 1990), and (6) supports cognitive flexibility (Spiro & Jehng, 1990). It was also claimed that (7) hypertext does not only *offer high levels of learner control* but is (8) also helpful for *improving learner control* (Marchionini, 1988). On the other hand, it was postulated from the very beginning (e.g., Conklin, 1987; Marchionini, 1988) that interacting with hypertext can easily lead to severe usability problems, for instance (1) spatial and conceptual *disorientation* ("lost in hyperspace": e.g., not knowing enough about the structure of the network), (2) *cognitive overload* due to navigation demands, and (3) *distraction* due to easily accessible information that is interesting but currently irrelevant for task accomplishment (for more details, see Scheiter & Gerjets, 2007).

Promises and drawbacks of hypertext-assisted learning. In line with the impression that hypertext comes with remarkable promises but also with critical drawbacks, early reviews from the 1990s on hypertext-assisted learning provided mixed conclusions on the educational value of hypermedia (e.g., Chen & Rada, 1996; Dillon & Gabbard, 1998; Nielsen, 1989). Dillon and Gabbard (1998) concluded that "clearly, the benefits gained from the use of hypermedia technology in learning scenarios appear to be very limited and not in keeping with the generally euphoric reaction to this technology in the professional arena" (p. 345). The main reason for this disappointing situation, as Rouet and Levonen (1996) have put it, seems to be that "hypertext efficiency involves a trade-off between the power of the linking and the searching tools it provides and the cognitive demands or costs these tools impose on the reader" (p. 20). Many authors postulated that these extra demands cannot be avoided because they result from one of the most beneficial features of hypermedia environments—the freedom to decide when and which information to access (e.g., Mayes, Kibby, & Anderson, 1990). In other words, hypermedia environments are inevitably characterized by certain advantages and drawbacks for learners at the same time. Research on hypertext efficiency seems to indicate that the general promises and the general drawbacks of hypertext are quite counterbalanced (see Fig. 4.1). This trade-off may explain why global comparisons of learning from hypertext and linear presentation formats usually failed to show major advantages concerning the effectiveness of hypertext learning.

Beyond this quite disappointing finding, the early reviews on hypertext-assisted learning also made very clear that there is considerable interindividual variability in hypertext efficiency. This is due to learner characteristics such as domain-specific prior knowledge, self-regulatory skills, spatial abilities, or cognitive styles that play an important role as moderators (e.g., Dillon & Gabbard, 1998, for an overview cf. Scheiter & Gerjets, 2007). Therefore, the role of learner prerequisites remains one of the most researched topics in the field of hypermedia learning. Although it was initially assumed that increased learner control would accommodate individual dif-

General Promises of Hypertext	General Drawbacks of Hypertext
- Access to huge amounts of information	- Spatial and conceptual disorientation
- In depth exploration on demand	- Cognitive overload (navigation demands)
- Engaging to use	- Distraction (irrelevant information)
- Cognitively plausible structure	
- Enables situated learning	
- Supports cognitive flexibility	
- Offers and improves learner control	

Fig. 4.1 General promises and drawbacks of hypertext seem to be counterbalanced

ferences by enabling learners to adapt instructions to their individual preferences and needs, the opposite turned out to be true: Hypertext was found to be particularly effective for students with favorable learner characteristics, thereby increasing the gap between good and poor students. In a nutshell, the general insight from this early period was that just using an arbitrarily designed hypertext for instruction would most likely not improve learning more strongly than an equivalent linear text document, particularly not for learners with less favorable learner characteristics.

Improving the theoretical foundations of hypertext design. Based on the insights from this early research on hypertext, many authors—including those in our own lab—realized that much more theoretical, methodological, and instructional sophistication would be needed to (1) capitalize on the instructional potential of hypertext and to (2) reduce the usability problems hypertext inevitably comes with (cf. Dillon & Gabbard, 1998; Gerjets & Scheiter, 2003; Scheiter & Gerjets, 2007; Shapiro & Niederhauser, 2004; Tergan, 1997a, 1997b). One of the strongest criticisms of early hypertext research was that the conceptual foundations of most hypertext designs and hypertext studies were rather shallow, relying on overly simplistic theoretical ideas that turned out to be wrong (e.g., that hypertext mimics the structure of the human mind or that hypertext automatically supports self-regulated learning, cf., Tergan, 1997b). Accordingly, in more recent research, usually more sophisticated comparisons of different hypertext designs are deployed that allow for answering more specific question on which aspects of hypertext environments have the most pronounced influence on learning (cf. Dillon & Jobst, 2005). There are two main lines of research on how to improve the design of hypertext environments for learning in the 2000s. One line of research focuses on generic design aspects of hypertext and their potential to reduce general usability problems like disorientation. Here, for instance, different types of information structures, graphical overviews, or advanced organizers are compared (for a review cf. Dillon & Jobst, 2005; Shapiro & Niederhauser, 2004). A second and from our perspective theoretically more specific line of research aims at improving the foundations of hypertext designs by combining elaborated instructional models with cognitive task analyses to tailor hypertext designs to well-defined instructional purposes and learning contents. For this purpose, different instructional models have been applied, most of which were originally developed in the context of linear instructions (e.g., *cognitive load theory*, Gerjets &

Hesse, 2004; Gerjets & Scheiter, 2003; *cognitive flexibility theory*, Jacobson & Spiro, 1995; *construction integration model*, Shapiro & Niederhauser, 2004; *elaboration theory*, Hoffmann, 1997). In the context of this chapter, it is not necessary to explain all of these models and their application to hypertext design in detail. Rather, the important point is that grounding hypertext designs in these types of theoretical models of instruction has a principled advantage, namely that the linking structure can be well aligned to specific instructional purposes and learning contents. Thus, the power of the linking can be exploited more directly for learning. Therefore, this approach can be considered a fruitful way of going beyond approaching hypertext design in rather general terms like the overall promises and drawbacks of hypertext. An example from our own research may illustrate this theoretical advantage:

In a series of experiments, we investigated how hyperlinks can be used to support a specific learning approach, namely, the acquisition of problem schemas from worked-out examples. For this learning approach, there is a rich literature available that is theoretically based in cognitive load theory, schema theory, and cognitive task analysis. This theoretical foundation allows for identifying pivotal cognitive processes as well as other learning resources required for successful learning (for an overview cf. Atkinson, Derry, Renkl, & Wortham, 2000). For instance, the most important processes that need to be supported in example-based learning are *example elaborations* (i.e., integrating information about abstract solution principles and concrete examples to identify the structural problem features of examples) and *example comparisons* (i.e., contrasting examples that belong to identical and different problem categories to identify important commonalities and differences). Based on these process assumptions, we designed a hypertext environment in the mathematical domain of combinatorics (HYPERCOMB). This environment provided learners on the one hand with the necessary information (e.g., abstract information on structural problem features and different types of worked-out examples). On the other hand, a theory-driven linking structure was implemented to support crucial example processing strategies (Gerjets, Scheiter, & Schuh, 2008). In particular, hyperlinks were designed (depending on experimental conditions) to allow learners to (1) quickly switch between the six different problem categories conveyed in the environment (navigation bar), to (2) directly connect abstract information on a problem category with a concrete example for that category and an instruction on how to process that example (processing prompts), and to (3) easily contrast multiple examples for each problem category that differ in their superficial cover stories but not in their structural problem features (comparison tool). Experimental comparisons of different HYPERCOMB-Versions revealed that both hyperlinks with processing prompts and the hyperlinked comparison tool improved students example processing, learning outcomes and transfer performance (Gerjets et al., 2008). We interpreted these findings as evidence that a specific and theoretically informed hypertext design can be used effectively to facilitate and afford pivotal learning processes.

The need for augmented theories of instructional design. As demonstrated in the last paragraph, instructional theories that were originally developed in the context of linear instructions can obviously be used to inform the design of hypertext environments. However, it should be noted that there are no dedicated theories of hypertext design or hypertext reading. Theories developed in the context of linear instruction usually ignore the most characteristic feature of hypertext environments, namely the high level of learner control reflected by the freedom of the learner to decide when and which information to access. Most theories of instructional design, on the contrary, assume that teachers or instructors can control which information is presented to learners at a particular point in time. Therefore, it is important to incorporate aspects of learner control into instructional design theories in order to be able to understand how learners actually use hypertext environments for learning. In this line of reasoning, Gerjets and Scheiter (2003) and Gerjets and Hesse (2004) proposed some augmentations of *cognitive load theory* inspired by evidence from hypertext-based instruction. In particular, these augmentations focused on the role of goal configurations and processing strategies as moderators between instructional design and cognitive load. Traditionally, cognitive load theory assumes a one-to-one mapping between instructional design, learner activities, and the associated pattern of cognitive load that determines the resulting learning outcomes (e.g., Sweller, van Merriënboer, & Paas, 1998). A basic level of cognitive load will result from the relational complexity of the learning materials in relation to learners' expertise (intrinsic cognitive load). Furthermore, learner activities resulting from the instructional design will determine how much unnecessary (extraneous) or elaborative (germane) cognitive load will be imposed onto learners. Moderating variables that might interfere with this direct mapping are usually not taken into account. Implicit premises that justify this neglect are that (1) the goals of using instructional materials are fixed (e.g., schema acquisition) and that (2) a particular instructional design is strongly associated with a specific type of learner activity in the sense that it elicits, encourages, or induces this activity. Both assumptions might be wrong in the context of hypertext environments. In our view, the relation between instructional design and cognitive load (and therefore learning outcome) is far less deterministic in hypertext environments than suggested by cognitive load theory. In particular, in learner-controlled settings, the relation is moderated by the configuration of the *instructional goals* a hypertext environment is designed for and by self-directed activities of the learner. The latter can be analyzed in terms of the configuration of *learner goals* and the *processing strategies* that are employed to accomplish these goals. In our view, adding these augmentations to cognitive load theory (for illustration, see Fig. 4.2) is necessary to account for the rather weak relation between instructional design and patterns of cognitive load or learning outcomes that were observed in the context of self-controlled hypertext learning. Three examples from our own research can illustrate this claim.

Configurations of instructional goals and learner goals. First, as hypertexts per definition can deliver multiple texts on the same topic, the same hypertext may be designed to serve a multitude of different *instructional goals* that can potentially be adopted by learners and then guide information utilization (e.g., getting a quick overview, fact learning, connecting different contents in a flexible way, and exploring information in depth). Depending on the instructional goals that a hypertext can be used for, different mappings between the instructional design, learner activities, and the resulting pattern of cognitive load will emerge. We were able to demonstrate this in a hypertext experiment on example-based learning in which different instructional goals could be achieved (i.e., learning to solve equivalent problems versus learning

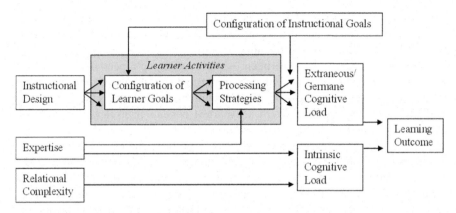

Fig. 4.2 Goals and strategies as moderators between instructional design and cognitive load (figure adapted from Gerjets & Scheiter, 2003)

to solve transfer problems; Schorr, Gerjets, Scheiter, & Laouris, 2002). Second, when it comes to *learner goals* as an important moderator, not only the instructional goals that a learner might adopt (e.g., provided by a teacher), but also task-unrelated pending goals may become relevant for learner activities in a hypertext environment. In these environments, students are often confronted with potential sources of distraction arising from hyperlinked information that, albeit interesting or related to a pending goal, is unrelated to the current task goal (e.g., browsing Wikipedia might provide a good example for the potential of hypertext to distract learners). To demonstrate that the presence of pending goals can influence the resulting pattern of cognitive load during hypertext learning, we manipulated learners' pending goals during the interaction with a hypertext environment that contained distracting information (Scheiter, Gerjets, & Heise, 2014). We assumed that the presence of hyperlinks referring to interesting but task-irrelevant information would interfere with task performance (due to increased extraneous cognitive load), in particular they are related to a pending goal. Based on previous work on volitional action control (Heise, Gerjets, & Westermann, 1997), we further hypothesized that this would primarily be the case when working on easy, but not on difficult tasks with a high level of intrinsic cognitive load. In two hypertext experiments, students learned about probability theory using an example-based hypertext and solved corresponding test problems, for which task difficulty was manipulated. As a second factor, the presence of hyperlinks referring to interesting information unrelated to the primary task was varied. In one experiment, a pending goal related to the task-irrelevant information was set up beforehand. This resulted in decreasing problem-solving performance while working on easy problems as expected, whereas no interference was observed for difficult problems. Beyond impeding performance, the presence of hyperlinks related to the pending goal also reduced time spent on task-relevant information and increased time spent on task-irrelevant information while working on easy tasks. However, as revealed by mediation analyses these changes in overt information processing behavior did not explain the decrease in problem-solving performance. As an alternative explanation, we suggested that goal conflicts resulting from hyperlinks related to pending goals may have claimed cognitive resources, which are then no longer available for learning and problem-solving.

When we replicated the experiment without setting up a pending goal beforehand, no decline in problem-solving performance due to the presence of irrelevant hyperlinks was observed. However, this does not imply that in this case there are no cognitive costs of reading through a hypertext containing irrelevant hyperlinks. When using more fine-grained analyses we still found indications of increased cognitive load due to irrelevant hyperlinks even when these links are not related to a pending goal. For instance, Scharinger, Kammerer, and Gerjets (2015) studied whether additional cognitive load is imposed onto executive working-memory functions by link-selection processes during reading. In this study, we compared pure text reading with hyperlink-like selection processes in an online reading situation in which some of the available links were relevant for the reading task while others were irrelevant. By using a methodology of combined electroencephalographic (EEG) and eye-tracking data recording we demonstrated in a series of three experiments that deciding on the relevance of links in a text yields physiological signatures that indicate an increased level of cognitive load (e.g., decreased alpha frequency band power and increased pupil dilation). We found similar neural signatures of increased cognitive load in a search task when searchers fixated hyperlinks that did not or did only partially match the search goal (as compared to matching hyperlinks, Scharinger, Kammerer, & Gerjets, 2016). Thus, hyperlinks available in a hypermedia environment that do not match the current goal seem to increase workload. Therefore, providing additional hyperlinks might lead to increased cognitive load even when these links are neither related to a current task nor to a pending goal. Moreover, when hyperlinks are related to pending learner goals competing with a learning task, even stronger effects of distraction and extraneous cognitive load can be demonstrated, eventually leading to performance impairments. Therefore, the resulting pattern of cognitive load when navigating a hypertext environment can be expected to strongly depend on learners' current and pending goals.

Learners' processing strategies. Third, the variability of *learners' processing strategies* plays a more pronounced role in hypertext environments than is usually assumed in instructional design theories. For instance, in cognitive load theory, no large variability of learner activities is expected as a reaction towards a specific instructional design, thus yielding a rather deterministic relation between instructional design and cognitive load pattern. However, processing strategies may act as important moderators between instructional design and cognitive load—especially in self-controlled learning situations. For instance, in a study by Gerjets, Scheiter, and Tack (2000), we compared three different instructional designs of an example-based hypertext environment, providing either three, one, or no worked examples per problem category. At the same time, we analyzed different strategies of using the information provided in these designs. We observed that processing strategies were good predictors of learning outcomes, whereas features of the learning environment were not. Thus, although the *mere provision* of one or three examples was obviously not sufficient to improve learning, using particular strategies of processing either one or three examples was strongly predictive of learning outcomes. In turn, this implies that learners' strategies of using hypertext environments seem to be more important predictors of learning outcomes than the hypertext design itself. In case that the learners do not take a chance on using the learning opportunities provided by a particular design, the disadvantages of the additional control requirements for handling the enriched instructional environment (e.g., decisions related to the selection and sequencing of hyperlinks) might even outweigh the benefits. Therefore, it is important to incorporate learners' processing strategies into instructional design theories in order to be able to better predict when learners will benefit from a hypertext environment and when not. For the prediction of learning outcomes it will of course also be necessary to better understand which learners will engage in fruitful learning strategies and which will not. In our augmented version of cognitive load theory (cf. Fig. 4.2), we primarily assumed that prior knowledge (as part of learners' level of expertise) will determine strategy choice, but there might be numerous other learner characteristics involved. We addressed this issue in a study by Scheiter, Gerjets, Vollmann, and Catrambone (2009) in which we provided learners with an example-based hypertext environment on combinatorics with a rich set of strategic choices (i.e., four problem categories, two example problems per category, eight formats for the presentation of the solution procedure per example). Based on theories of example-based learning and on our own previous findings (cf. Gerjets, Scheiter, & Catrambone, 2006), different types of promising example processing strategies could be specified for this set of learning materials (e.g., comparing different types of examples, focusing on examples that present solution procedures in the most intelligible way, investing time in example selection). To investigate the impact of different learner characteristics on example utilization strategies and learning outcomes in this hypertext environment, five clusters of students were identified according to their domain-specific prior knowledge, self-regulation abilities, preferences for amount of instruction, and epistemological beliefs. In line with prior research (Azevedo, 2005; Bendixen & Hartley, 2003; Chen, Fan, & Macredie, 2006), we found that learners with more favorable characteristics (i.e., higher prior knowledge, more complex epistemological beliefs, more positive attitudes towards mathematics, better cognitive and metacognitive strategy use) tended to show more successful example utilization behavior and better learning outcomes than learners with less favorable characteristics. In particular, students' attitudes towards mathematics were very important for defining clusters. Interestingly, there were three "good" clusters with regard to learning outcomes that where characterized by three specific combinations of favorable learner characteristics as well as by specific types of "good" example processing strategies enabled by the environment (see above). The navigation behavior of the two "bad" clusters, on the other hand, seemed to indicate that learners in these clusters either suffered from navigational problems (e.g., unsystematic retrieval of examples) or from illusions of understanding (e.g., not enough examples retrieved). In sum, this study provided further support for necessary augmentations of cognitive load theory (Gerjets & Hesse, 2004; Gerjets & Scheiter, 2003) in learner-controlled settings as it demonstrated that there are other variables beyond prior knowledge and instructional design features that may affect strategy selection and thereby the emerging pattern of cognitive load and learning outcomes.

Hypermedia: Interacting with Multiple External Representations

The previous section focused on our research on text-based hypermedia environments. However, many of the research issues addressed in this section also apply to other hypermedia environments utilizing a richer set of external representations. In fact, when hypermedia environments become more complex by incorporating static and dynamic multimedia materials such as pictures, animations, or spoken text, many of these issues become even more important. Additionally, instructional decisions of hypermedia designers as well as the selection decisions of hypermedia users become more complicated. Beyond the question of which text contents and which hyperlinks to present or to select, they now also need to consider which type of external representation to provide or to use for learning. Therefore, additional research questions arise when multimedia materials are embedded in hypermedia environments. In our own research in this field, we mainly focused on dynamic representations such as spoken text or animations, which are in fact two of the most interesting types of external representations for incorporation into hypermedia environments because they go beyond what can be done with printed multimedia materials alone (e.g., written text with static visualizations). We addressed mainly two pivotal questions, namely, (1) whether multimedia design theories do apply to hypermedia and (2) how to design dynamic representations such as animations or spoken text for hypermedia environments. Due to space restrictions, however, most of our research on the use of spoken text in hypermedia environments cannot be reviewed in this chapter (cf. Kühl, Scheiter, Gerjets, & Edelmann, 2011; Linek, Gerjets, & Scheiter, 2010; Schüler, Scheiter, & Gerjets, 2011, 2013; Schüler, Scheiter, Rummer, & Gerjets, 2012). As a result of our research, it turned out that good instructional hypermedia design comprising dynamic representations is a much greater challenge and a much more subtle design task than initially considered. In particular, it turned out that hypermedia design based on a set of simple and plausible principles borrowed from adjacent research fields like multimedia will probably not work well.

Application of multimedia design theories to hypermedia. While several theory-based design recommendations exist with regard to multimedia learning (e.g., multimedia design principles, Mayer, 2009; cf. Scheiter, Schüler & Eitel 2017), there is hardly any such advice for hypermedia environments because they come with higher learner control (Gerjets & Kirschner, 2009). Moreover, although multimedia design principles have been validated empirically in controlled laboratory studies, their transfer to hypermedia environments is not trivial. In fact, there is first evidence that specific multimedia design principles, for instance the modality principle in favor of spoken instead of written text, might not work under a high level of learner control (Tabbers, Martens, & van Merriënboer, 2004). Therefore, we directly investigated the question whether multimedia design principles would also hold for hypermedia environments and found that this is not the case (Gerjets, Scheiter, Opfermann, Hesse, & Eysink, 2009). In a first experiment, learners were presented with different versions of a hypermedia environment on probability word problems with only a low level of learner control. A control condition included arithmetical representations and written text only to describe problem statements and solutions procedures of example problems. This condition was compared to four different conditions with dynamic multimedia materials (spoken text instead of written text, written text together with spoken text, animations for the illustration of solutions together with spoken text, animations together with written text). To implement a basic level of learner control, all dynamic multimedia materials did not play automatically but had to be actively selected by clicking on a link. Existing multimedia design principles (Mayer, 2009) would provide clear predictions for these learning materials when presented without learner control to students: For instance, according to the multimedia principle, augmenting spoken or written text with visual representations such as animations should improve learning. According to the modality principle, using different modalities, for example, by combining animations or arithmetical representations with spoken instead of written text should also improve learning.

In our experiment, however, these predictions could by no means be confirmed: The option to augment spoken or written explanations with animations yielded worse performance than not being given this option, indicating a reversed multimedia effect. Moreover, there was no evidence in favor of accompanying the arithmetical information or the animations with spoken rather than written text; thus, there was also no modality effect. We assumed that these results go back to learner control and might be explained best by learners' navigational decisions. For instance, we found that learners did not sufficiently use the representations responsible for the respective effects in the multimedia literature (i.e., spoken text or animations). Hence, these potentially useful representations seemed to have only minor affordances for using them, resulting in an unfavorable "information diet." Moreover, when learners decide against using spoken text or an animation, they may nevertheless have to invest cognitive resources and time for reaching these decisions, which are no longer available for learning (cf. Niederhauser, Reynolds, Salmen, & Skolmoski, 2000). As a result, the situation for learners may be worse than in a situation in which these helpful external representations are not made available to them in the hypermedia environment in the first place.

The situation becomes even worse, when the level of learner control is increased, as the second experiment by Gerjets et al. (2009) demonstrates: In this study, all materials from the first experiments were integrated into a single hypermedia environment so that learners were given the opportunity to select among all representational formats that students in the different experimental conditions of the first experiment had been assigned to. When comparing the efficiency of this highly learner controlled environment with the mean performance of all groups from the first experiment, a strong effect in favor of a low level of learner control was observed. Moreover, as in the first experiment, we found that dynamic representations (i.e., spoken text and animations) did not seem to have sufficient affordances for selection so that they were not used to a sufficient extent. Thus, the idea of directly transferring multimedia design principles to inform hypermedia learning environments seems to be too simple. It does not seem advisable to simply equate hypermedia learning with multimedia learning as suggested by Dillon and Jobst (2005). Good instructional materials (e.g., combinations of animations with spoken explanations) might not attract learners and accordingly might not be selected. Multimedia learning and hypermedia learning may comprise very different information utilization and processing strategies and therefore require very different research agendas and instructional support measures (cf. Scheiter & Gerjets, 2007). This is very much in line with our theoretical model depicted in Fig. 4.2, which postulates a pivotal role for learners' strategies of selecting and processing hypermedia materials in predicting learning outcomes.

Designing animations for hypermedia environments. The disappointing findings obtained by our and other labs with regard to the instructional efficiency of dynamic representations such as animations in hypermedia environments clearly showed that more specific research on animation design for hypermedia was required. In particular, animation design needs to fulfill two constraints at the same time, namely, being useful for learning and providing affordances for learners to use them (which might be partially a function of the first constraint). In our research, we found that the differences between animations for hypermedia learning that do work and those that do not might be quite subtle. In the study by Gerjets et al. (2009) that we have just discussed we used probability problems such as "What is the chance to correctly guess the winner of the gold, the silver, and the bronze medal in a race with seven runners?". The animations that we designed for this type of problem were neither very concrete nor very abstract and used a standard visualization from probability theory, namely, an urn model, where marbles of different colors are taken out one after another. However, learners only retrieved about one-third of the available animations. Thus, the animations might not have been very attractive for them. However, it also turned out that designing the animations more realistically to make them more appealing to students was not successful either. When we, for instance, depicted a race of seven runners more realistically, showing in three animated sequences how the first, the second, and the third runner crossed the goal line in a study by Scheiter, Gerjets, and Catrambone (2006), learners still only retrieved about one-third of the available animations. Even worse, when distinguishing between frequent and sparse users of the animations we found that frequency of animations was not associated with better learning. Thus, the mere availability of realistic animations in a hypermedia environment on probability problems seemed to be neither more attractive for learners than the availability of more abstract urn animations nor was their retrieval helpful for learning. The prima facie plausible idea that animations, which make abstract learning materials more concrete, would not only be attractive for learners but also helpful for learning turned out to be fundamentally flawed (for similar findings with regard to realistic dynamic visualizations in natural science domains, see also Brucker, Scheiter & Gerjets, 2014; Scheiter, Gerjets, Huk, Imhof & Kammerer, 2009; cf. Schwan, 2017).

In the further course of our research program, it turned out to be helpful to base animation design not on the idea of providing learners with a vivid representation of a situation or event described in a math problem. Rather, the idea to support learners in necessary representational transitions from a concrete cover story of a mathematical word problem to more abstract geometrical and algebraic representations turned out to be useful. Theoretically, this approach can be based on detailed task analyses of the steps involved in solving mathematical word problems (e.g., Nathan, Kintsch, & Young, 1992). Using this approach, we came up with designing animations that can be described as hybrid animations because they comprise a switch from realistic to abstract visualizations (Scheiter, Gerjets, & Schuh, 2010), a principle that Goldstone and Son (2005) have described in other contexts as concreteness fading. Hybrid animations start with realistic visualizations of concrete problem situations described in word problems and subsequently morph these visualizations into geometric and algebraic representations. Thereby, these animations exclude irrelevant surface features and highlight structural features of problems at the same time. In terms of Nathan et al. (1992) task analysis, hybrid animations support all necessary processing steps: First, constructing a situation model with realistic visualizations, second, extracting relevant structural problem features for constructing a problem model by morphing these visualizations into geometric representations, and third, translating the problem model into a solution procedure by connecting geometric to algebraic representations. As we could demonstrate in an experimental study (Scheiter et al., 2010), learners not only retrieved about two-thirds of the hybrid animations but also strongly benefited from them with regard to learning outcomes as compared to a text-only condition. Most importantly, the effects in favor of hybrid animations became even stronger with increasing transfer distance between learning materials and test problems. Thus, hybrid animations were not only useful for learning but also provided sufficient affordances for learners to retrieve them (which might be attributed to learners' recognition that these representations were helpful to support their learning and understanding).

Based on these and other research findings, Scheiter and Gerjets (2010) concluded that design recommendations for the instructional use of animations in hypermedia environments need to be much more refined and have to take into account more moderating variables than they usually do within dominating theories of multimedia learning (for another illustration of this point, see also Brucker, Ehlis, Häußinger, Fallgatter, & Gerjets, 2015). Hypermedia-specific augmentations of instructional design models together with cognitive task analyses are helpful to derive these design recommendations.

Up to now, we have been mostly discussing the advantages and drawbacks of hypertext and hypermedia environments that have been intentionally developed by an instructional designer to support learning processes. However, in the next step of the technological development of hypermedia environments, this picture changed quite radically. When using distributed hypermedia environments such as the World Wide Web for educational purposes, learners typically are not using a single instructional information source any more. Therefore, evaluating multiple information sources and selecting appropriate sources for learning became a novel challenge for learners as well as a novel field of study in hypermedia research.

The World Wide Web: Evaluating Multiple Information Sources

When we switch our focus from using instructional hypermedia environments as discussed in the previous sections to using the WWW for learning and problem-solving, the evaluation of information sources, which has hardly played a role before, now becomes crucial for hypermedia navigation. With the exponential growth of information available on the WWW, it has evolved into one of the most important hypermedia environments for educational purposes. Besides searching for simple and uncontroversial facts, the WWW increasingly serves as a rich information source for conducting research on more complex academic or science-related topics (cf. Horrigan, 2006). Contrary to traditional educational hypertext and hypermedia applications that are designed by a small number of instructors to support specific learning goals, the WWW and particularly the Web 2.0 are characterized by multiple information sources as well as by numerous different purposes for putting information online. On the WWW not only scientific, educational and other institutions, but also journalists, instructors, companies, and laypeople provide information on complex domains, yielding a substantial variability in terms of quality and reliability of Web information. As anyone can publish virtually any information on the WWW, it is characterized by a large variability of information quality with information sources differing dramatically with regard to authors' expertise, motives, and vested interests. Moreover, there is hardly any kind of quality assurance on the Web as it is the case when expert knowledge was obtained from academic or educational professionals or publishers. As a result, Web users are required to appropriately evaluate diverse, potentially diffuse, or even contradictory sources of information.

Hence, using the WWW for educational purposes goes beyond traditional hypermedia learning and can better be described as "hypermedia learning in the wild." Accordingly, adequate strategies for the critical evaluation of information quality while searching for complex contents on the Web have become pivotal. Therefore, they need to be included into theoretical models aiming to describe how learners successfully select important and valid information for learning from hypermedia environments (Gerjets, Kammerer, & Werner, 2011). In the literature, it has been shown repeatedly that learners usually face difficulties in appropriately evaluating information during Web search (Brand-Gruwel, Wopereis, & Vermetten, 2005; Gerjets & Hellenthal-Schorr, 2008; OECD, 2011). Therefore, our own research in this area focuses not only on identifying variables that influence learners' critical evaluation of Web sources but also on support measures for stimulating appropriate strategies of source evaluation. In relation to the model depicted in Fig. 4.2, our main research questions boil down to identifying factors that elicit source evaluations as a particular type of processing strategies. These factors can be relevant aspects of learners' Web search expertise as well as features of the interface design used for Web navigation.

When do source evaluation processes occur? In a first step, we experimentally compared an explicit evaluation instruction to a neutral thinking-aloud instruction to better understand which evaluation processes students are able to apply and which they would spontaneously apply when provided with the task to investigate a complex scientific topic based on a set of different Web sources (Gerjets et al., 2011). Data from thinking-aloud protocols, eye-tracking, and information problem-solving revealed that the instructed evaluation resulted in much more verbal utterances of quality-related evaluation criteria, in an increased attention focus on user ratings displayed on Web pages, and in a better quality of decision-making than the spontaneous evaluation. These findings support the assumption that the critical evaluation of Web information is not a common event during Web navigation although students could do better than they spontaneously do. When it comes to the question why learners do not apply source evaluation strategies more often, one important learner characteristic that might be relevant is learners' personal epistemology (epistemological beliefs about the nature of knowledge). Particularly interesting in this context are internet-specific epistemic beliefs, that is, individuals' personal beliefs about what knowledge and knowing is like on the WWW. Our own research provides some evidence that sophisticated internet-specific epistemic beliefs positively predict source evaluation behaviors (Kammerer, Amann, & Gerjets, 2015; Kammerer, Bråten, Gerjets, & Strømsø, 2013; Kammerer & Gerjets, 2012). For instance, Kammerer et al. (2015) could show that (1) beliefs that internet-based knowledge claims need to be critically evaluated by cross-checking multiple Web sources and (2) beliefs that the internet is a reliable knowledge resource that contains correct and detailed information were both positively related to the time spent on reliable over less reliable Web pages and to the quality of knowledge acquired from the Web search. Thus, learners' personal epistemology with regard to the WWW might be an important part of their Web search expertise determining the occurrence of spontaneous evaluations of Web sources. Additionally, personal epistemology might also be a potential target for interventions that improve learners' Web competencies.

Beyond learner characteristics, also context variables might influence when source evaluation processes occur during Web navigation. For instance, according to the discrepancy-induced source comprehension (D-ISC) assumption proposed by Braasch, Rouet, Vibert, and Britt (2012), perceived contradictions between sources should prompt readers to attend more strategically to source information during encoding and to integrate sources into their memory representations. In our own research, we found support for these predictions. In two experiments, we systematically examined whether contradictions between two Web pages—of which one was commercially biased as stated in an "about us" section—stimulated the consideration of source information both during and after reading (Kammerer, Kalbfell, & Gerjets, 2016). In the first experiment, the "about us" information of the Web pages was presented directly below their content; in the second experiment, it needed to be accessed by clicking on an "about us" link. Results of both experiments showed consistently that after having encountered contradicting information, students attended longer to the' "about us" statements, more frequently included this information in their written reports and judged the commercially biased page as less trustworthy than after having encountered consistent (positive or negative) information. Therefore, with regard to potential interventions for improving learners' spontaneous source evaluation activities on the Web, interface designs might be considered that—other than current designs—maximize the chance that learners process multiple sources and perceive contradictions among them.

How can source evaluation processes be stimulated? Stimulating learners to engage in quality-related evaluation processes of Web sources is an important aspect of improving their Web search performance in educational contexts. A way to directly help learners to improve their evaluation strategies is to provide specific Web trainings (cf. Brand-Gruwel & Gerjets, 2008). In our own research, we developed and evaluated different Web trainings, ranging from rather broad interventions with several sessions and targeting a wide range of skills (e.g., Gerjets &

Hellenthal-Schorr, 2008) to very focused interventions mainly aiming at improving individuals' beliefs about what knowledge is like on the WWW. In a study by Kammerer et al. (2015), we developed and evaluated a very brief source evaluation intervention of about 20 min with a focus on raising awareness for the following aspects of source information and on teaching how to evaluate information sources according to these aspects (see also Wiley et al., 2009): The type of website (e.g., websites from official institutions, forum websites, commercial websites) and the potential motives of the respective information providers (e.g., to inform, to exchange experiences, or to persuade), the expertise of the information provider (i.e., experts vs. laypersons), and the availability (or lack) of source references to identify whether the information is based on scientific evidence. The intervention yielded positive results on learners' subsequent navigation behavior (i.e., they spent more time on reliable over less reliable Web pages) and the quality of the knowledge acquired from a Web search in a medical domain. Moreover, even 1 week after the source evaluation intervention, individuals' beliefs that internet-based knowledge need to be critically evaluated by comparing multiple Web pages were stronger than before the intervention. Thus, it seems that even a very short training with regard to crucial contents improved learners' source evaluation strategies as well as their internet-specific epistemic beliefs.

An alternative approach to directly stimulating learners to apply better source evaluation strategies might be to change the design of search interfaces in a way that more affordances for evaluation processes are provided. For instance, in one study, we compared a standard Google-like list interface to a tabular interface that presented search results grouped according to objective, subjective, or commercial information in order to provide users with affordances for source evaluations (Kammerer & Gerjets, 2012). Results revealed that learners investigating a medical topic using the tabular interface paid less attention to commercial search results and selected objective search results more often and commercial ones less often than students using the list interface. Moreover, epistemic beliefs moderated the effects of the search interface such that students with strong beliefs that the Web contains (among other types of information) reliable knowledge showed a more focused information selection and better search outcomes in terms of their argumentative summaries when using the tabular interface than when using the list interface. Thus, in line with the model depicted in Fig. 4.2, particular aspects of learners' expertise as well as features of the interface design used for Web navigation might together determine learners' processing strategies in hypermedia environments. In another study (Kammerer & Gerjets, 2014), we investigated a similar, but technologically less demanding interface design, namely a grid format, which presented search results in multiple rows and columns (but without grouping them according to source types). We could show that the grid interface encourages users to engage in their own evaluations in order to decide which search results to select. This might be due to the fact that, contrary to a Google-like list interface, in a grid interface the decision about reading order is left open to the user and the ranking is less salient. Thus, search interfaces in educational contexts could potentially be improved by introducing source categories making different types of sources more salient or by introducing a grid interface making the ranking of links less salient. Our results show that even rather simple changes in the design of Web search interfaces might help to substantially increase learners' spontaneous use of source evaluation strategies when encountering Web resources in educational contexts.

Each technological milestone reviewed up to now (hypertext, hypermedia, and WWW) was fundamentally characterized by increasing the number of options for users to select, utilize, and manipulate information (i.e., selecting from multiple text links, multiple representations, and finally from multiple information sources). For each of these evolutionary steps, the question of whether the new options provided to learners would improve learning processes was critically dependent on learners' abilities to capitalize on the technological opportunities. However, as the research reported in this chapter clearly shows, new technological options seem to always impose new psychological challenges onto users. Learners experience difficulties in using navigational options appropriately and in selecting useful instructional materials. Moreover, they get easily overloaded and distracted from too many navigational options. As the examples from our own research show, counteracting these problems usually requires to carefully aligning instructional designs of materials and interfaces designs of hypermedia environments to various aspects of learners' expertise in order to achieve good results. These alignments might involve instructional measures like prompts or trainings as well as theory-based developments of new types of search interfaces, instructional animations, or linking structures.

Interestingly, the most recent milestone in the technological development of hypermedia environments, namely the paradigm shift to multimodality and mobility, might be somewhat different than all the milestones before. This technological step seems not to be characterized by providing more information and more complex navigational structures but by reducing the amount of available information due to context adaptation and by making navigation easier for learners due to multimodality. A brief overview of these developments will be given in the concluding section of this chapter.

Multimodal Adaptivity: Navigating Hypermedia with Mind and Body

In recent years, a paradigm shift towards multimodality and mobility in human interface interaction has taken place due to the establishment of mobile devices as the dominant interfaces for hypermedia exploration (Oviatt & Cohen, 2015). In this final section, some of our very recent research will be reviewed on how the innovative characteristics of mobile and multimodal hypermedia environments might be used to support learning. We will, however, not address the potential of these environments to support mobile and situated learning scenarios, which is a research tradition on its own (cf. Pfeiffer, Gemballa, Jarodzka, Scheiter, & Gerjets, 2009). Rather, we will focus on how new forms of multimodal interaction with hypermedia might solve some of the old issues that have been discussed throughout this chapter, namely issues of affording suitable navigation strategies, of selecting useful instructional materials, and of avoiding cognitive overload.

Intuitive ways of navigating complex hypermedia environments. Multimodal devices used for exploring hypermedia environments such as smartphones or tablets are usually equipped with built-in sensors such as multi-touch screens, cameras, and so forth, and are controlled directly by the body, for instance, by means of intuitive gesture-based interactions such as touching or swiping representations. Due to these intuitive interaction modalities, complex hypermedia environments might become much easier to navigate than before, so that they could even be used by very young groups of learners such as primary school children, who may not yet be able to use such environments on traditional desktop PCs (Lane & Ziviani, 2010). For instance, we used gesture-based interactions to design a rather complex multi-perspective hypermedia environment for fourth graders (Kornmann, Kammerer, Zettler, Trautwein & Gerjets, 2016). The multi-perspective hypermedia environment based on cognitive flexibility theory (Spiro & Jehng, 1990) conveyed information about the biodiversity of fish species and required learners to explore contents autonomously while at the same time switching between different perspectives on these contents (e.g., comparing the different fish species with regard to their size, living environment, eating habits, social behavior, or swimming style). The environment comprised interactive perspective pages showing different overviews of the different fish species, depending on the perspective chosen, as well as content pages for each of the species. We designed the environment for tablets, so that the navigation needed for exploring contents and for switching perspectives could be implemented by simple interaction gestures such as touches, swipes, and pinches to zoom. Additionally, all interactions were supported by animated visualizations showing the results of the interaction—for instance, the reordering of contents when the perspective was changed. An experimental comparison of this hypermedia environment to an information-equivalent linear multimedia-book on the tablet indicated that the hypermedia environment better supported children's ability to engage in multi-perspective scientific reasoning during the test phase, at least for children that had sufficient working-memory capacity at their disposal. Furthermore, Kornmann, Kammerer, Anjewerden, Zettler, Trautwein, and Gerjets (2016) analyzed learners' navigational behavior in this environment and observed that specific processing strategies afforded by the gesture-based interaction used in the environment (e.g., focusing on perspective pages rather than content pages) were responsible for superior learning outcomes. We concluded that intuitive multi-touch navigation could make it easier than ever before to afford suitable navigation strategies in hypermedia environments, thereby even enabling primary school children to successfully use complex multi-perspective hypermedia environments.

How do interactions with touches and swipes affect the learning mind? Beyond the obvious advantage that interaction gestures might allow for an intuitive navigation of complex hypermedia environments, touch-based interaction might also affect the mental processing of information during learning more deeply. For instance, Abrams, Davoli, Du, Knapp, and Paull (2008) postulated an enhancement of visual processing near the hand due to mechanisms involved in manipulating objects with the hands. Therefore, we investigate how the proximity of the hand during touch interaction influences the acquisition of visuospatial and verbal information as well as the processing of emotional stimuli. In a series of experiments, learners interacted with pictures of paintings together with text boxes containing additional information on a multi-touch table. Participants either touched the objects on the multi-touch table directly (i.e., the object was near the hand) or manipulated the objects indirectly by touching placeholders or goal positions of the objects (i.e., the object was further away from the hand). We could show that learning of visuo-spatial information was fostered near the hands, whereas hand proximity had no influence on learning verbal information (Brucker, Ehrmann, Edelmann, & Gerjets, 2016; Kranz, Imhof, Schwan, Kaup, & Gerjets, 2012). Thus, we concluded that touch interaction is not only an easy way to navigate hypermedia environments but might also be helpful for learning the contents one has interacted with.

This "near-hand effect" can be directly used by hypermedia designers, for instance by providing affordances for learners to touch important visuospatial infor-mation during interaction. In several touch-based hypermedia environments that we designed for tablets (e.g., the multi-perspective environment on fish biodiversity discussed in the last paragraph) and multi-touch tables (e.g., an interactive visitor information system called EyeVisit for an art museum, Gerjets, 2014), we exploited this principle extensively. In these environments, we made sure that the most impor-tant pictorial elements (instead of the corresponding words) are used as hyperlinks (i.e., "hyperpictures"), thereby affording learners to touch relevant visuospatial information. These examples show how touch navigation in hypermedia environ-ments can make it easier to afford suitable interaction strategies.

Beyond the cognitive advantages, we also found emotional influences of touch interaction. When we presented positive pictures to participants either near to the hand or further away from the hand after a sad mood induction (Ruiz Fernández, Lachmair, Rahona, & Gerjets, 2016b), we observed that participants in the near-hand condition showed a faster mood recovery than participants in the far-hand condition. We assumed that hand proximity increased attention allocation to the positive visuospatial information, thereby helping participants to improve their mood. We also found emotional influences of interaction gestures like swipes. For instance, in a study on the embodiment of abstract concepts (e.g., Casasanto, 2009), we asked participants to swipe pictures of neutral valence with their dominant right hand either to their left with a flexion movement or to their right with an extension movement (Ruiz Fernández, Lachmair, Rahona, & Gerjets, 2016a). When asking participants to rate the valence of the pictures, it turned out that pictures moved with an arm flexion to the left were evaluated more positive than pictures moved with an arm extension to the right. In line with embodiment theories, these findings provide evidence that specific types of interaction gestures might be associated with more abstract mental processes. Accordingly, interaction gestures in hypermedia environ-ments might carry "hidden meanings" beyond their explicit functions and beyond the intentions of the interaction designers—thereby exerting subtle influences on the processing of the information interacted with. This shows that there is much more to say about exploiting touch and interaction gestures for hypermedia learning than just that they allow for novel forms of intuitive navigation.

Sensor-based adaptivity and cognitive-load monitoring. In this chapter, we have been repeatedly discussing issues of cognitive overload during hypermedia learn-ing. For instance, navigational demands and distracting hyperlinks might impose cognitive load onto learners. Moreover, poor navigational decisions might lead to additional cognitive load when learners select instructional materials that are not appropriate in relation to their current level of expertise (see Fig. 4.2). Multimodal devices might enable novel approaches to avoid cognitive overload during hypermedia navigation due to their built-in touch sensors, cameras, and so forth. These sensors enable hypermedia environments, in principle, to adapt to learners' current physical, social, and even mental context (e.g., current workload), without the necessity for an explicit interaction on the part of the learner (implicit interaction, Schmidt, 2000). For instance, many apps for smartphones already use sensor information such as the GPS coordinates of users' current location to display relevant information for this location automatically. In our research, we concentrated on how prospective hypermedia learning environments might use sensor data to track learners' cognitive workload during learning in order to adaptively present learning materials or instructional support in relation to learners either being overwhelmed, underwhelmed or in an optimal zone of their cognitive capacity (cf. Gerjets, Walter, Rosenstiel, Bogdan, & Zander, 2014).

For instance, we collected interaction patterns of primary school children solving math tasks on a multi-touch device in a study evaluating the potential of high-resolution touch-sensor data (Mock et al., 2016). Based on these data, we investigated how machine-learning algorithms can be applied to predict cognitive workload associated with tasks of varying difficulty. Our results show that touchscreen interaction patterns can be used to predict high levels of working-memory load even without knowing anything about learners' speed and accuracy of task accomplishment. In another series of experiments where we used camera data to measure the pupil diameter, we found that this measure was responsive to different types of working-memory load in basic tasks as well as in instructional contexts. As an example, pupil diameter could be used to detect updating and inhibition demands in simple working-memory tasks (Scharinger, Soutschek, Schubert & Gerjets, 2015). In instructional settings, we found this measure to reliably reflect working-memory load due to link-selection processes when reading text (Scharinger, Kammerer, et al., 2015) as well as due to text-picture integration processes when studying multimedia materials (Scharinger, Schüler, & Gerjets, 2016).

The most advanced approach to using sensor-based cognitive-load monitoring for adaptive hypermedia environments would probably be to rely on neurophysiological data (e.g., data from skin electrodes on the scalp) that might become accessible for practical purposes in the near future. In our own lab we used approaches from brain–computer interfaces to investigate the potentials of using EEG data for designing future hypermedia learning environments. We could demonstrate that quite simple frequency band measures from a handful of EEG electrodes might be helpful to substantially improve the detection of working-memory load in tasks ranging from working-memory tasks, math tasks, reading tasks, Web search tasks to multimedia learning (Gerjets et al., 2014; Scharinger, Kammerer, et al., 2015, 2016; Scharinger, Schüler, et al., 2016, Scharinger, Soutschek, et al., 2015, 2017). As expected, cognitive-load monitoring based on EEG data seems to be more exact than monitoring based on touch or camera data. For instance, we could systematically distinguish different components of working-memory load (i.e., updating demands versus inhibition demands) in EEG-based neural signatures (Krumpe, Scharinger, Gerjets, Rosenstiel, & Spüler, 2016). With regard to instructional applications, we were able to differentiate several levels of cognitive workload in arithmetic tasks by means of machine-learning algorithms (Spüler et al., 2016). In the future, this method of graded workload detection might be used to develop math learning environments that improve arithmetic learning by means of real-time EEG-based workload adaption of the learning tasks provided (Walter, Rosenstiel, Bogdan, Gerjets, & Spüler, 2016).

Although in this "brain–computer interface" type of hypermedia environment the learner no longer explicitly controls information selection, it is nevertheless controlled by learners' current mental state. These learning environments are literally navigated by learners' minds but without requiring their conscious attention. In the future, there might be hypermedia environments in which sensor-based adaptations are able to replace at least some of learners' choices with regard to learning materials or instructional support measures. This might be considered to be a positive development as many research findings reported in "Hypertext: Learning from Nonlinear Text," "Hypermedia: Interacting with Multiple External Representations," "The World Wide Web: Evaluating Multiple Information Sources," and "Multimodal Adaptivity: Navigating Hypermedia with Mind and Body" sections of this chapter show that learners perform poorly in selecting appropriate learning materials and additionally become easily distracted and cognitively overloaded when given the option to select materials.

Conclusion. To conclude this chapter with venturing a glimpse in the future, it might well be that navigating prospective hypermedia environments with mind and body due to gesture-based and sensor-based forms of interaction might solve some long-standing problems of hypermedia learning, for instance by allowing for an easier navigation or by finding a better balance between learner-controlled and system-controlled learning. Looking back to the beginning of this chapter, hypermedia-assisted learning has obviously been coming a long way from its very beginnings as nonlinear text to its current form, where the information universe of the WWW can be intuitively navigated by touch interaction on mobile and context-aware devices. Nevertheless, each step of this enormous technological development has also raised numerous psychological research questions that kept our lab as well as many other labs worldwide busy in the past 15 years. One of the main messages that should become clear from the research reported in this chapter is that technology without psychology will probably not be sufficient to substantially improve hypermedia environments for learning. For the future, it can be expected that prospective technological developments might lead to an even closer connection between cognition and technology, for instance, based on further developments in sensor technologies, display technologies (e.g., head-mounted virtual reality displays), and machine-learning algorithms, together potentially enabling completely new and hopefully useful forms of interaction with hypermedia learning materials.

References

Abrams, R. A., Davoli, C. C., Du, F., Knapp, W. H., & Paull, D. (2008). Altered vision near the hands. *Cognition, 107*(3), 1035–1047. doi:10.1016/j.cognition.2007.09.006.

Atkinson, R. K., Derry, S. J., Renkl, A., & Wortham, D. (2000). Learning from examples: Instructional principles from the worked examples research. *Review of Educational Research, 70*(2), 181–214.

Azevedo, R. (2005). Using hypermedia as a metacognitive tool for enhancing student learning? The role of self-regulated learning. *Educational Psychologist, 40*(4), 199–209.

Bendixen, L. D., & Hartley, K. (2003). Sucessful learning with hypermedia: The role of epistemological beliefs and metacognitive awareness. *Journal of Educational Computing Research, 28*(1), 15–30.

Braasch, J. L. G., Rouet, J.-F., Vibert, N., & Britt, M. A. (2012). Readers' use of source information in text comprehension. *Memory & Cognition, 40*, 450–465. doi:10.3758/s13421-011-0160-6.

Brand-Gruwel, S., & Gerjets, P. (2008). Instructional support for enhancing students' information problem solving ability. *Computers in Human Behavior, 24*, 615–622.

Brand-Gruwel, S., Wopereis, I., & Vermetten, Y. (2005). Information problem solving by experts and novices: Analysis of a complex cognitive skill. *Computers in Human Behavior, 21*, 487–508. doi:10.1016/j.chb.2004.10.005.

Brucker, B., Ehlis, A.-C., Häußinger, F. B., Fallgatter, A. J., & Gerjets, P. (2015). Watching corresponding gestures facilitates learning with animations by activating human mirror-neurons: An fNIRS study. *Learning and Instruction, 36*, 27–37.

Brucker, B., Ehrmann, A., Edelmann, J., & Gerjets, P. (2016). Near-hand-attention on multi-touch devices: Touching digital information fosters visuospatial learning (manuscript submitted for publication).

Brucker, B., Scheiter, K., & Gerjets, P. (2014). Learning with dynamic and static visualizations: Realistic details only benefit learners with high visuospatial abilities. *Computers in Human Behavior, 36*, 330–339. doi:10.1016/j.chb.2014.03.077.

Bush, V. (1945). As we may think. *Atlantic Monthly, 176*, 101–108.

Casasanto, D. (2009). Embodiment of abstract concepts: Good and bad in right- and left-handers. *Journal of Experimental Psychology: General, 138*(3), 351–367. doi:10.1037/a0015854.

Chen, S. Y., Fan, J.-P., & Macredie, R. D. (2006). Navigation in hypermedia learning systems: Experts vs. novices. *Computers in Human Behavior, 22*(2), 251–266. doi:10.1016/j.chb.2004.06.004.

Chen, C., & Rada, R. (1996). Interacting with hypertext: A meta-analysis of experimental studies. *Human Computer Interaction, 11*, 125–156.

Collier, G. H. (1987). Thoth-II: Hypertext with explicit semantics. In *Proceedings of the ACM Conference on Hypertext* (pp. 269–289). ACM: New York. doi:10.1145/317426.317446

Conklin, J. (1987). Hypertext: An introduction and survey. *Computer, 20*, 17–41.

Cormode, G., & Krishnamurthy, B. (2008). Key differences between web 1.0 and web 2.0. *First Monday, 13*(6). Retrieved from http://firstmonday.org/ojs/index.php/fm/article/view/2125/1972

Dillon, A., & Gabbard, R. (1998). Hypermedia as an educational technology: A review of the quantitative research literature on learner comprehension, control, and style. *Review of Educational Research, 68*(3), 322–349.

Dillon, A., & Jobst, J. (2005). Multimedia learning in hypermedia. In R. Mayer (Ed.), *Cambridge handbook of multimedia learning* (pp. 569–588). Cambridge: Cambridge University Press.

Duffy, T. M., & Knuth, R. (1990). Hypermedia and instruction: Where is the match? In D. Jonassen & H. Mandl (Eds.), *Designing hypermedia for learning*. Berlin: Springer.

Gerjets, P. (2014). Vom Nutzen psychologischer Forschung für das Kunstmuseum. In L. von Stieglitz & T. Brune (Eds.), *Hin und Her – Dialoge in Museen zur Alltagskultur (Edition Museum, Band 9)* (pp. 113–124). Bielefeld: Transcript Verlag.

Gerjets, P., & Hellenthal-Schorr, T. (2008). Competent information search in the World Wide Web: Development and evaluation of a web training for pupils. *Computers in Human Behavior, 24*, 693–715.

Gerjets, P., & Hesse, F. W. (2004). When are powerful learning environments effective? The role of learning activities and of students' conceptions of educational technology. *International Journal of Educational Research, 41*, 445–465.

Gerjets, P., Kammerer, Y., & Werner, B. (2011). Measuring spontaneous and instructed evaluation processes during web search: Integrating concurrent thinking-aloud protocols and eye-tracking data. *Learning and Instruction, 21*, 220–231.

Gerjets, P., & Kirschner, P. (2009). Learning from multimedia and hypermedia. In S. Ludvigsen, N. Balacheff, T. de Jong, A. Lazonder, & S. Barnes (Eds.), *Technology-enhanced learning: Principles and products* (pp. 251–272). Berlin: Springer.

Gerjets, P., & Scheiter, K. (2003). Goal configurations and processing strategies as moderators between instructional design and cognitive load: Evidence from hypertext-based instruction. *Educational Psychologist, 38*, 33–41.

Gerjets, P., Scheiter, K., & Catrambone, R. (2006). Can learning from molar and modular worked-out examples be enhanced by providing instructional explanations and prompting self-explanations? *Learning and Instruction, 16*, 104–121.

Gerjets, P., Scheiter, K., Opfermann, M., Hesse, F. W., & Eysink, T. H. S. (2009). Learning with hypermedia: The influence of representational formats and different levels of learner control on performance and learning behavior. *Computers in Human Behavior, 25*(2), 360–370.

Gerjets, P., Scheiter, K., & Schuh, J. (2008). Information comparisons in example-based hypermedia environments: Supporting learners with processing prompts and an interactive comparison tool. *Educational Technology, Research & Development, 56*, 73–92.

Gerjets, P., Scheiter, K., & Tack, W. H. (2000). Resource-adaptive selection of strategies in learning from worked-out examples. In L. R. Gleitman & A. K. Joshi (Eds.), *Proceedings of the 22nd Annual Conference of the Cognitive Science Society* (pp. 166–171). Mahwah, NJ: Erlbaum.

Gerjets, P., Walter, C., Rosenstiel, W., Bogdan, M., & Zander, T. O. (2014). Cognitive state monitoring and the design of adaptive instruction in digital environments: Lessons learned from cognitive workload assessment using a passive brain-computer interface approach. *Frontiers in Neuroscience, 8*, 385. doi:10.3389/fnins.2014.00385.

Goldstone, R. L., & Son, J. Y. (2005). The transfer of scientific principles using concrete and idealized simulations. *The Journal of the Learning Sciences, 14*(1), 69–110.

Heise, E., Gerjets, P., & Westermann, R. (1997). The influence of a waiting intention on action performance: Efficiency impairment and volitional protection in tasks of varying difficulty. *Acta Psychologica, 97*, 167–182. doi: 10.1016/S00016918(97)000279.

Hoffmann, S. (1997). Elaboration theory and hypermedia: Is there a link? *Educational Technology, 37*(1), 57–64.

Horrigan, J. (2006). The internet as a resource for news and information about science. *Pew Internet & American Life Project*. Retrieved from http://www.pewinternet.org/Reports/2006/The-Internet-as-a-Resource-for-News-and-Information-about-Science.aspx

Jacobson, M. J., & Spiro, R. J. (1995). Hypertext learning environments, cognitive flexibility, and the transfer of complex knowledge: An empirical investigation. *Journal of Educational Computing Research, 12*, 301–333.

Jonassen, D. H. (1986). Hypertext principles for text and courseware design. *Educational Psychologist, 21*, 269–292.

Jonassen, D. H. (1989). *Hypertext/hypermedia*. Englewood Cliffs, NJ: Educational Technology Publications.

Kammerer, Y., Amann, D., & Gerjets, P. (2015). When adults without university education search the Internet for health information: The roles of Internet-specific epistemic beliefs and a source evaluation intervention. *Computers in Human Behavior, 48*, 297–309.

Kammerer, Y., Bråten, I., Gerjets, P., & Strømsø, H. I. (2013). The role of Internet-specific epistemic beliefs in laypersons' source evaluations and decisions during Web search on a medical issue. *Computers in Human Behavior, 29*, 1193–1203. doi:10.1016/j.chb.2012.10.012.

Kammerer, Y., & Gerjets, P. (2012). Effects of search interface and internet-specific epistemic beliefs on source evaluations during web search for medical information: An eye-tracking study. *Behaviour & Information Technology, 31*, 83–97. doi:10.1016/j.chb.2012.10.012.

Kammerer, Y., & Gerjets, P. (2014). The role of search result position and source trustworthiness in the selection of Web search results when using a list or a grid interface. *International Journal of Human-Computer-Interaction, 30*, 177–191.

Kammerer, Y., Kalbfell, E., & Gerjets, P. (2016). Is this information source commercially biased? How contradictions between web pages stimulate the consideration of source information. *Discourse Processes, 53*(5/6), 430–456. doi:10.1080/0163853X.2016.1169968.

Kornmann, J., Kammerer, Y., Anjewierden, A., Zettler, I., Trautwein, U., & Gerjets, P. (2016). How children navigate a multiperspective hypermedia environment: The role of spatial working memory capacity. *Computers in Human Behavior, 55*, 145–158.

Kornmann, J., Kammerer, Y., Zettler, I., Trautwein, U., & Gerjets, P. (2016). Hypermedia exploration stimulates multiperspective reasoning in elementary school children with high working memory capacity: A tablet computer study. *Learning and Individual Differences, 51*, 277–283.

Kranz, J., Imhof, B., Schwan, S., Kaup, B., & Gerjets, P. (2012). Learning art history on multi-touch-tables: Metaphorical meaning of interaction gestures matters. In E. de Vries & K. Scheiter (Eds.), *Proceedings of the EARLI Special Interest Group Text and Graphics: Staging Knowledge and Experience: How to Take Advantage of Representational Technologies in Education and Training?* (pp. 109–111). Grenoble, France: Université Pierre-Mendès-France.

Krumpe, T., Scharinger, C., Gerjets, P., Rosenstiel, W., & Spüler, M. (2016). Disentangeling working memory load—Finding inhibition and updating components in EEG data. In G. R. Müller-Putz, J. E. Huggins, & D. Steyrl (Eds.), *Proceedings of the 6th International Brain-Computer Interface Meeting: BCI Past, Present, and Future* (p. 174). Graz: Verlag der Technischen Universität Graz.

Kühl, T., Scheiter, K., Gerjets, P., & Edelmann, J. (2011). The influence of text modality on learning with static and dynamic visualizations. *Computers in Human Behavior, 27*, 29–35. doi:10.1016/j.chb.2010.05.008.

Landow, G. P. (1992). *Hypertext. The convergence of contemporary literary theory and technology*. Baltimore, MD: John Hopkins University Press.

Lane, A. E., & Ziviani, J. M. (2010). Factors influencing skilled use of the computer mouse by school-aged children. *Computers & Education, 55*, 1112–1122 http://dx.doi.org/10.1016/j.compedu.2010.05.008.

Linek, S., Gerjets, P., & Scheiter, K. (2010). The speaker/gender effect: Does the speaker's gender matter when presenting auditory text in multimedia messages? *Instructional Science, 38*, 503–521.

Marchionini, G. (1988). Hypermedia and learning: Freedom and chaos. *Educational Technology, 28*(11), 8–12.

Mayer, R. E. (2009). *Multimedia learning* (2nd ed.). New York, NY: Cambridge University Press.

Mayes, T., Kibby, M., & Anderson, T. (1990). Learning about learning from hypertext. In D. H. Jonassen & H. Mandl (Eds.), *Designing hypermedia for learning* (pp. 227–250). Berlin: Springer.

Mock, P., Gerjets, P., Tibus, M., Trautwein, U., Möller, K., & Rosenstiel, W. (2016). Using touchscreen interaction data to predict cognitive workload. In Y. I. Nakano, E. André, T. Nishida, L.-P. Morency, C. Busso, & C. Pelachaud (Eds.), *Proceedings of the 18th ACM International Conference on Multimodal Interaction* (pp. 349-356). New York, NY: ACM.

Nathan, M. J., Kintsch, W., & Young, E. (1992). A theory of algebra-word-problem comprehension and its implications for the design of learning environments. *Cognition and Instruction, 9*, 329–389.

Nelson, T. H. (1965). Complex information processing: A file structure for the complex, the changing and the indeterminate. In *ACM'65—Proceedings of the 1965 20th National Conference* (pp. 84–100). New York: ACM. doi:10.1145/800197.806036.

Niederhauser, D. S., Reynolds, R. E., Salmen, D. L., & Skolmoski, P. (2000). The influence of cognitive load on learning from hypertext. *Journal of Educational Computing Research, 23*, 237–255.

Nielsen, J. (1989). The matters that really matter for hypertext usability. In *Proceedings of the ACM Conference on Hypertext—Hypertext'89* (pp. 239–248). New York: ACM.

Nielsen, J. (1990). *Hypertext and hypermedia.* London: Academic.

OECD. (2011). *PISA 2009 results: Students on line: Digital technologies and performance* (Vol. VI). Paris: OECD.

Oviatt, S., & Cohen, P. R. (2015). *The paradigm shift to multimodality in contemporary computer interfaces.* San Rafael, CA: Morgan & Claypool.

Pfeiffer, V. D. I., Gemballa, S., Jarodzka, H., Scheiter, K., & Gerjets, P. (2009). Situated learning in the mobile age: Mobile devices on a field trip to the sea. *Research in Learning Technology, 17,* 187–199.

Rouet, J.-F., & Levonen, J. J. (1996). Studying and learning with hypertext: Empirical studies and their implications. In J.-F. Rouet, J. J. Levonen, A. Dillon, & R. J. Spiro (Eds.), *Hypertext and cognition* (pp. 9–23). Mahwah, NJ: Lawrence Erlbaum Associates.

Rouet, J.-F., Levonen, J. J., Dillon, A., & Spiro, R. J. (1996). *Hypertext and cognition.* Mahwah, NJ: Erlbaum.

Ruiz Fernández, S., Lachmair, M., Rahona, J. J., & Gerjets, P. (2016a). Flexing to the left, extending to the right: Disambiguating motor from spatial grounding mechanisms for valáence judgements (manuscript submitted for publication).

Ruiz Fernández, S., Lachmair, M., Rahona, J. J., & Gerjets, P. (2016b). Hands on positive pictures: Hand proximity to positive pictures influences emotional regulation (manuscript submitted for publication).

Scharinger, C., Kammerer, Y., & Gerjets, P. (2015). Pupil dilation and EEG alpha frequency band power reveal load on executive functions for link-selection processes during text reading. *PLoS ONE, 10*(6), e0130608.

Scharinger, C., Kammerer, Y., & Gerjets, P. (2016). Fixation-related EEG frequency band power analysis: A promising neuro-cognitive methodology to evaluate the matching-quality of web search results? In C. Stephanidis (Ed.), Communications in computer and information science series, Vol. 617 (pp. 245–250). Cham, Switzerland: Springer International Publishing.

Scharinger, C., Schüler, A., & Gerjets, P. (2016). *Text-picture integration during learning—EEG frequency band power correlates of congruency effects, 4th Meeting of the EARLI SIG 22 Neuroscience and Education.* Amsterdam: Netherlands.

Scharinger, C., Soutschek, A., Schubert, T., & Gerjets, P. (2015). When flanker meets the n-back: What EEG and pupil dilation data reveal about the interplay between the two central-executive working memory functions inhibition and updating. *Psychophysiology, 52,* 1293–1304.

Scharinger, C., Soutschek, A., Schubert, T., & Gerjets, P. (2017). Comparison of the working memory load in n-back and working memory span tasks by means of EEG frequency band power and P300 amplitude. *Frontiers in Human Neuroscience, 11*:6.

Scheiter, K., & Gerjets, P. (2007). Learner control in hypermedia environments. *Educational Psychology Review, 19*(3), 285–307.

Scheiter, K., & Gerjets, P. (2010). Cognitive and socio-motivational aspects in learning with animations: There is more to it than "do they aid learning or not". *Instructional Science, 38,* 435–440. doi:10.1007/s11251-009-9118-5.

Scheiter, K., Gerjets, P., & Catrambone, R. (2006). Making the abstract concrete: Visualizing mathematical solution procedures. *Computers in Human Behavior, 22,* 9–26.

Scheiter, K., Gerjets, P., & Heise, E. (2014). Distraction during learning with hypermedia: Difficult tasks help to keep task goals on track. *Frontiers in Psychology, 5,* 268.

Scheiter, K., Gerjets, P., Huk, T., Imhof, B., & Kammerer, Y. (2009). The effects of realism in learning with dynamic visualizations. Learning and Instruction, 19(6), 481–494. doi:10.1016/j. learninstruc.2008.08.001

Scheiter, K., Gerjets, P., & Schuh, J. (2010). The acquisition of problem-solving skills in mathematics: How animations can aid understanding of structural problem features and solution procedures. *Instructional Science, 38,* 487–502.

Scheiter, K., Gerjets, P., Vollmann, B., & Catrambone, R. (2009). The impact of learner characteristics on information utilization strategies, cognitive load experienced, and performance in hypermedia learning. Learning and Instruction, 19, 387–401.

Scheiter, K., Schüler, A., & Eitel, A. (2017). Learning from multimedia: Cognitive processes and instructional support. In S. Schwan & U. Cress (Eds.), The psychology of digital learning: Constructing, exchanging, and acquiring knowledge with digital media. New York: Springer.

Schmidt, A. (2000). Implicit human computer interaction through context. *Personal Technologies, 4*(2–3), 191–199.

Schorr, T., Gerjets, P., Scheiter, K., & Laouris, Y. (2002). Designing sets of instructional examples to accomplish different goals of instruction. In W. D. Gray & C. D. Schunn (Eds.), *Proceedings of the 24th Annual Conference of the Cognitive Science Society* (pp. 810–815). Mahwah, NJ: Erlbaum.

Schüler, A., Scheiter, K., & Gerjets, P. (2011). Does the modality effect in multimedia learning appear only with text containing spatial information? *Zeitschrift für Pädagogische Psychologie, 25*(4), 257–267. doi:10.1024/1010-0652/a00005.

Schüler, A., Scheiter, K., Rummer, R., & Gerjets, P. (2012). Explaining the modality effect in multimedia learning: Is it due to a lack of temporal contiguity with written text and pictures? *Learning and Instruction, 22*, 92–102.

Schüler, A., Scheiter, K., & Gerjets, P. (2013). Is spoken text always better? Investigating the modality and redundancy effect with longer text presentation. *Computers in Human Behavior, 29*, 1590–1601. doi:10.1016/j.chb.2013.01.047.

Schwan, S. (2017). Digital pictures, videos, and beyond: Knowledge acquisition with realistic images. In S. Schwan & U. Cress (Eds.), The psychology of digital learning: Constructing, exchanging, and acquiring knowledge with digital media. New York: Springer.

Shapiro, A. M., & Niederhauser, D. S. (2004). Learning from hypertext: Research issues and findings. In D. H. Jonassen (Ed.), *Handbook of research for educational communications and technology* (pp. 605–622). Mahwah, NJ: Erlbaum.

Spiro, R. J., & Jehng, J.-C. (1990). Cognitive flexibility and hypertext: Theory and technology for the nonlinear and multidimensional traversal of complex subject matter. In D. Nix & R. J. Spiro (Eds.), *Cognition, education, and multimedia* (pp. 163–205). Hillsdale, NJ: Erlbaum.

Spüler, M., Walter, C., Rosenstiel, W., Gerjets, P., Moeller, K., & Klein, E. (2016). EEG-based prediction of cognitive workload induced by arithmetic: A step towards online adaptation in numerical learning. *ZDM Mathematics Education, 48*(3), 267–278. doi:10.1007/s11858-015-0754-8.

Sweller, J., van Merriënboer, J. J. G., & Paas, F. G. W. C. (1998). Cognitive architecture and instructional design. *Educational Psychology Review, 10*, 251–296.

Tabbers, H. K., Martens, R. L., & van Merriënboer, J. J. G. (2004). Multimedia instructions and cognitive load theory: Effects of modality and cueing. *British Journal of Educational Psychology, 71*, 71–81.

Tergan, S.-O. (1997a). Conceptual and methodological shortcomings in hypertext/hypermedia design and research. *Journal of Educational Computing Research, 16*(3), 209–235.

Tergan, S.-O. (1997b). Misleading theoretical assumptions in hypertext/hypermedia research. *Journal of Educational Multimedia and Hypermedia, 6*(3/4), 395–412.

Walter, C., Rosenstiel, W., Bogdan, M., Gerjets, P., & Spüler, M. (2016). Improving arithmetic learning by real-time EEG-based workload adaptation (manuscript submitted for publication).

Wiley, J., Goldman, S., Graesser, A., Sanchez, C., Ash, I., & Hemmerich, J. (2009). Source evaluation, comprehension, and learning in internet science inquiry tasks. *American Educational Research Journal., 46*, 1060–1106.

Chapter 5
Knowledge Exchange as a Motivated Social Process

Annika Scholl, Florian Landkammer, and Kai Sassenberg

Abstract Be it in the case of learning together or cooperating with each other at universities, in schools, at work or during leisure time, individuals usually need to exchange knowledge in order to achieve their goals. Knowledge exchange contributes to joint performance, provided that the knowledge is, indeed, effectively exchanged. Such knowledge exchange often occurs via computer-mediated communication (cmc): e-mails, online chats, blogs, or social networks provide an easy opportunity to exchange information at all times and with a wide range of users. Yet, people do not always exchange knowledge via digital media effectively– although digital media would technically allow them to do so. Why is this the case and how can we foster exchange? This chapter considers knowledge exchange as a socially motivated process. We argue that, at times, people may be motivated to share their information with others, such as when trying to reach a decision together as a group; yet, at other times, people might strategically withhold information from others, such as when trying to keep a personal advantage. This chapter outlines from an experimental, social–psychological approach how specific social constellations between users can elicit such group- or self-serving motives and how these can enhance or hinder knowledge exchange. Finally, we discuss how barriers for knowledge exchange may be overcome in order to facilitate collaboration in cmc (or face-to-face) contexts.

Keywords Information sharing • Information exchange • Social processes • Motivation

No matter whether individuals learn together or cooperate at universities, in schools, at work or during leisure time, they usually need to exchange knowledge in order to achieve their goals. For instance, project teams implementing innovations in a company have to share their knowledge to reach an optimal outcome. Students learning together

A. Scholl (✉) • F. Landkammer • K. Sassenberg
Leibniz-Institut für Wissensmedien (IWM), Schleichstraße 6, 72076 Tübingen, Germany
e-mail: a.scholl@iwm-tuebingen.de; f.landkammer@iwm-tuebingen.de;
k.sassenberg@iwm-tuebingen.de

© Springer International Publishing AG 2017
S. Schwan, U. Cress (eds.), *The Psychology of Digital Learning*,
DOI 10.1007/978-3-319-49077-9_5

for an exam or preparing a joint presentation need to exchange information and build upon each other's input to achieve a good grade. As these examples demonstrate, knowledge exchange is a central factor in everyday cooperations that contributes to joint performance—provided that the knowledge is, indeed, effectively exchanged.

Nowadays, information exchange often occurs via computer-mediated communication (cmc): e-mails, online chats, blogs, or social networks provide an easy opportunity to exchange information at all times and with a wide range of users. Yet, individuals do not always exchange information via digital media *effectively* although digital media would technically allow them to do so. Research investigating preconditions of successful information exchange in cmc largely focused on the design of the medium, user characteristics (e.g., personality), or the interaction of both (cf. Buder, this volume; Sassenberg, 2013). However, particularly in cmc, the *social constellation* (e.g., competitive or hierarchical relations) between communication partners should affect communication behavior and its outcomes (see Postmes, Spears, & Lea, 1998). The impact of such social constellations between users has often been neglected (but see, e.g., Cress, 2005; Kimmerle, Wodzicki, & Cress, 2008; Matschke, Moskaliuk, Bokhorst, Schümmer, & Cress, 2014).

To extend this research, a number of our studies over the last years tested the impact of a variety of characteristics of social constellations on information exchange in cmc contexts. This research, summarized in this chapter, considers information exchange as a socially motivated process. Specifically, we argue that individuals will be motivated to share their information with others, for instance, when trying to reach a decision together as a group—yet, they will strategically withhold information from others when trying to keep a personal advantage. In this chapter, we outline how specific social constellations between users can elicit such *group-* or *self*-serving motives and, subsequently, guide information exchange. Taking an experimental, social–psychological approach, we investigate information exchange in (standardized) cmc contexts in most studies. We here differentiate two aspects of information exchange, namely, *sharing* information with others (e.g., by mentioning a piece of information in an e-mail discussion) and *using* information from others (e.g., integrating another person's information into a decision).

In what follows, we first discuss why social constellations are important in cmc. We then outline how central dimensions of social constellations between users in cmc can activate group- or self-serving tendencies and, thereby, help or hinder information exchange, respectively. Finally, we provide an outlook how aspects of these social constellations can be effectively combined in order to overcome self-serving motives and, ultimately, facilitate information sharing in social contexts.

The Relevance of Social Constellations for Information Exchange in cmc

"Social constellation" refers to the (perceived or actual) social relation between two or more individuals. The term covers a broad range of factors, including the perceived quality of an interpersonal relationship (e.g., subjective closeness to one's communication partner) or to a group (e.g., one's team), the perceived or actual interdependence structure of a situation, such as competition or differences in social power, as well as joint or different goals between communication partners. Considering these social constellations is particularly relevant in cmc because less social cues (e.g., person characteristics or nonverbal signals between users) are transmitted (compared to face-to-face communication). Early Internet research (e.g., Kiesler, Siegel, & McGuire, 1984) was dominated by the assumption that the transmission of less social cues should render social factors (e.g., social constellations) less important in cmc than face-to-face communication. Empirical evidence supported this assumption only in some cases, but contradicted it in other cases (for a summary, see Sassenberg & Jonas, 2007).

Integrating these inconsistent findings, the Social Identity Model of Deindividuation Effects (SIDE; Postmes et al., 1998) posits that a social constellation, as it is perceived *before* cmc takes place, especially influences perceptions and behavior during a subsequent communication. That is, power relations, competitive situations, or differences in prior knowledge, but also group goals and shared identification that communication partners experience beforehand should particularly guide subsequent behavior in cmc. This is because the lack of social cues and, thus, relatively higher anonymity during cmc strengthens these initially perceived social constellations. Empirical evidence supported these ideas (for an overview, see also Sassenberg & Jonas, 2007). This suggests that investigating the role of social constellations for information exchange is important in cmc.

This chapter summarizes research based on different (facets of) social constellations (for an overview, see Fig. 5.1). These studies are conducted in line with core social psychological methods—that is, in experimental setting using cmc—because work in this tradition often implements cmc. It thus is ideally suited to facilitate the understanding of the impact of social constellations in cmc. We first focus on preconditions *fostering* information exchange—that is, social constellations highlighting commonalities with others that activate group-serving tendencies. Specifically,

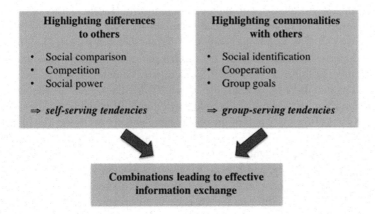

Fig. 5.1 Overview of social constellations summarized in this chapter that affect information exchange

we outline how social identification motivates individuals to actively contribute information to their group and how making each other's expertise explicit can improve information exchange. We then turn to factors *undermining* information exchange—that is, social constellations highlighting differences to others that activate *self*-serving tendencies. Here, we explain the role of social comparisons with others, competition (vs. cooperation), individual (vs. group) goals, and power hierarchies. For each of these predictors, potentially useful strategies on how to circumvent the detrimental consequences for information exchange will be outlined.

Preconditions Fostering Information Exchange

When Others Are Part of the Self: Social Identification with a Joint Group

Sharing information with others is, oftentimes, not strictly or formally required. In other words, it may be considered a behavior that individuals more or less voluntarily engage in—such as in the case of an employee sharing her lessons learned from a project with current and future colleagues on the intranet, or a student summarizing important details about an exam for future generations within a social network.

At the same time, sharing information with others requires some time and effort. Accordingly, an individual's motivation to take this extra step and actively engage in such behavior partly depends on who the recipients are, or how *socially close* these recipients seem to the individual. Here, a close personal relationship to communication partners can contribute to individuals' willingness to share information (see Sassenberg & Scholl, 2010). Yet, not all communication partners know each other well in person, especially in cmc—for instance, when exchanging information with group members at different locations or with (potentially unknown) colleagues on an organization's internal communication platform. Hence, factors beyond high-quality interpersonal relationships need to be considered.

A positive relation to a joint group that communication partners belong to can much easier be established (Utz, 2003). Such a *shared social identity* with the other group members (Tajfel & Turner, 1979) facilitates voluntary effort in favor of the group and its members (e.g., Matschke et al., 2014; Riketta, 2002). The more individuals identify with the group of people they communicate with, the more they are willing to exert effort on behalf of the group's interests (Ouwerkerk, de Gilder, & de Vries, 2000); this should include a higher willingness to share information with members of a group one identifies with.

Behringer, Sassenberg, and Scholl (in press) investigated this idea in an organizational cmc context. Specifically, we examined the relation between social identification and employees' information sharing on an organization's intranet (i.e., an internal wiki). A common problem with platforms like these is that, despite their purpose to provide tools for exchanging work-related information, individuals often do not use them much (Pirkkalainen & Pawlowski, 2014). We assumed that social identification with the organization should predict a greater willingness to actively share information on the platform. Besides social identification, however, the expected usefulness of such behavior should moderate the effect (see Vroom, 1964): Social identification with the organization should only predict more information sharing if individuals consider the platform to be useful. The results supported these predictions, indicating how social identification with the group and media perception (here: perceived usefulness of the platform) jointly guide information sharing in a real-life context.

Adding to these findings, Woltin and Sassenberg (2015) performed a controlled lab experiment and tested the impact of social identification on computer-mediated information sharing among undergraduates. Here, we investigated information sharing by means of the time individuals invested into providing group members with hints to solve a joint group task. The results indicated that individuals invested more time to give hints, the more they identified with their group; however, this was only the case if participants were informed that their hints would be useful in potentially contributing to the group's success (compared to when they were informed that the hints were, most likely, not instrumental).

Taken together, these findings suggest that social identification with a joint group can motivate individuals to take the extra step and invest effort into actively sharing information with their group. Specifically, social identification with a joint group motivates information sharing, as long as such sharing is (subjectively) benefitting the group within the current context. Hence, the (subjective) social constellation and media perceptions (e.g., the perceived usefulness of a cmc tool) can jointly foster information exchange among group members.

Expert Roles and Knowledge Awareness: Making Knowledge Differences Explicit

Another factor contributing to information sharing is the extent to which communication partners become *aware* of their knowledge differences and, therefore, can adaptively share the specific information that the other person does not possess. Consider, for instance, two students learning together for an exam. Both students might possess specific knowledge. One learning partner may be an "expert" in one domain and be able to explain corresponding topics, in which the other learning partner lacks understanding, and vice versa. Here, collaborative learning can improve both students' performance—provided that the students realize that they each possess individual expertise that is worth sharing with each other (Crommelinck & Anseel, 2013).

Investigating this idea, Sassenberg, Boos, and Klapproth (2001) tested how assigning communication partners to *roles as experts*, which make each other's knowledge explicit, contributes to information exchange in a group decision context via cmc.

Particularly, this research investigated the impact of differently introduced expert roles for information sharing. One role involved being an "information"-based expert to make differences in the possessed information explicit; the other role implied being a "decision-making" expert possessing specific competencies rather than information. The results indicated that assigning participants the role of "information"-based (but not "decision-making") expert facilitated their willingness to share information with others. In line with the idea that perceived social constellations particularly affect behavior in cmc, these assigned expert roles seemed to promote information sharing much stronger in this study, using cmc, than in earlier research, using face-to-face groups (Stasser, Stewart, & Wittenbaum, 1995).

Beyond such role assignments, the so-called knowledge awareness tools in cmc make individuals' knowledge explicit. These tools graphically depict each communication partner's knowledge on a respective topic. In doing so, knowledge awareness tools enable individuals to effectively adapt their information sharing—it helps individuals to identify which information they should best provide to whom, resulting in better learning outcomes (e.g., Dehler, Bodemer, Buder, & Hesse, 2011).

In sum, this research indicates that creating an *awareness* of each other's knowledge—indicated by assigned expert roles or digital awareness tools in cmc—can facilitate information sharing. Yet, one can wonder if such an awareness of knowledge differences is, indeed, always beneficial. Knowing more than others can also boost self-esteem (Festinger, 1954). Hence, individuals may sometimes be tempted not to share their superior knowledge as a means to *protect* their self-esteem and maintain their status. The following section targets such cases.

Preconditions Diminishing Information Exchange and Potential Solutions

Social Comparisons: Keeping One's Superior Knowledge

Students learning together might not be willing to share their unique information under all circumstances. Rather, they may strive to keep information to themselves, if knowledge awareness tools provide them with the opportunity to compare with learning partners. If individuals recognize, in such a social comparison, that they possess superior information, this is beneficial for their self-esteem (Tesser, 1988). As an outcome, learners might prefer *not* to share their superior information in order to protect their self-esteem (i.e., not to lose the basis for the positive social comparison). Importantly, social comparison during collaborative learning is only possible in cases when individuals are (made) aware of the learning partner's state of knowledge—for instance, by means of a Knowledge Awareness tool. Accordingly, superior students who are provided with knowledge awareness could harm their self-esteem if they share their information to help the learning partner. They might, thus, rather keep their information and protect their (indicated) relative advantage over the other person.

In two experiments, Ray, Neugebauer, Sassenberg, Buder, and Hesse (2013) investigated a chronic or induced predisposition for social comparison and information sharing in collaborative learning settings with and without Knowledge Awareness tools. We assumed that the stronger individuals' predisposition for social comparison is, the more they should be motivated to keep an advantage over their learning partner when a knowledge awareness tool was available. In a collaborative learning context with knowledge awareness, this can be achieved by withholding (i.e., *not* sharing) one's information.

In Ray et al.'s (2013) studies, participants became aware that a learning partner was less knowledgeable than they were themselves by means of a graphical Knowledge Awareness tool. It depicted the participant's own knowledge and the learning partner's (comparatively lower) knowledge on a number of topics. Participants could then provide their learning partner with information, or more specifically, with explanations about the learning topics they were more knowledgeable about. Before providing their explanations, participants' social comparison orientation was either measured or experimentally manipulated. We found that, although Knowledge Awareness facilitated matching the *explained topics* to the learning partner's needs (i.e., their partner's knowledge gaps), the *extent* of these explanations differed, depending on Knowledge awareness and participants' social comparison orientation: Participants high in social comparison orientation put much less *effort* into their explanations when Knowledge Awareness was given (and they were, by means of this tool, informed about the positive outcome of social comparison) than when Knowledge Awareness was not given. No such effect was found for participants low in social comparison orientation.

Notably, these detrimental effects of social comparison in combination with Knowledge Awareness pertained to situations in which participants interacted with *less* knowledgeable partners—the so-called *downward* social comparisons—and, thus, the individuals who should share information during collaborative learning. What happens, however, to less knowledgeable partners—those who should receive information—when using Knowledge Awareness tools? These tools make less knowledgeable individuals aware that their partners know more than themselves—representing the so-called *upward* social comparison. In such upward social comparisons in information exchange, the less knowledgeable individuals *receive* information from others and can use (or neglect) this information. Upward comparisons may constitute a threat to less knowledgeable individuals' self-esteem (Buchs & Butera, 2009); however, more knowledgeable partners can likewise serve as role models, motivating their partners to keep up and improve. Indeed, Neugebauer, Ray, and Sassenberg (2015) showed that learning partners profited most from upward social comparisons if (a) Knowledge Awareness was provided and (b) they were predisposed to attend to the knowledge differences (i.e., were high in social comparison orientation).

Put together, making differences in communication partners' state of knowledge salient provides the opportunity for social comparisons between the self and others. Among individuals that are predisposed to compare themselves to others (i.e., those high in social comparison orientation), such comparisons (i.e., whether oneself is the more or less knowledgeable partner) might elicit a strategic motivation—either to protect the self and *not* to share one's information, or to improve one's own performance by learning from others and *using* the others' superior information. Considering the interplay between individual tendencies to socially compare and the tools provided could help both individual learners and organizations (e.g., universities creating learning environments) to implement optimal conditions for information exchange.

Thinking Competitively, Cooperatively, or Both: The Role of Cognitive Schemata

Social comparisons are not only initiated by learning partners (as in the research summarized in the preceding section), but can also be inherent in the social constellation itself. In this vein, *competition* can be defined as a situation in which an individual's success is negatively related to the success of others (i.e., negative interdependence). Examples for a competition include two coworkers applying for the same job, or several students trying to outperform others to get a university place. In cooperative situations, on the contrary, the success of one person renders the success of others more likely (i.e., positive interdependence).

Research consistently demonstrated that competition (compared to cooperation) leads to negative interpersonal behavior—including less information exchange (e.g., Toma & Butera, 2009). Indeed, competition even enhances the distortion of information, that is, the sharing of information intentionally changed to be incorrect (e.g., Poortvliet, Janssen, Van Yperen, & Van de Vliert, 2007). On a social-cognitive level, such detrimental effects of competition can be explained with a specific, self-serving thinking style: Because the described behavior is, per se, functional for winning (e.g., to be the first to know the solution for a group task), the underlying strategies and thoughts (e.g., to keep information to oneself) become activated as soon as he/she perceives a situation as competitive. One important characteristic of such automatic thinking styles—or cognitive schemata (cf. Fiske & Taylor, 1991)—is that they remain active beyond a specific context, as long as they are not interrupted. Therefore, an activated competition schema can also be applied to subsequent, *unrelated* situations and interaction partners. This means that after being in a competition, even subsequent, unrelated situations will be perceived as more competitive (than after a cooperative or neutral situation; Sassenberg, Moskowitz, Jacoby, & Hansen, 2007).

These effects of competition—both within a situation and from one context to another—are relevant for information exchange. In competitive work environments, less information exchange and more information distortion (i.e., misleading others) should occur (compared to neutral or cooperative environments). In line with this notion, Landkammer and Sassenberg (2015) showed that competition (vs. cooperation and control) also enhances the distortion of information with uninvolved others (i.e., a carry-over effect of competition on information exchange).

Given that competition is particularly widespread in work environments, this calls for possible interventions. Reducing competition might result in the desired effect—yet, this is most likely not feasible in all contexts. *Combining* competition with cooperation might provide a more feasible workaround. Indeed, competition and cooperation are often not mutually exclusive, but many situations require both (Deutsch, 1949). Team members, for instance, might compete for a job promotion that only one of them will get. While trying to get the promotion, they need to cooperate on a project to which has been assigned to their team and for which every member's contribution is required. This context requires the team members to cooperate and compete at the same time. Situations like this have been called co-opetition (see Luo, Slotegraaf, & Pan, 2006 for co-opetition between a company's units).

How do these co-opetition contexts affect information sharing? Landkammer and Sassenberg (2016) argued that experiencing co-opetition activates mixed demands ("cooperate *and* compete") that are often considered contradictory. As a consequence, schematic competitive thinking cannot be applied and, thus, cannot guide behavior. In other words, co-opetition should *not* lead to schematic competitive thinking. Therefore, co-opetition should *not* have the same detrimental effects on information sharing as competition does. In line with this prediction, only competition enhanced the distortion of information in a subsequent task compared to cooperation, whereas co-opetition did not. Although co-opetition has been perceived to require competing, it did not elicit information distortion (i.e., behavior usually associated with competition) in our studies.

This indicates that competitive incentives do not impair information sharing, as long as other aspects of the situation, such as cooperative demands, prevent schematic competitive thinking. In line with this reasoning, we assumed that some individuals might have learned better than others to combine competition with cooperation. We examined this in the sports domain with team and individual athletes. Compared to individual athletes, team athletes have to compete (e.g., for starting positions) and to cooperate (e.g., to win games) with their teammates (i.e., one and the same social target). Hence, they may deal differently with competitive situations. Indeed, we found that whereas individual athletes reduce information sharing after performing a competitive task, team athletes do not (Landkammer, Sassenberg, & Thiel, 2015). In other words, team athletes, who frequently experience co-opetition, do not show carry-over effects of competition—presumably because they have learnt in their sports context to reconcile competition and cooperation.

In a nutshell, competitive situations can give rise to self-serving tendencies—that is, attempts to keep one's superior knowledge status. Importantly, a competition can carry over to subsequent situations, such that individuals may distort information or withhold information from communication partners who are, actually, completely uninvolved in the competition. On a positive note, these detrimental effects of competition can be remedied when competition and cooperation are combined in one-and-the-same situation, that is, by means of co-opetition. Similarly, frequent experiences of co-opetition seem to reduce the negative effects of competition. This provides crucial insights for potentially ideal conditions fostering information exchange in cmc.

Confirming Own Opinions When Receiving Information from Other Group Members

Beyond the problem that information is often insufficiently *shared* among group members, individuals tend to protect their own point of view when receiving and using information from others. Imagine, for instance, a group of personnel recruiters making decisions about the most suitable candidate for a job opening. Each group member may have formed a personal opinion before entering the discussion. If another group member voices new information that speaks in favor of another candidate, the other group members are likely to neglect this new information in order to protect their initial choice (Nickerson, 1998)—unless they are motivated to reach the best decision *together* as a group.

Research on group discussions suggests that after forming an initial opinion, individuals tend to judge the relevance of new information depending on whether it supports their initial opinion or not. As an outcome, they are likely to stick with this opinion (Greitemeyer & Schulz-Hardt, 2003). Resulting from this so-called confirmation bias (for a review, see Nickerson, 1998), group members often do not adequately receive and integrate information in their individual decisions (Greitemeyer & Schulz-Hardt, 2003).

Yet, this confirmation bias especially occurs under specific circumstances. In this regard, Sassenberg, Landkammer, and Jacoby (2014) investigated motivational conditions that enhance or diminish this confirmation bias when receiving information from others during e-mail communication. Specifically, we focused on individuals' (a) defensive vs. eager strategies and (b) the individual vs. group goals provided to perform a task. We expected the confirmation bias to be stronger when individuals apply *defensive* strategies (i.e., strive for security in a prevention focus; Higgins, 1997) compared to eager strategies (i.e., strive for advancement in a promotion focus). Applying defensive strategies means that individuals strive to prevent making mistakes and act more conservatively. In case of a group discussion that members enter with an initial opinion, this implies holding on to this initial opinion in order not to give it up prematurely (cf. Butera & Mugny, 2001). Hence, individuals applying defensive (rather than eager) strategies are less open to new information once they have formed an initial opinion (in contrast to when they have not formed such an opinion yet; Ditrich, Landkammer, Sassenberg, & Jacoby, 2014). As predicted, a set of studies showed that individuals applying a defensive (versus eager) strategy, indeed, exhibited a stronger confirmation bias towards new information that others shared via e-mail within their group (Sassenberg et al., 2014). Importantly, this higher confirmation bias, in turn, diminished receivers' memory of the new pieces of information presented in others' e-mails. Moreover, because of their confirmation bias, receivers showed fewer correct decision changes towards the correct alternative after reading others' e-mails.

Notably, this effect of defensive vs. eager strategies should only occur when individuals pursue an individual goal (e.g., to prevent personal errors, to demonstrate their own competencies)—which is usually the "standard" goal individuals pursue (Wittenbaum, Hollingshead, & Botero, 2004). In contrast, when individuals are given a *group goal*, this should heighten the importance of group (rather than individual) errors and group performance (DeShon, Kozlowski, Schmidt, Milner, & Wiechmann, 2004). Thus, in combination with a group goal, a defensive strategy should lead to a focus on the avoidance of errors *as a group*. Here, individual errors, such as giving up one's own opinion prematurely, should become less relevant and thus, the confirmation bias should be reduced. In other words, group goals should serve to compensate for individuals' defensive strategies. As expected, Sassenberg et al.'s (2014) studies found support for this assumption: Providing "defensive" individuals with the group goal to "solve a task successfully together as a team" (rather than an individual goal) did diminish the confirmation bias. When pursuing the group goal, the defensive (compared to the eager) strategy did no longer lead to heightened confirmation bias.

To conclude, individuals often tend to protect their own opinion when receiving new information from others (i.e., they show a confirmation bias). In particular, a defensive (vs. eager) strategy can impair the reception and use of information provided by others and, thereby, diminishes decision quality in social contexts. Yet, holding a group goal (i.e., to "move in the same direction") in cmc wipes out these detriments. Notably, although these defensive tendencies can already pose a risk for information exchange in equally powerful groups, the more severe risks can come from the selfish tendencies that can be found within power hierarchies, as we discuss in the following.

The Focus on Own Goals and the Selfishness of Those High in Power

Many social relations are characterized by (factual or perceived) hierarchical structures, that is, differences in *social power*. Going beyond the previous paragraphs that focused on equally powerful communication partners, this section examines hierarchical differences as another type of social constellation that can evoke self-serving motives.

Social power comprises asymmetric control over resources (e.g., money, social appreciation, social contacts; Fiske & Berdahl, 2007) and represents a characteristic of a social relation between at least two individuals. As such, the power-holder controls resources that the powerless person(s) depend(s) on and is relatively independent from others. Resulting from this independence, power provides freedom to act and to focus on currently activated goals (Guinote, 2007; Keltner, Gruenfeld, & Anderson, 2003).

Our own research investigated how (high versus low) social power guides (a) the (mental) effort individuals put into preparing an information exchange with others and (b) their willingness to share important information. First, we focused on their preparation when composing e-mails to communication partners. Due to its asynchronous nature, e-mail provides the opportunity to think one's actions through: Individuals can carefully construct and revise a message before sending it off, which can contribute to effective communication (Walther, 1996, 2007). Imagine, for instance, a professor and her student exchanging e-mails about a class. While the student will likely think extensively on how to best frame her requests, the professor might promptly compose a reply without thinking too much about how to respond. As social power facilitates goal-directed behavior (Guinote, 2007), we expected power to reduce preparation times during e-mail cmc though potentially without diminishing communication effectiveness. Results of an experiment confirmed this prediction: Participants in a high (versus low) power role thought less about their actions while composing their e-mail requests. Interestingly, this did, indeed, not harm the quality of their messages; in contrast, powerful individuals communicated their requests more persuasively than those low in power (Scholl & Sassenberg, 2014b).

Notably, this does not imply that power always diminishes such mental preparation for information exchange. In follow-up studies, we found that power-holders better adapt to the task at hand: More than the powerless, power-holders think their actions through when the task at hand requires them to do so (Scholl & Sassenberg, 2015), or when a prior exchange failed to produce the desired outcome (Scholl & Sassenberg, 2014a). In sum, power seems to enable individuals to better prepare for cmc with others.

Beyond such preparation for information exchange, power alters the willingness to share information with others. Due to their independence, power-holders often tend to act selfishly and in their own interest (for an overview, see Lammers, Dubois, Rucker, & Galinsky, 2015). Moreover, individuals high in power aim to keep the status quo, for instance, by protecting their resources against potential exploitation by the powerless (Inesi, Lee, & Rios, 2014). This implies that those high in power (e.g., team leaders) may tend to withhold important information more than powerless individuals, in order to take care of their resources and retain the status quo (i.e., their superior knowledge). Landkammer and Scholl (2015) tested this hypothesis and also examined a potential condition under which those high in power could be less selfish, but willing to share their important information with others. As described in the previous section, group goals are a potential means to strengthen the importance of joint (rather than individual) performance and thereby reduce self-serving tendencies (see Sassenberg et al., 2014).

We hypothesized that social power triggers self-serving motives and, thereby, reduces sharing of important information when individuals simply seek to "solve the task." In contrast, this effect should disappear when individuals receive the group goal to "solve the task *together as a team*," because such a group goal should reduce the self-serving motives social power comes with. Three experiments tested and confirmed this prediction: power-holders withheld more of their important information from others than the powerless when pursuing a task goal, but they shared as much important information as the powerless when pursuing a group goal. Indeed, the reduced willingness to share important information (in case of a task goal) was explained by a heightened self-serving orientation among the powerful (compared to the powerless; Landkammer & Scholl, 2015).

Once again, this demonstrates how self-serving motives can impair information exchange in social situations—here in the context of hierarchical relations. However, our research also outlines a potential solution to be implemented in team contexts: Group goals can buffer these selfish tendencies in the powerful and motivate them to share their important information with others.

Conclusion

Information exchange is crucial for effective cooperation and a group's success—be it at school, at the university, at work or in leisure contexts. Yet, individuals do not always share and receive information effectively—neither via cmc nor in face-to-face interactions. This chapter took a social psychological perspective on the conditions that may promote or hinder information exchange via digital media. More specifically, the chapter outlined preconditions that either motivate individuals to actively contribute information or motivate them to keep their information as well as to distort information. We focused on social constellations (on the individual and contextual level) as predictors of such tendencies because these constellations are of particular importance in cmc.

Indeed, our research demonstrates that some social constellations that highlight closeness to or *commonalities* with communication partners can foster information exchange: social identification (understanding a group as an essential part of the self), cooperation (in which a goal can, factually, only be achieved together), and group goals (which specifically imply the task to perform together). These constellations can activate group-serving motives and improve information exchange among communication partners (for an overview, see Fig. 5.1).

Yet, other social constellations can trigger self-serving motives, namely, those that provoke individuals to focus on the *self* and their *differences* to others, such as their own success and personal advantage relative to their communication partners (see Fig. 5.1). These social constellations include (opportunities for) social comparison (in which one individual tends to compare the self, relative to the other, striving for a positive outcome for one's self-esteem), competition (in which one individual needs to win against the other), and social power (in which one individual is relatively independent providing the opportunity to be selfish and not to care about others).

Understanding the effects of all these social constellations can help us to explain why some communication partners may be especially motivated (not) to engage in knowledge exchange, for instance, via e-mail or on a wiki. It can also provide crucial insights for the design and implementation of potential interventions boosting information sharing across contexts. On a cautious note, however, it may not always be possible to completely replace social constellations hindering information sharing—like competition—with contexts fostering it—like cooperation. Similarly, power hierarchies cannot be reduced in all contexts. Hence, our research suggests that specific *combinations* of such constellations may provide a useful intervention to overcome barriers for information sharing: Competition combined with cooperation (i.e., co-opetition) can successfully reduce the detrimental, self-serving tendencies the former comes with. Likewise, a powerful position or defensive strategies combined with a group goal can compensate for the usually negative, self-serving outcomes of (high) power or defensive proceeding.

In short, social constellations can help or hinder information sharing in cmc. Those dimensions hindering information sharing, like competitive relations or power hierarchies, cannot be resolved at all times. Yet, helping individuals who exchange information with each other to see these constellations through the new "lens" of serving the group might, in turn, prevent that such social constellations (e.g., competition or social power) pose a threat to effective information exchange.

References

Behringer, N., Sassenberg, K., & Scholl, A. (in press). Knowledge contribution in organizations via social media: The interplay of identification and perceived usefulness. Journal of Personnel Psychology. doi: 10.1027/1866-5888/a000169

Buchs, C., & Butera, F. (2009). Is a partner's competence threatening during dyadic cooperative work? It depends on resource interdependence. *European Journal of Psychology of Education, 24*, 145–154. doi:10.1007/BF03173007.

Buder, J. (2017). A conceptual framework of knowledge exchange. In S. Schwan, & U. Cress (Eds.), The psychology of digital learning: Constructing, exchanging, and acquiring knowledge with digital media (pp. xxx–xxx). New York: Springer.

Butera, F., & Mugny, G. (2001). Conflicts and social influences in hypothesis testing. In C. De Dreu & N. De Vries (Eds.), *Group consensus and minority influence: Implications for innovation* (pp. 160–182). Oxford: Blackwell.

Cress, U. (2005). Ambivalent effect of member portraits in virtual groups. *Journal of Computer Assisted Learning, 21*, 281–291.

Crommelinck, M., & Anseel, F. (2013). Understanding and encouraging feedback-seeking behavior: A literature review. *Medical Education, 47*, 232–241. doi:10.1111/medu.12075.

Dehler, J., Bodemer, D., Buder, J., & Hesse, F. W. (2011). Guiding knowledge communication in CSCL via group knowledge awareness. *Computers in Human Behavior, 27*, 1068–1078.

DeShon, R. P., Kozlowski, W. J., Schmidt, A. M., Milner, K. R., & Wiechmann, D. (2004). Multiple-goal, multilevel model of feedback effects on the regulation of individual and team performance. *Journal of Applied Psychology, 89*, 1035–1056.

Deutsch, M. (1949). A theory of cooperation and competition. *Human Relations, 2*, 129–152.

Ditrich, L., Landkammer, F., Sassenberg, K., & Jacoby, J. (2014). *The impact of regulatory focus and initial opinions on decision making.* Poster presented at the 17th General Meeting der European Association of Social Psychology (EASP), Amsterdam, The Netherlands.

Festinger, L. (1954). A theory of social comparison processes. *Human Relations, 7*, 117–140.

Fiske, S. T., & Berdahl, J. (2007). Social power. In A. W. Kruglanski & E. T. Higgins (Eds.), *Social psychology: Handbook of basic principles* (2nd ed., pp. 678–692). New York, NY: Guilford Press.

Fiske, S. T., & Taylor, S. E. (1991). *Social cognition* (2nd ed.). New York: McGraw-Hill.

Greitemeyer, T., & Schulz-Hardt, S. (2003). Preference-consistent evaluation of information in the hidden profile paradigm: Beyond group-level explanations for the dominance of shared information in group decisions. *Journal of Personality and Social Psychology, 84*, 322–339.

Guinote, A. (2007). Behaviour variability and the situated focus theory of power. *European Review of Social Psychology, 18*, 256–295.

Higgins, E. T. (1997). Beyond pleasure and pain. *American Psychologist, 52*, 1280–1300.

Inesi, M. E., Lee, S. Y., & Rios, K. (2014). Objects of desire: Subordinate ingratiation triggers self-objectification among powerful. *Journal of Experimental Social Psychology, 53*, 19–30.

Keltner, D., Gruenfeld, D. H., & Anderson, C. (2003). Power, approach, and inhibition. *Psychological Review, 110*, 265–284.

Kiesler, S., Siegel, J., & McGuire, T. W. (1984). Social psychological aspects of computer-mediated communication. *American Psychologist, 39*, 1123–1134.

Kimmerle, J., Wodzicki, K., & Cress, U. (2008). The social psychology of knowledge management. *Team Performance Management, 14*, 381–401. doi:10.1108/13527590810912340.

Lammers, J., Dubois, D., Rucker, D. D., & Galinsky, A. D. (2015). Power and morality. *Current Opinion in Psychology, 6*, 15–19.

Landkammer, F., & Scholl, A. (2015). *Group goals compensate for the corrupting effect of power on strategic information sharing.* Unpublished manuscript.

Landkammer, F., Sassenberg, K., & Thiel, A. (2015). *Team sports off the field: Competing excludes cooperating for individual but not for team athletes.* Unpublished manuscript.

Landkammer, F., & Sassenberg, K. (2016). Competing while cooperating with the same others: The consequences of conflicting demands in co-opetition. Journal of Experimental Psychology: General, 145, 1670–1686.

Luo, X., Slotegraaf, R. J., & Pan, X. (2006). Cross-functional 'coopetition': The simultaneous role of cooperation and competition within firms. *Journal of Marketing, 70*(2), 67–80. doi:10.1509/jmkg.70.2.67.

Matschke, C., Moskaliuk, J., Bokhorst, F., Schümmer, T., & Cress, U. (2014). Motivational factors of information exchange in social information spaces. *Computers in Human Behavior, 36*, 549–558. doi:10.1016/j.chb.2014.04.044.

Neugebauer, J., Ray, D. G., & Sassenberg, K. (2015). *When being worse helps: The influence of upward social comparisons and knowledge awareness on learner engagement and learning in collaborative settings.* Unpublished manuscript.

Nickerson, R. S. (1998). Confirmation bias: A ubiquitous phenomenon in many guises. *Review of General Psychology, 2*, 175–220.

Ouwerkerk, J. W., de Gilder, D., & de Vries, N. K. (2000). When the going gets tough, the tough get going: Social identification and individual effort in intergroup competition. *Personality and Social Psychology Bulletin, 26*, 1550–1559. doi:10.1177/01461672002612009.

Pirkkalainen, H., & Pawlowski, J. M. (2014). Global social knowledge management—Understanding barriers for global workers utilizing social software. *Computers in Human Behavior, 30*, 637–647. doi:10.1016/j.chb.2013.07.041.

Poortvliet, P. M., Janssen, O., Van Yperen, N. W., & Van de Vliert, E. (2007). Achievement goals and interpersonal behavior: How mastery and performance goals shape information exchange. *Personality and Social Psychology Bulletin, 33*(10), 1435–1447.

Postmes, T., Spears, R., & Lea, M. (1998). Breaching or building social boundaries? SIDE-effects of computer-mediated communication. *Communication Research, 25*, 689–715.

Ray, D. G., Neugebauer, J., Sassenberg, K., Buder, J., & Hesse, F. W. (2013). Motivated shortcomings in explanation: The role of comparative self-evaluation and awareness of explanation recipient's knowledge. *Journal of Experimental Psychology: General, 142*, 445–457.

Riketta, M. (2002). Attitudinal organizational commitment and job performance: A meta-analysis. *Journal of Organizational Behavior, 23*, 257–266. doi:10.1002/job.141.

Sassenberg, K. (2013). It is about the web and the user: The effects of web use depend on person characteristics. *Psychological Inquiry, 24*, 333–340.

Sassenberg, K., & Jonas, K. J. (2007). Attitude change and social influence on the net. In A. Joinson, K. A. McKenna, T. Postmes, & U.-D. Reips (Eds.), *Oxford handbook of internet psychology* (pp. 273–288). Oxford, UK: Oxford University Press.

Sassenberg, K., & Scholl, A. (2010). Soziale Bindung von Usern an Web 2.0-Angebote. In G. Walsh, B. H. Haas, & T. Killian (Eds.), Web 2.0—Neue Perspektiven für Marketing und Medien (2nd rev. ed., pp. 49–64). Heidelberg: Springer.

Sassenberg, K., Boos, M., & Klapproth, F. (2001). Wissen und Glaubwürdigkeit als zentrale Merkmale von Experten: Der Einfluss von Expertise auf den Informationsaustausch in computervermittelter Kommunikation. *Zeitschrift für Sozialpsychologie, 32*, 45–56.

Sassenberg, K., Landkammer, F., & Jacoby, J. (2014). The influence of regulatory focus and group vs. individual goals on the evaluation bias in the context of group decision making. *Journal of Experimental Social Psychology, 54*, 153–164.

Sassenberg, K., Moskowitz, G. B., Jacoby, J., & Hansen, N. (2007). The carry-over effect of competition: The impact of competition on prejudice towards uninvolved outgroups. *Journal of Experimental Social Psychology, 43*, 529–538.

Scholl, A., & Sassenberg, K. (2014a). Where could we stand if I had…? How social power impacts counterfactual thinking after failure. *Journal of Experimental Social Psychology, 53*, 51–61.

Scholl, A., & Sassenberg, K. (2014b). "While you still think, I already type": Experienced social power reduces deliberation during e-mail communication. *Cyberpsychology, Behavior, and Social Networking, 17*, 692–696.

Scholl, A., & Sassenberg, K. (2015). Better know when (not) to think twice: How social power impacts prefactual thought. *Personality and Social Psychology Bulletin, 41*, 159–170.

Stasser, G., Stewart, D. D., & Wittenbaum, G. M. (1995). Expert roles and information exchange during discussion: The importance of knowing who knows what. *Journal of Experimental Social Psychology, 31*, 244–265.

Tajfel, H., & Turner, J. C. (1979). An integrative theory of intergroup conflict. In W. G. Austin & S. Worchel (Eds.), *The social psychology of intergroup relations* (pp. 33–47). Monterey, CA: Books/Cole.

Tesser, A. (1988). Toward a self-evaluation maintenance model of social behavior. *Advances in Experimental Social Psychology, 21*, 181–227.

Toma, C., & Butera, F. (2009). Hidden profiles and concealed information: Strategic information sharing and use in group decision making. *Personality and Social Psychology Bulletin, 35*(6), 793–806.

Utz, S. (2003). Social identification and interpersonal attraction in MUDs. *Swiss Journal of Psychology, 62*, 91–101.

Vroom, V. H. (1964). *Work and motivation*. New York: Wiley.

Walther, J. B. (1996). Computer-mediated communication: Impersonal, interpersonal, and hyperpersonal interaction. *Communication Research, 23*, 3–43.

Walther, J. B. (2007). Selective self-presentation in computer-mediated communication: Hyperpersonal dimensions of technology, language, and cognition. *Computers in Human Behavior, 23*, 2538–2557.

Wittenbaum, G. M., Hollingshead, A. B., & Botero, I. C. (2004). From cooperative to motivated information sharing in groups: Moving beyond the hidden profile paradigm. *Communication Monographs, 71*, 286–310.

Woltin, K.-A., & Sassenberg, K. (2015). Showing engagement or not: The influence of social identification and group deadlines on individual control strategies. *Group Processes & Intergroup Relations, 18*, 24–44.

Chapter 6
A Conceptual Framework of Knowledge Exchange

Jürgen Buder

Abstract Knowledge exchange, defined as interpersonal interactions that change knowledge in the heads and/or knowledge in the world, is a topic of interest in many research fields. This chapter outlines a conceptual framework which captures many variables that play a role in knowledge exchange. The conceptual framework draws a distinction between input variables, process variables, and output variables. Moreover, the framework stresses the importance of taking both individual-level variables and group-level variables into account in order to describe and explain knowledge exchange. These variables can be used to describe and categorize a broad range of empirical studies from various scholarly fields. Patterns of covariation that are discovered in the network of variables have the potential to transform the conceptual framework of knowledge exchange into a theoretical framework.

Keywords Communication • Learning • Attitudes • Conflict • Elaboration

Introduction

There is hardly any activity that persons are engaged in that does not have a social component. Humans are interwoven in a constant net of coordinating with others (e.g., moving at traffic lights), communicating with others (e.g., ordering food in a restaurant), cooperating with others (e.g., distributing the workload in a team), or collaborating with others (e.g., jointly solving a math problem) in a social surrounding. Understanding these dynamics is part of many research fields, for instance, communication science, learning sciences, social psychology, computer-supported collaborative learning (CSCL), or computer-supported cooperative work (CSCW). In this chapter, the term "knowledge exchange" serves as a common denominator to describe work from these different research fields.

J. Buder (✉)
Leibniz-Institut für Wissensmedien, Schleichstrasse 6, 72076 Tübingen, Germany
e-mail: j.buder@iwm-tuebingen.de

© Springer International Publishing AG 2017
S. Schwan, U. Cress (eds.), *The Psychology of Digital Learning*,
DOI 10.1007/978-3-319-49077-9_6

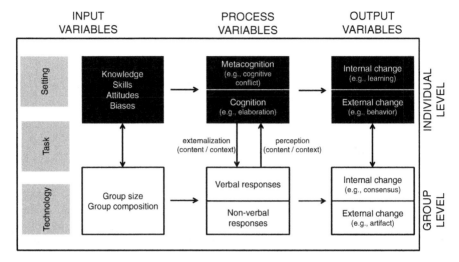

Fig. 6.1 The IPO framework of knowledge exchange

This chapter has a distinctly cognitive focus on knowledge-related processes (see the chapter by Scholl et al. (2017), for a discussion of motivational processes in knowledge exchange). That being said, this chapter defines knowledge exchange as social interactions (coordination, communication, cooperation, collaboration) among two or more persons which change knowledge "in the heads" of the persons or change knowledge in their environment. Learning or knowledge acquisition through collaboration would be an example of the former, and collaboratively writing a document or making a decision would be examples of the latter.

This chapter outlines a conceptual framework of knowledge exchange. The framework takes a look at crucial variables in knowledge exchange. It describes knowledge exchange as an IPO (input-process-output) model involving the interaction of many variables on the individual and the group level.

The IPO Framework of Knowledge Exchange

It has become quite common in the social sciences to describe complex dependencies among variables in so-called IPO models, where I stands for input variables, P for process variables, and O for output variables. The framework of knowledge exchange (see Fig. 6.1) follows this logic.

As can be seen from Fig. 6.1, the three layers (input-process-output) are represented as vertical columns. Moreover, blocks of variables are represented using three different colors. Grey boxes on Fig. 6.1 (in the leftmost column) refer to general factors that describe the environment in which knowledge exchange unfolds. These variables cannot be attributed to specific individuals or groups. Most of the variables in this framework, however, are represented in black or white boxes, and are arranged along two horizontal rows. The upper row (black boxes) represents individual-level variables, and the lower row (white boxes) represents group-level variables.

Input Variables

In terms of statistical analysis, input variables are often independent variables, i.e., factors whose natural or induced variations are supposed to have specific effects. Applied to the conceptual framework of knowledge exchange, input variables are those variables that are supposed to have specific effects on the processes of knowledge exchange and its outcome. The framework makes a distinction between environmental input variables (represented as grey boxes in Fig. 6.1) and human input variables (represented as black or white boxes in Fig. 6.1).

Environmental Input Variables

Environmental input variables are those variables that impact knowledge exchange, but cannot be directly attributed to individuals or groups. The conceptual framework of knowledge exchange distinguishes between three clusters of environmental input variables: setting, task, and technology.

Setting

While the term setting could refer to many different things (e.g., formal vs. informal learning settings; school vs. workplace settings), the conceptual framework refers to setting only with regard to general spatial and temporal characteristics. For instance, one of the most basic distinctions of knowledge exchange refers to the question of whether participants share the same physical space (face-to-face communication) or whether they are distributed over different locations (e.g., computer-mediated communication). In the 1980s and 1990s, there has been quite a lot of research about this distinction, basically holding that communication over the distance lacks the richness of face-to-face communication and should be associated with greater anonymity (Lea & Spears, 1991) which leads to stronger depersonalization, more group polarization, and more uninhibited speech (Kiesler, Siegel, & McGuire, 1984). Modern technologies can provide some of the richness of face-to-face communication, so the notion that communicating over the distance is always anonymous and impersonal is rather outdated. Still, interacting face-to-face has the benefit that participants can see each other, can see the same objects in their environment, and they can refer to these objects by deictic means, thus increasing common ground in communication (Clark & Brennan, 1991).

A second dimension along which different settings for knowledge exchange can be distinguished refers not to spatial, but to temporal characteristics. For instance, knowledge exchange in an air traffic control setting requires very efficient communication and well-placed timing of utterances over the range of seconds (Hutchins, 1995). If knowledge exchange episodes have a longer duration (e.g., in a meeting, in a school lesson), individuals and groups have more time for reflection. In asynchronous settings, knowledge exchange cannot be accomplished directly, but requires some kind of record (e.g., a letter, an online forum discussion). This preservation of content allows knowledge exchange to unfold over much larger time spans: the knowledge exchange in the editing history of a Wikipedia article may cover years, and the knowledge exchange in science may cover centuries.

Task

There are many conceptualizations of how to distinguish tasks (for an overview, see Zigurs & Buckland, 1998). For current purposes, it is suggested to align tasks on a dimension ranging from cooperation to competition, adapting a taxonomy proposed by McGrath and Hollingshead (1994). In cooperative tasks, the goals of the individual and the goals of the group align. Cooperative tasks can be further divided into creativity tasks and intellective tasks. Brainstorming is the quintessential creativity task where group members try to generate new ideas. How well groups perform this task depends on the setting. For instance, brainstorming in synchronous face-to-face settings yields less ideas than brainstorming among spatially separated people because in face-to-face scenarios people have to wait for their turn (Diehl & Stroebe, 1987). Intellective tasks also rely on cooperation among group members, but they differ in that they have a demonstrably correct solution. Most cases of collaborative learning and collaborative problem-solving fall under this rubric. For instance, in a typical collaborative problem-solving task investigated by Engelmann and Hesse (2010, 2011), groups of three were facing a fictitious problem which involved finding the best set of pesticides to save a forest. In order to arrive at the best solution, group members had to share their individual knowledge by adding elements to a digital concept map.

While cooperative tasks like brainstorming or collaborative problem-solving are characterized by an alignment between individual goals and group goals, the goals of group members misalign in competitive tasks—what is a good outcome for one interactor might be a bad outcome for another communication partner. Competitive tasks can be further divided into decision-making tasks and cognitive conflict tasks. When groups have to make a decision, different viewpoints might emerge that prevent an immediate solution. For example, in a study by Buder and Bodemer (2008), four-person groups had to arrive at a decision whether light dies out or goes on forever. Evidence for these two conflicting hypotheses was distributed across the group in a way that one member—the minority—was favoring the correct hypothesis (light goes on forever), but was confronted with a majority of three members who favored the incorrect hypothesis (light dies out). This study showed that digital technologies can facilitate the decision-making process by making the minority viewpoint more salient. In a cognitive conflict task, competition among group members is even stronger than in decision-making tasks, because a gain for one group member is frequently mirrored by a loss for another group member. Bargaining among two stakeholders is an example of a cognitive conflict task. However, even in cognitive conflict tasks, stakeholders can often achieve mutual benefit when they are aware of their individual priorities. For instance, an individual negotiator might give in on an issue that is less important, but in return might be insistent with regard to an issue that has top priority. Kolodziej, Hesse, and Engelmann (2016) investigated how negotiations among car sellers and car buyers could lead to better joint outcomes if the stakeholders were aware of the priorities of the other party.

Technology

The third set of environmental input variables in the conceptual framework is comprised of the technologies used for knowledge exchange. For the purposes of this chapter, a distinction is made between three functions that digital technologies serve in knowledge exchange: as channels, as external representations of content, and as external representations of context. The first function for technologies is to act as a channel for communication. As discussed with regard to the setting variable, a lot of knowledge exchange is among people at different locations, and of course technology is needed to even enable social interaction over the distance. Whether it is through telephones, videoconferencing, e-mail, texting, social networks, Twitter, online discussion forums, or wikis—technology creates a platform to connect people. However, digital technologies can also be used to support knowledge exchange in face-to-face communication.

The second function, therefore, is to provide external content representations for groups to interact with. External representations can be physical (e.g., pieces of paper), digital (e.g., elements of a concept map), or hybrid (tangibles). While many external representations (e.g., pictures and diagrams) are passive and non-manipulable, for the current purposes those representations that can be created and/ or manipulated are of prime importance to knowledge exchange. A particularly interesting technology to support this is through interactive surfaces like multi-touch tables. They provide face-to-face groups with a means to manipulate digital objects (moving them around, resizing them, organizing them, annotating them, combining them). External representations serve as reference points to individuals and groups, i.e., members can point at them, thus grounding knowledge exchange processes (Suthers, Girardeau, & Hundhausen, 2003). External representations may also contain elements of machine intelligence, thus creating feedback loops between users and systems. This is the case for simulation environments (de Jong & van Joolingen, 1998): individuals or groups can change parameters, and the system produces an output based on these changes, thus creating quasi-conversational turns.

Technologies can also be used to represent contextual information—both among spatially distributed groups and among people interacting face-to-face (Engelmann,

Dehler, Bodemer, & Buder, 2009). Providing contextual information lies at the heart of many group awareness tools (Buder, 2011). These tools collect contextual information about a group and its members, and feed this information back to the interacting group. The Knowledge Exchange Lab at the Leibniz-Institut für Wissensmedien (IWM) at Tübingen has a long tradition of developing and empirically testing these types of tools for a variety of tasks: intellective tasks like collaborative learning and collaborative problem-solving were supported through tools that provide information about the knowledge level of group members (Dehler-Zufferey, Bodemer, Buder, & Hesse, 2011) or directly provide the relevant knowledge via concept mapping (Engelmann & Hesse, 2010). Decision-making tasks could be facilitated when a group awareness tool provided group members with a means to express how novel a given discussion contribution was (Buder & Bodemer, 2008). Finally, cognitive conflict tasks can also benefit from group awareness tools. Examples are tools that capture group member ratings of quality of, and agreement with contributions in an online forum discussion (Buder, Schwind, Rudat, & Bodemer, 2015); tools that make stakeholders' priority in a negotiation salient (Kolodziej et al., 2016); or tools that assist in group members' pre-negotiation activities (Thiemann & Engelmann, 2015).

Human Input Variables

The conceptual framework of knowledge exchange draws a distinction between individual-level input variables and group-level input variables. Individual and group data are often statistically dependent on one another (e.g., the amount of utterances a group member makes depends on the total amount of utterances that the group makes). By stressing a distinction between individual level and group level, the framework therefore highlights the necessity to use multilevel statistical analyses in order to properly address many research questions about knowledge exchange.

Individual-Level Input

Of course, there is a wide range of variables that can be used to describe a person, for instance, the knowledge, the personality, the motivation, and the emotional state. As this chapter focuses on knowledge exchange (i.e., interactions which lead to a change of knowledge in heads or knowledge in the environment), particular emphasis is on cognitive variables. First, there is the amount of prior knowledge that a person brings into an episode of knowledge change. Second, there is a set of skills that a person brings into the situation. Third, there are attitudes that a person has, i.e., the person's evaluation of a piece of knowledge. And fourth, there are all kinds of biases in information processing that shape how people develop their knowledge and attitudes. Typical examples are confirmation bias, a tendency to interpret and remember ambiguous pieces of evidence in a way that favors their pre-existing attitudes (Nickerson, 1998), or congeniality bias, a tendency to select preference-consistent pieces of information (Hart et al., 2009).

Group-Level Input

As with individual-level input variables, there are many different variables to describe groups. However, this section will only discuss two very prominent features: group size and group composition. Knowledge exchange strongly differs for different group sizes. For instance, in dyadic knowledge exchange, both interaction partners are likely to have quite similar amounts of participation. However, the bigger the group becomes, the bigger the differences among the most active and least active member will be. For instance, van Mierlo (2014) looked at participation rates in different online medical health groups, and reported that 1 % of members posted frequently, 24 % posted sporadically, and 75 % never posted in these groups. Group size does not only change participation patterns, but might also require different technologies. For instance, group awareness tools for dyads or small groups typically provide information about each individual member (e.g., Dehler, Bodemer, Buder, & Hesse, 2011; Engelmann, Kozlov, Kolodziej, & Clariana, 2014; Kolodziej et al., 2016; Kozlov, Engelmann, Buder, & Hesse, 2015). In contrast, group awareness tools for larger groups aggregate the data from many individual users, thus only feeding back group averages (e.g., Buder & Bodemer, 2008; Buder et al., 2015; Rudat & Buder, 2015). For a detailed treatment on knowledge exchange in large groups, see also the chapter by Cress & Kimmerle (2017).

The second prominent feature beyond group size is group composition. From a conceptual point of view, many approaches of knowledge exchange do not necessarily make predictions on the basis of individual variables (e.g., individual knowledge, individual attitudes), but rather about the *distribution* of knowledge and the *distribution* of attitudes in a group. An underlying (but also contested) assumption holds that a heterogeneous distribution of groups with regard to knowledge or attitudes is superior to a homogeneous group composition. For instance, when pairing learners with different amounts of knowledge, one learner becomes more advanced than the other. This might lead to a situation where the learner on the higher level provides scaffolding for the one on a lower level (Vygotsky, 1978). Further evidence for the benefits of heterogeneity comes from Webb (1991) who reported that both learners on a high level and learners on a low level benefit most from collaborating with a medium-level learner. Heterogeneity of expertise with regard to the topic is at the heart of Piagetian approaches to learning (Doise & Mugny, 1984), or to the notion of transactive memory systems (Wegner, 1987). Finally, indirect evidence comes from social psychological studies on the hidden profile paradigm where small groups typically fail to make the best possible decision if all members share the same pre-discussion preference and are too homogeneous in this respect (Stasser & Titus, 2003).

Process Variables

Process variables describe the centerpiece of knowledge exchange. Once again, it is suggested to differentiate between individual-level and group-level variables, and it is with regard to different epistemologies that this distinction fully plays out. For instance, many scholars in the field of CSCL use a methodological approach based on dense narrative accounts of what takes place in isolated episodes of knowledge exchange (e.g., Roschelle, 1992; Stahl, 2005). These scholars try to explain episodes of knowledge exchange only by virtue of observable actions: things that group members say, how these utterances relate to earlier utterances, how the words are accompanied by gestures, and how they are modulated in intonations and temporal rhythms. The conceptual framework of knowledge exchange counts all these observable variables as group-level variables. Many of the scholars who favor narrative accounts make little or no assumptions about individual-level variables. In contrast, many other scholars in CSCL feel closer to cognitivist epistemologies, and they try to explain the processes of knowledge exchange by means of cognitive and social processes that take place in the heads of individuals. For these scholars, the observable actions are often just a complement to address basic causal mechanisms between input variables, individual-level cognitive variables, and outcome variables. The conceptual framework of knowledge exchange stresses the importance of both individual-level and group-level processes to fully grasp the complex interaction between individual minds and their contribution to a group-level endeavor.

Before going to discuss crucial variables on the individual and the group level, two additional assumptions will be made. The first refers to the ways in which individual-level and group-level processes connect to each other. As can be seen in Fig. 6.1, connections between these two levels are represented by two arrows, named "externalization" and "perception" (see the chapter by Cress & Kimmerle (2017), for a similar approach). Through perception, the individual cognitive apparatus takes up observable group-level activities. Through externalization, the cognitive apparatus takes action by making internal information observable to others. A second point that bears mentioning refers to the assumption that the processes of perception and externalization do not only refer to content information, but also to contextual information. For example, a verbal utterance (content) that is made in a self-assured manner plays a different role in knowledge exchange than the same utterance externalized in a hesitant manner. While the content is the same, contextual cues reveal something about the individual-level processes of the speaker, and these cues become observable to other participants in knowledge exchange.

Individual-Level Processes

What goes on in an individual's mind during knowledge exchange? First of all, observable activities (words, gestures, etc.) from the environment must be processed, i.e., translated into a language of thought (Fodor, 1975). However, knowledge exchange is not an automatic, reflex-like process—it also has evaluative and strategic elements. Therefore, the conceptual framework of knowledge exchange does not only look at cognition, but also at metacognition.

Cognition

On a very basic level, perceived information from the observable group-level must be processed, i.e., attended to, and semantically parsed. Most theories in cognitive science agree that this type of processing occurs in a limited working memory (Baddeley & Hitch, 1974; Mayer, 2001). Within working memory, attention is allocated (selection), information is organized and maintained (e.g., through memorization), information is retrieved from long-term memory, and information from the environment and from long-term memory might be integrated. These basic forms of information flow give rise to broader processes, and the conceptual framework specifically focuses on three of them: attention, comprehension, and elaboration. Attention requires that information will actually be processed by the cognitive apparatus. For instance, social psychological literature suggests that attitudinally consistent information receives more attention than counterattitudinal information, a phenomenon that is known as congeniality bias (Hart et al., 2009). Attention can also be influenced by the way that content information and context information are represented. For instance, Buder et al. (2015) showed how the visual display of an online discussion forum can have a strong influence on what pieces of information readers will actually attend to. The second process, comprehension, refers to the ability to properly understand content-related and contextual information from the environment. While comprehension of content might be diminished by a lack of expertise (individual-level input variable), failure to comprehend contextual cues can also have detrimental effects, as is exemplified in the inability of many people to understand sarcasm in online communication (Kruger, Epley, Parker, & Ng, 2005). The third cognitive process that bears mentioning is elaboration. Generally, elaboration is associated with deeper processing, better retention, better learning, better thinking, and better decision-making—in short, fostering elaboration is assumed to be the key to effective knowledge exchange. For instance, many group awareness tools are supposed to have a direct influence on elaboration (Buder & Bodemer, 2008; Dehler-Zufferey et al., 2011; Engelmann & Hesse, 2011). Elaboration should also be fostered by making counterattitudinal information salient (Schwind & Buder, 2012; Schwind, Buder, Cress, & Hesse, 2012), or by engaging small groups in collaborative design tasks (see the chapter of Zahn (2017)).

Metacognition

Based on a metacognitive model from Efklides (2008), the conceptual framework of knowledge exchange draws a distinction between metacognitive knowledge, metacognitive experiences, and metacognitive processes. The first component, metacognitive knowledge, implies that individuals possess mental representations about themselves, and that an evaluation and constant updating of this knowledge gives rise to metacognitive experiences which inform cognitive processes as well as behavioral actions (Efklides, 2008). Moreover, many scholars have suggested that individuals possess mental representations about the cognitive states of others, variously termed as metacognitive judgments about others (Efklides, 2008), transactive memory systems (Wegner, 1987), team mental models (Mohammed & Dumville, 2001), or group awareness (Engelmann et al., 2009). Many empirical studies on knowledge exchange are built on the assumption that group awareness—knowledge about the cognitive properties of others—can be supported through technological means (e.g., through group awareness tools), and this in turn will improve outcomes in learning (Dehler et al., 2011; Engelmann & Hesse, 2010; Kozlov et al., 2015), information dissemination (Rudat, Buder, & Hesse, 2014), or decision-making (Buder & Bodemer, 2008).

However, individuals do not only possess metacognitive knowledge about the current state of knowledge of themselves and others, but also about an intended, or goal state of themselves and others (Flavell, 1979). One of the strongest empirical claims of the conceptual framework of knowledge exchange holds that discrepancies between current state and goal state are the driving force for knowledge exchange. For instance, if an individual experiences a discrepancy between her current knowledge level and a desired goal level, the likelihood rises that this will lead to corresponding acts of externalization (e.g., asking for help). Similarly, if an individual experiences a discrepancy between the current knowledge level and the assumed goal level of a communication partner, this will also be associated with characteristic acts of externalizations (e.g., explaining a concept to another learner).

The second component of metacognition refers to metacognitive experiences. Classical examples from research on individual metacognition are judgments of learning (Nelson, 1996) or feelings of knowing (Hart, 1965). It is an intriguing question whether individuals also possess judgments of learning or feelings of knowing about others (Schubert, Buder, & Hesse, 2014). Social psychological literature suggests that this could be the case, as individuals are often engaged in processes of social comparison with others (Festinger, 1954; see Ray, Neugebauer, Sassenberg, Buder, & Hesse, 2013, for a study that addresses social comparison and group awareness). The conceptual framework of knowledge exchange also subsumes cognitive conflict under the rubric of metacognitive experiences. Ever since Piaget, cognitive conflicts between an individual and her environment are an integral mechanism of cognitive and behavioral change (Piaget & Inhelder, 1969). Doise and Mugny (1984) built on the Piagetian notion to express that cognitive conflicts between individuals can be highly conducive to learning, an assumption that was also expressed in the development of teaching methods that create socio-cognitive conflict in order to facilitate learning (structured controversy; Johnson & Johnson, 1979). Organizational psychology also holds that cognitive conflicts may facilitate team performance (Jehn, 1995). As a consequence, many empirical investigations into knowledge exchange have stressed the importance of cognitive conflict, going so far to develop technologies that make conflict highly salient (Buder & Bodemer, 2008; Buder et al., 2015; Schwind & Buder, 2012; Schwind et al., 2012). The framework of knowledge exchange posits that cognitive conflicts arise as metacognitive experiences based on discrepancies between current state and goal state.

Metacognitive knowledge and metacognitive experiences are updated through metacognitive processes. Based on the well-established notion from Nelson and Narens (1994), a distinction is made between processes of monitoring and processes of control. Through monitoring, metacognitive experiences (judgments of learning, feeling of knowing, discrepancies between current state and goal state, cognitive conflicts) are created. Control processes seek to reduce goal discrepancies and act on cognition (e.g., further elaboration of content) as well as on behavior (e.g., externalizations).

Group-Level Processes

The conceptual framework of knowledge exchange regards all observable activities in an interaction space as group-level processes. As mentioned before, observable activities play a different role for scholars adhering to different epistemologies. Those who take a narrative or historiographic stance try to explain knowledge exchange only by reference to observable activities, interpreting fine modulations of speech or accompanying gestures, and studying intricate sets of interrelated activities (Medina & Suthers, 2013; Roschelle, 1992; Stahl, 2005). In contrast, scholars from cognitivist schools of thought often try to categorize observable activities into coding schemes (Baker, Andriessen, Lund, van Amelsvoort, & Quignard, 2007). A common criticism of the latter approach is that sequential dependencies which might be crucial to knowledge exchange cannot be captured by a summary "coding-and-counting" approach (Stahl, 2005), which has led some interesting suggestions to treat chains of observable activities in an event-based approach (Reimann, Yacef, & Kay, 2011). The conceptual framework of knowledge exchange does not take a particular stance on this contentious topic, but rather provides a basic categorization of observable activities (verbal vs. nonverbal responses). It does, however, take a stance in suggesting that all these observable activities are like different languages that help participants in knowledge exchange to express and externalize both content and contextual information.

Verbal Responses

Knowledge exchange is hardly conceivable without the use of words. Words are a typical, but not the only way to express content-related information in knowledge exchange; they can also be used to express contextual information, e.g., by explicitly informing about the cognitive state of the sender. When participants of knowledge exchange are colocated, they typically communicate via spoken words (face-to-face communication). However, this is sometimes complemented by written words (e.g., making annotations on content representations). In distributed settings, both spoken and written words are prevalent, depending on the communication channel being used. Sign language represents a special case where words are communicated through gestures.

Nonverbal Responses

Nonverbal means are often used to express contextual information. However, some nonverbal activities can also be used to express content-related information (e.g., drawing, connecting links in a concept map). Typically, the expression of nonverbal means is somewhat limited in spatially distributed settings. Nonverbal responses can be loosely grouped into four categories, depending on whether things are expressed with one's face, one's voice, one's hands, or with the entire body. Gaze and eye movements provide contextual information about a person's attention, whereas facial expressions and mimics often convey information about the emotional context of a content-related message. Intensity and pitch of a voice can be used to express contextual information, and small modulations in intensity and pitch are used to shape questions or express commands. Temporal patterns of speech productions (pauses etc.) also express contextual information about the speaker. Gestural responses often play a very crucial role in knowledge exchange. For instance, by pointing at an object, senders guide the attention of their recipients. Manipulating physical or digital objects (rearranging, resizing, connecting, drawing) becomes a form of expression that is used in technological environments using touch surfaces (e.g., multi-touch tables). These explicit manipulations are often used to convey content-related information. Turning an analog or digital knob and pressing a "Like" button are also examples of how gestures can be explicitly used to express information. Finally, information can be conveyed by bodily means: bodily postures might be indicative of emotional states while bodily distances can be used to express not only attentional focus, but also to express social relations (Monge & Kirste, 1980).

Output Variables

Output variables of knowledge exchange typically reflect goal states that participants achieve in the course of interaction. In technical-statistical terms, output variables often can be conceived of as dependent variables. As was the case with input and process variables, the conceptual framework of knowledge exchange draws a distinction between individual-level and group-level output variables.

Individual-Level Output

The definition of knowledge exchange holds that knowledge exchange leads to changes of knowledge "in the heads" or changes of knowledge in the environment. Therefore, a further distinction can be made between internal and external changes.

Internal Change

Knowledge exchange might lead to learning, i.e., to the acquisition or restructuring of declarative and procedural knowledge (skill acquisition). How much an individual learnt is at the heart of many empirical studies on knowledge exchange. For instance, Dehler-Zufferey et al. (2011) showed that explaining concepts to a learning partner improved the learning performance of the explainer. In another study, Kozlov et al. (2015) reported that individuals had better learning outcomes when they had access to the entirety of the learning material than when material was distributed across members of a dyad. Another facet of internal change refers to the change of attitudes. For example, Schwind et al. (2012) showed that creating cognitive conflict by recommending counterattitudinal pieces of information led to a more moderate view on a controversial topic. Apart from changes in internal knowledge structures, knowledge exchange also might have an effect on emotional variables: satisfaction with a task or affect towards a partner (Kozlov et al., 2015) might be beneficial outcomes of knowledge exchange.

External Change

Knowledge exchange can have an effect on individual observable behavior. For instance, Thiemann and Engelmann (2015) had individuals act as representatives of a group for an upcoming negotiation. By analyzing the concrete negotiation issues that representatives suggested, the study showed that individuals were better able to integrate the diversity of group member preferences if they were supported by a group awareness tool. Individual behavior was also targeted in a study by Rudat and Buder (2015) which showed that retweeting behavior of individuals is influenced by tools that mirror the tweeting behavior of similar other individuals.

Group-Level Output

As with individual-level output, group-level output can be loosely categorized into internal changes that are brought about in the heads of group members, and external changes that are brought about in the physical environment.

Internal Change

The group-level counterpart to individual learning is shared understanding through collaborative learning. For instance, Dehler et al. (2011) investigated an awareness tool that made differences between the levels of comprehension of dyads highly salient, and found that such a tool leads to better joint outcomes in the dyads. In a similar vein, there is a group-level counterpart to attitude change, and that would be consensus or conflict resolution. For instance, in Thiemann and Engelmann's (2015) study about pre-negotiation preferences in groups participants were required to indicate their group's joint preferences after discussion. It was found that these joint preferences became more similar and consensual among group members when they were supported by a group awareness tool.

External Change

Collaboratively solving a problem is a group-level outcome. The KIA (Knowledge and Information Awareness) approach of Engelmann and colleagues showed how the visibility and awareness of individual content representations (concept maps) improved problem-solving performance (Engelmann & Hesse, 2010), how it can help to highlight unshared information (Engelmann & Hesse, 2011), how it can serve as a transactive memory system (Schreiber & Engelmann, 2010), how it can lead to group norms (Engelmann, Kozlov et al., 2014), and how it can counteract levels of mutual trust that are too high for the groups' own good (Engelmann, Kolodziej, & Hesse, 2014). Another form of external change is brought about by group decision-making (Buder & Bodemer, 2008). The joint payoff is a group-level metric that indicates how far stakeholders negotiated in a way that optimized the individual payoffs. By making potentials for integrative negotiation options salient through a priority awareness tool, Kolodziej et al. (2016) could improve the joint payoff of bargaining dyads. Last, but not least, jointly created artifacts provide examples of external group-level output. This was exemplified by work of Zahn (see her chapter in Zahn (2017)) that investigated how video tools could be used by groups to collaboratively design video artifacts.

Conclusions and Outlook

The current chapter proposes a conceptual framework of knowledge exchange. It defines knowledge exchange as interpersonal, interactive episodes in which knowledge is changed in the heads of group members and/or in the physical environment of groups. The framework itself groups crucial variables of knowledge exchange into input, process, and output variables which are broadly impacted by context variables. Moreover, for input, process, and output variables it emphasizes that both the individual level and the group level of knowledge exchange can and indeed should be taken into account.

The framework is admittedly quite complex, listing dozens of variables that can be taken into account. While in its current version it lacks the elegance of refined and specific frameworks, this approach also has some potential advantages. For instance, it can be used to integrate empirical studies from a very wide spectrum of research fields, e.g., from educational psychology, social psychology, organizational psychology, CSCL, and CSCW. Later versions could focus on more specific parts of the general framework and investigate particular relations among variables in more detail. What the current framework does is to provide a joint language to describe knowledge exchange. This joint language could be used to code empirical studies on varying degrees of detail for meta-analytic purposes. For instance, the framework could help to code the broad range of studies in which group awareness tools were employed. Results of such meta-analyses would also help to uncover typical and robust patterns of covariations among input, process, and output variables.

Once a conceptual understanding of patterns of covariations is achieved, the conceptual framework of knowledge exchange would gradually develop into a theoretical framework of knowledge exchange. Such a theoretical framework would focus on those covariations that are commonly found in the literature, and could provide valuable hints at covariations that haven't been tested so far. Ultimately, the conceptual framework could be a tool to improve knowledge exchange among scientists who have an interest in the topic of knowledge exchange.

Acknowledgments This chapter constitutes the summary (output variable) of many discussions (process variable) that were conducted during Lab meetings of the Tübingen IWM Knowledge Exchange Lab between 2012 and 2015. Therefore, the author would like to thank previous and current members of the Lab (in alphabetical order) for their input: Inga Bause, Carmen Biel, Moritz Borchers, Irina Brich, Brett Buttliere, Gabriele Cierniak, Tanja Engelmann, Friedrich W. Hesse, Katrin König, Richard Kolodziej, Michail Kozlov, Karsten Krauskopf, Anja Rudat, Michael Schubert, Julien Schweitzer, Christina Schwind, Irene Skuballa, Daniel Thiemann, and Daniel Wessel.

References

Baddeley, A. D., & Hitch, G. (1974). Working memory. In G. H. Bower (Ed.), *The psychology of learning and motivation: Advances in research and theory* (pp. 47–89). New York: Academic Press.

Baker, M. J., Andriessen, J., Lund, K., van Amelsvoort, M., & Quignard, M. (2007). Rainbow: a framework for analysing computer-mediated pedagogical debates. *International Journal of Computer-Supported Collaborative Learning, 2*, 315–357.

Buder, J. (2011). Group awareness tools for learning: Current and future directions. *Computers in Human Behavior, 27*, 1114–1117.

Buder, J., & Bodemer, D. (2008). Supporting controversial CSCL discussions with augmented group awareness tools. *International Journal of Computer-Supported Collaborative Learning, 3*, 123–139.

Buder, J., Schwind, C., Rudat, A., & Bodemer, D. (2015). Selective reading of large online forum discussions: The impact of rating visualizations on navigation and learning. *Computers in Human Behavior, 44*, 191–201.

Clark, H., & Brennan, S. (1991). Grounding in communication. In L. B. Resnick, J. M. Levine, & S. D. Teasley (Eds.), *Perspectives on socially shared cognition* (pp. 127–149). Washington, DC: American Psychological Association.

Cress, U., & Kimmerle, J. (2017). The interrelations of individual learning and collective knowledge construction: A cognitive-systemic framework. In S. Schwan & U. Cress (Eds.), *The psychology of digital learning: Constructing, exchanging, and acquiring knowledge with digital media*. New York: Springer.

De Jong, T., & van Joolingen, W. (1998). Scientific discovery learning with computer simulations of conceptual domains. *Review of Educational Research, 68*, 179–201.

Dehler, J., Bodemer, D., Buder, J., & Hesse, F. W. (2011). Guiding knowledge communication in CSCL via group knowledge awareness. *Computers in Human Behavior, 27*, 1068–1078.

Dehler-Zufferey, J., Bodemer, D., Buder, J., & Hesse, F. W. (2011). Partner knowledge awareness in knowledge communication: Learning by adapting to the partner. *The Journal of Experimental Education, 79*, 102–125.

Diehl, M., & Stroebe, W. (1987). Productivity loss in brainstorming groups: Toward the solution of a riddle. *Journal of Personality and Social Psychology, 53*, 497–509.

Doise, W., & Mugny, G. (1984). *The social development of the intellect*. Oxford: Pergamon.

Efklides, A. (2008). Metacognition: Defining its facets and levels of functioning in relation to self-regulation and co-regulation. *European Psychologist, 13*, 277–287.

Engelmann, T., & Hesse, F. W. (2010). How digital concept maps about the collaborators' knowledge and information influence computer-supported collaborative problem solving. *International Journal of Computer-Supported Collaborative Learning, 5*, 299–320.

Engelmann, T., & Hesse, F. W. (2011). Fostering sharing of unshared knowledge by having access to the collaborators' meta-knowledge structures. *Computers in Human Behavior, 27*, 2078–2087.

Engelmann, T., Kolodziej, R., & Hesse, F. W.Preventing undesirable effects of mutual trust and the development of skepticism in virtual groups by applying the knowledge and information awareness approach. *International Journal of Computer-Supported Collaborative Learning, 9*, 211–235.

Engelmann, T., Kozlov, M. D., Kolodziej, R., & Clariana, R. B. (2014). Fostering group norm development and orientation while creating awareness contents for improving net-based collaborative problem solving. *Computers in Human Behavior, 37*, 298–306.

Engelmann, T., Dehler, J., Bodemer, D., & Buder, J. (2009). Knowledge awareness in CSCL: a psychological perspective. *Computers in Human Behavior, 25*, 949–960.

Festinger, L. (1954). A theory of social comparison processes. *Human Relations, 7*, 117–140.

Flavell, J. H. (1979). Metacognition and cognitive monitoring: A new area of cognitive-developmental inquiry. *American Psychologist, 34*, 906–911.

Fodor, J. (1975). *The language of thought*. Cambridge: Harvard University Press.

Hart, J. T. (1965). Memory and the feeling-of-knowing experience. *Journal of Educational Psychology, 56*, 208–216.

Hart, W., Albarracin, D., Eagly, A. H., Brechan, I., Lindberg, M. J., & Merrill, L. (2009). Feeling validated versus being correct: A meta-analysis of selective exposure to information. *Psychological Bulletin, 135*, 555–588.

Hutchins, E. (1995). *Cognition in the wild*. Cambridge, MA: MIT Press.

Jehn, K. (1995). A multimethod examination of the benefits and detriments of intragroup conflict. *Administrative Science Quarterly, 40*, 256–282.

Johnson, D. W., & Johnson, R. T. (1979). Conflict in the classroom: Controversy and learning. *Review of Educational Research, 49*, 51–69.

Kiesler, S., Siegel, J., & McGuire, T. W. (1984). Social psychological aspects of computer-mediated communication. *American Psychologist, 39*, 1123–1134.

Kolodziej, R., Hesse, F. W., & Engelmann, T. (2016). Improving negotiations with bar charts: The advantages of priority awareness. *Computers in Human Behavior, 60*, 351–360.

Kozlov, M. D., Engelmann, T., Buder, J., & Hesse, F. W. (2015). Is knowledge best shared or given to individuals? Expanding the content-based knowledge awareness paradigm. *Computers in Human Behavior, 37*, 298–306.

Kruger, J., Epley, N., Parker, J., & Ng, Z. W. (2005). Egocentrism over e-mail: Can we communicate as well as we think? *Journal of Personality and Social Psychology, 89*, 925–936.

Lea, M., & Spears, R. (1991). Computer-mediated communication, de-individuation and group decision-making. *International Journal of Man-Machine Studies, 34*, 283–301.

Mayer, R. E. (2001). *Multimedia learning*. New York: Cambridge University Press.

McGrath, J. E., & Hollingshead, A. B. (1994). *Groups interacting with technology*. Newbury Park: Sage.

Medina, R., & Suthers, D. D. (2013). Inscriptions becoming representations in representational practices. *Journal of the Learning Sciences, 22*, 33–69.

van Mierlo, T. (2014). The 1 % rule in four digital health social networks: An observational study. *Journal of Medical Internet Research, 16*, e33.

Mohammed, S., & Dumville, B. C. (2001). Team mental models in a team knowledge framework: Expanding theory and measurement across disciplinary boundaries. *Journal of Organizational Behavior, 22*, 89–106.

Monge, P. R., & Kirste, K. K. (1980). Measuring proximity in human organization. *Social Psychology Quarterly, 43*, 110–115.

Nelson, T. O. (1996). Consciousness and metacognition. *American Psychologist, 51*, 102–116.

Nelson, T. O., & Narens, L. (1994). Why investigate metacognition? In J. Metcalfe & A. Shimamura (Eds.), *Metacognition: Knowing about knowing* (pp. 1–25). Cambridge, MA: MIT.

Nickerson, R. S. (1998). Confirmation bias: A ubiquitous phenomenon in many guises. *Review of General Psychology, 2*, 175–220.

Piaget, J., & Inhelder, B. (1969). *The psychology of the child*. New York: Basic Books.

Ray, D., Neugebauer, J., Sassenberg, K., Buder, J., & Hesse, F. W. (2013). Motivated shortcomings in explanation: The role of comparative self-evaluation and awareness of explanation recipient knowledge. *Journal of Experimental Psychology: General, 142*, 445–457.

Reimann, P., Yacef, K., & Kay, J. (2011). Analyzing collaborative interactions with data mining methods for the benefit of learning. In S. Puntambekar, G. Erkens, & C. Hmelo-Silver (Eds.), *Analyzing Interactions in CSCL* (pp. 161–185). Berlin: Springer.

Roschelle, J. (1992). Learning by collaborating: Convergent conceptual change. *The Journal of the Learning Sciences, 2*, 235–276.

Rudat, A., & Buder, J. (2015). Making retweeting social: The influence of content and context information on sharing news in Twitter. *Computers in Human Behavior, 46*, 75–84.

Rudat, A., Buder, J., & Hesse, F. W. (2014). Audience design in Twitter: Retweeting behavior between informational value and followers' interests. *Computers in Human Behavior, 35*, 132–139.

Scholl, A., Landkammer, F., & Sassenberg, K. (2017). Knowledge exchange as a motivated social process. In S. Schwan & U. Cress (Eds.), *The psychology of digital learning: Constructing, exchanging, and acquiring knowledge with digital media*. New York: Springer.

Schreiber, M., & Engelmann, T. (2010). Knowledge and information awareness for initiating transactive memory system processes of computer-supported collaborating ad hoc groups. *Computers in Human Behavior, 26*, 1701–1709.

Schubert, M., Buder, J., & Hesse, F. W. (2014). What should I say now? A metacognitive model on the regulation of information exchange in group learning. *Meeting of the EARLI SIG 16 Metacognition*. Istanbul, Turkey.

Schwind, C., & Buder, J. (2012). Reducing confirmation bias and evaluation bias: When are preference-inconsistent recommendations effective—and when not? *Computers in Human Behavior, 28*, 2280–2290.

Schwind, C., Buder, J., Cress, U., & Hesse, F. W. (2012). Preference-inconsistent recommendations: An effective approach for reducing confirmation bias and stimulating divergent thinking? *Computers & Education, 58*, 787–796.

Stahl, G. (2005). *Group cognition: Computer support for collaborative knowledge building*. Cambridge, MA: MIT Press.

Stasser, G., & Titus, W. (2003). Hidden profiles: A brief history. *Psychological Inquiry, 14*, 304–313.

Suthers, D., Girardeau, L., & Hundhausen, C. (2003). Deictic roles of external representations in face-to-face and online collaboration. In B. Wasson, S. Ludvigsen, & U. Hoppe (Eds.), *Designing for change* (pp. 173–182). Berlin: Springer.

Thiemann, D., & Engelmann, T. (2015). Computer-supported preference awareness in negotiation teams for fostering accurate joint priorities. In D. Cosley, A. Forte, C. Luigina, & D. McDonald (Eds.), *Proceedings of the 18th ACM Conference Companion on Computer Supported Cooperative Work & Social Computing (CSCW'15 Companion)* (pp. 227–230). New York, NY: ACM.

Vygotsky, L. S. (1978). *Mind in society: The development of higher psychological processes.* Cambridge: University Press.

Webb, N. M. (1991). Task-related verbal interaction and mathematics learning in small groups. *Journal for Research in Mathematics Education, 22,* 366–389.

Wegner, D. M. (1987). Transactive memory: A contemporary analysis of the group mind. In B. Mullen & G. R. Goethals (Eds.), *Theories of group behavior* (pp. 185–208). New York: Springer.

Zahn, C. (2017). Digital design and learning: Cognitive-constructivist perspectives on individual and group knowledge processes in design problem solving. In S. Schwan & U. Cress (Eds.), *The psychology of digital learning: Constructing, exchanging, and acquiring knowledge with digital media.* New York: Springer.

Zigurs, I., & Buckland, B. K. (1998). A theory of task/technology fit and group support systems effectiveness. *MIS Quarterly, 1998,* 313–334.

Chapter 7
The Interrelations of Individual Learning and Collective Knowledge Construction: A Cognitive-Systemic Framework

Ulrike Cress and Joachim Kimmerle

Abstract This chapter deals with the strong interdependence between individual learning and collective knowledge construction. In the first part, we show that research on collaborative learning needs to take both the level of the individual and the level of the group into consideration. Most current theories, however, focus solely either on the individual or on the group level and fall short of linking them to each other. In the second part, we present our "co-evolution model" that aims to integrate processes of individual learning and collective knowledge construction into a cognitive-systemic framework. We discuss how cognitive systems emerge in their attempt to comprehend their environment. We also discuss how social systems develop out of communication arising from the human need for social interaction. Finally, we point out how cognitive and social systems couple with and stimulate each other and how this process leads to a co-evolution of both systems. In this effect, individual learning results from the processes that go on in cognitive systems while collective knowledge construction unfolds due to the processes that occur in social systems. The third part of this chapter elaborates on how this cognitive-systemic framework contributes to our understanding of digital collaborative learning. We point out that our framework provides a descriptive, rather than a normative view of learning. Its main focus is not on formal learning settings where learning is explicitly intended, but on situations where people informally exchange knowledge and participate in knowledge-related communities. All forms of social media (wikis, blogs, or social networking services) may enable this type of interaction and knowledge development. Even though these tools were not explicitly designed for "learning," their use leads to knowledge exchange, knowledge acquisition, and knowledge construction. The quality of this knowledge depends on the norms of the social systems.

U. Cress (✉)
Knowledge Construction, Leibniz-Institut für Wissensmedien, Tübingen, Germany

J. Kimmerle
Leibniz-Institut für Wissensmedien, Schleichstrasse 6, 72076 Tübingen, Germany

University of Tuebingen, Department of Psychology, 72076 Tübingen, Germany
e-mail: u.cress@iwm-tuebingen.de; j.kimmerle@iwm-tuebingen.de

© Springer International Publishing AG 2017
S. Schwan, U. Cress (eds.), *The Psychology of Digital Learning*,
DOI 10.1007/978-3-319-49077-9_7

Keywords Collective knowledge construction • Social system • Cognitive system • Co-evolution • Social software

Introduction

As described in the previous chapters, digital environments provide people with access to digital content and digital learning material, and can thereby support and enhance individual learning (e.g., Chap. 1 by Scheiter (2017) and Chap. 3 by Schwan (2017)). Besides providing learners with particular *content*, digital environments also provide them with *access to other people*. By linking people they enable and support knowledge exchange and collaboration. Chapter 9 of this book (Utz & Levordashka, 2017), for example, shows how social media, such as Facebook, LinkedIn, or Twitter, support people in establishing and maintaining personal networks that enable the exchange of knowledge.

Still, learning together and learning from each other is much more than mere knowledge exchange. Since the 1990s, the research area of computer-supported collaborative learning (CSCL; see e.g., Koschmann, 1996) has focused on collaborative learning. In the first part of this chapter, we deal with the multilevel structure of collaborative learning and show that research in CSCL comprises two different theoretical and methodological traditions: The *cognitive approach* focuses on individuals and describes processes that take place in an individual. The *sociocultural approach* focuses on the group (with all its members and tools) and considers the group to be the relevant unit of analysis. These two approaches, however, result from quite different research traditions, and, to a large extent, they are adverse to each other. To date, attempts to combine or integrate both traditions into one model have been sparse.

In the second part of this chapter, we introduce our cognitive-systemic approach. Here, we propose that the general systems theory of the German sociologist Niklas Luhmann (1995) may be helpful in providing a meta-framework that allows for integrating the cognitive and the sociocultural approaches, and that describes how individual and collective processes are intertwined. From this perspective, individual learning and collective knowledge construction can be interpreted as being dynamic developments of individual cognitive systems and social systems that co-evolve.

Since the initial introduction of this co-evolution model (Cress & Kimmerle, 2007, 2008), we have continuously aimed to refine it (Kimmerle, Cress, & Held, 2010; Kimmerle, Moskaliuk, Cress, & Thiel, 2011; Kimmerle, Moskaliuk, Oeberst, & Cress, 2015; Kump, Moskaliuk, Cress, & Kimmerle, 2015; Oeberst, Halatchliyski, Kimmerle, & Cress, 2014). In various empirical studies, we have described the co-evolution of cognitive and social systems with regard to different technologies and communities (e.g., *social tagging*: Cress, Held, & Kimmerle, 2013; Schweiger, Oeberst, & Cress, 2014; *design patterns*: Bokhorst, Moskaliuk, & Cress, 2014; Moskaliuk, Bokhorst, & Cress, 2016; *Wikis*: Moskaliuk, Kimmerle, & Cress, 2009, 2012; Moskaliuk et al., 2011; *Wikipedia*: Kimmerle, Moskaliuk, Harrer, & Cress, 2010; Oeberst et al., 2014). In this chapter, our intent is to explain our approach on a more general level, since the model can be applied to all kinds of communities and technologies. In a narrative presentation, we describe how a cognitive system, without any knowledge at the outset, comes into existence and then starts to attempt to understand the world. We describe how the cognitive system builds mental structures that enable it to survive and to deal with the challenges of the world. We explain why it starts to connect with other cognitive systems and aims to "socialize." We show how social systems result from that interaction and how systems develop dynamically and build their own structures. The cognitive and the social systems then can couple and make use of each other, which leads to a co-evolution of the cognitive and the social systems. This co-evolution describes the dynamic interdependence between individual learning and collective knowledge construction and makes possible studying both systems in a combined context.

In the third part of this chapter, we describe how this cognitive-systemic framework contributes to our understanding of *learning and collaboration with technology*. Technology is part of our typical environment, when it comes to knowledge-related processes. People consult Internet forums to receive answers from other people to their personal questions; they use Wikipedia to gain a deeper insight into a topic, or they even contribute to this online encyclopedia; they read and write blogs or tweets; and they spend a lot of time using social networking services such as Facebook. The users may not be aware of it, but all of these tools provide platforms that constitute *social systems*. Each of these platforms not only delivers information but also processes information and deals with knowledge in a specific way. Whenever people interact with these systems—be it passively or actively—the social systems that become apparent in these digital environments influence people's thinking and understanding and lead in turn to individual learning.

In explicitly considering such nonformal learning situations, our co-evolution model holds a descriptive, not a normative view of learning. This approach makes us aware that "learning" and "knowledge construction" do not only happen as intentional and instructionally guided processes in classrooms or other settings of formal learning. Instead, we take into account that learning and knowledge construction happen consistently "in the wild," whenever and wherever people come in contact with groups and social environments. Individuals may not be aware of the collaborative phenomenon when they read Wikipedia articles or write tweets. Nevertheless, collaboration is an inherent part of these social systems.

The Multilevel Structure of Collaborative Learning

One of the most difficult issues in analyzing collaborative learning is that it involves processes and outcomes at two distinct levels: Processes that occur at the individual level and processes that occur at the group level (see also Oeberst, Kimmerle, & Cress, 2016). The demand that CSCL needs to consider both levels (e.g., Buder, 2017; Cress, 2008; Stahl, 2013) may sound trivial, but its realization is not simple at all. In CSCL research, different theoretical positions exist that focus on either one or the other level. These positions also reflect the different disciplines and methodological backgrounds in CSCL, and they are as yet only very coincidentally linked to each other.

The Cognitive Approach: Learning at the Individual Level

From the perspective of *cognitive psychology* individuals have more or less stable mental structures that describe their "knowledge." An individual "knows" what a table is, if she possesses a mental representation of a table. Whenever a person perceives something in the world, she may compare it with this mental representation in order to identify the object as a table or as something else. Knowledge, as it is regarded in this cognitive tradition, is something that exists *within* a person's mind. This concept refers to the internal representations that an individual possesses of the world. Based on this understanding, knowledge cannot exist outside someone's mind. It is part of a person's cognitive system. On the one hand, these internal mental structures are the basis of people's ability to make sense of the world around them; on the other hand, these structures are variable and can change through experiences. Such a change in mental concepts is considered to be "learning" or "conceptual change" (Carey, 1985; Vosniadou, 1994). Someone may have known that tables are made out of wood or metal, but through experiences with new technology, this person may learn that tables can also be interactive tools with a screen as its surface. So, on an abstract level, learning is the "delta" measured between two different points in time in one's acquisition of knowledge; and learning can be attributed to the experiences a person has made during that time span.

Consistent with this individual perspective, researchers who first dealt with collaborative learning (e.g., Johnson & Johnson, 1989; Slavin, 1990) considered it primarily as a means of fostering *individual* knowledge acquisition. They described, for instance, how collaboration between learners enhances their motivation and deepens their understanding. They focused on how learning as an individual's acquisition of knowledge can be stimulated or directed through collaboration. They described, for another example, how collaboration leads to an enhancement of the cognitive effort that people put into their learning activities. Collaboration motivates the individual learners to ask questions, explain their insights, search for help, or detect their own misunderstandings (e.g., King, 1989; Sharan, 1994; Webb, 1989). These processes might all simulate learning. What these researchers measure in the end is the *individual knowledge* that the different learners have acquired through collaboration. The effect of collaboration is the difference between the average learning outcome of people who learned independently and that of people who interacted with others. Figure 7.1 illustrates this with an abstract graphic.

The Sociocultural Approach: Learning at the Group Level

A second line of research is built by *sociocultural theories*, ranging from early approaches of Leontiev (1981) or Vygotsky (1978) to contemporary theorists like Engeström (2014). In sharp contrast to the cognitive tradition, these theories propose that knowledge is not something a person owns or acquires. It rather is

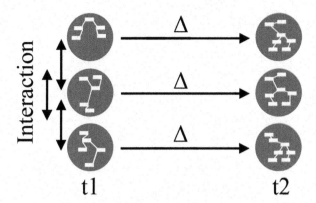

Fig. 7.1 Collaborative learning from the perspective of the individual cognitive approach: The learning of three inidividuals is shown by the change (delta) in their mental concepts between two points in time (t1 and t2). From this perspective, collaborative learning would be considered effective when the interaction between learners leads to higher deltas in the individual learners at t2, when compared to independent learning

something that is embedded into people's activities and cultural practices. Instead of focusing on individuals, Engeström (2014) describes entire "activity systems." Such an activity system not only consists of an actor (subject), but also of an object or goal, of mediating artifacts (tools), of the community of all actors involved, of the rules that regulate their activities, and of the division of activities within the community. From this sociocultural perspective, it would not be adequate to measure knowledge merely as a characteristic of an individual. It is not the individual that "owns" knowledge that is measured, but it is how effectively an individual behaves within the activity system. For example, a sociocultural study of medical knowledge would not only focus on an individual doctor and measure his/her expert knowledge in medicine. It would widen its focus to the whole activity system—consisting of this doctor, but also of the medical tools that are available for diagnoses, the nurses, the hospital ward, and the colleagues the doctor could consult. It is the entire activity system that is efficient or not, not only the individual doctor. The efficiency of this activity system may change if any of its parts change, for example, when new medical tools are available, when the doctor has new colleagues, or when new treatments are available. The sociocultural view would see the whole activity system as the unit of learning, not the individual. Figure 7.2 depicts an activity system as described by Engeström (2014).

The Need to Combine Both Levels

In current research on collaborative learning, the cognitive psychological tradition and the sociocultural tradition coexist without much overlap. If they refer to each other at all, they do it in a critical and opposing way (see also Anderson, Reder, &

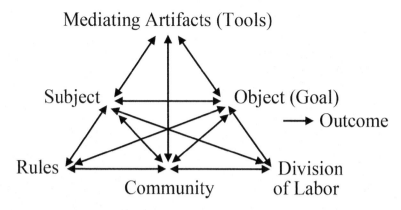

Fig. 7.2 Activity system in the notion of Engeström (2014)

Simon, 1996; Greeno, 1997). Besides differences in their theoretical approach, both research traditions also strongly differ with regard to the methodologies they use. Studies in psychology usually measure learning at the individual level. They regard the social situation primarily as stimulation for individual processes. They vary the social situation in *controlled experiments*, in order to see if and how it influences individual cognitive processes. If these studies take account of knowledge and learning processes at the group level at all, they typically simply aggregate the individual learning measures and regard them as group measures (see Fig. 7.1). In contrast to this, sociocultural studies primarily use *ethnomethodological methods* to analyze in great detail collaborative processes as they happen in single cases (e.g., Stahl, 2006). Sociocultural studies aim to take the whole complex situation (see Fig. 7.2) of an activity into consideration. They are not interested in measuring internal processes that take place in an individual.

Unfortunately, each of these research approaches only deals with one side of the coin of collaborative learning. We agree with the sociocultural approach that learning is more than an individual process; learning includes an enculturation that takes place in real, complex environments consisting of people, communities, and artifacts. And we agree that the experimental paradigm can hardly deal with that complexity. Experiments are suitable for segmenting complex situations into distinct processes and analyzing them separately. For this purpose, cognitive psychology has developed elaborate methods to measure knowledge and learning in individuals. Experimental methods reach their limits, however, when it comes to dealing with effects that occur in the very complex settings of collaboration situations. But we also agree with the cognitive approach's statement that an individual possesses knowledge and skills as stable characteristics that can and should be taken into account. People's individual cognitive processes are still the foundation for collaborative knowledge construction. So when examining collaborative learning, consideration of these individual mental processes and representations is indispensable.

With these strengths and weaknesses of the two opposing theoretical approaches, we see a strong need for further theoretical development in CSCL and for a model that considers equally both kinds of processes: internal processes that take place on the level of the individual learners and that describe their cognitions, as well as the group-level processes that describe knowledge as it is embedded in complex social situation along with the tools, communities, and division of labor in these communities. Individuals bring their distinct characteristics to this social situation. They influence others and are influenced by others. At the very same time, they are most probably part of activity systems which—in a feedback loop—influence their cognitions. Individual learning and collective knowledge construction are two sides of the same coin and both have to be considered concurrently.

We argue that Luhmann's (1995) "general systems theory" (he also refers to this approach as a "theory of autopoietic systems") might provide such a theoretical frame that allows observing and analyzing both sides adequately: the cognitive, intraindividual side of learning as well as the interindividual, sociocultural side of knowledge construction. With the notion of "systems," Luhmann provides a concept that allows considering the intraindividual as well as the interindividual processes and conceptualizing them as analogous, corresponding types of entities. In the following sections, we first present some conceptual clarifications about the nature of systems. We then provide a description of cognitive systems, explaining how they develop and how they contribute to the development of social systems. Finally, we show how cognitive and social systems interact and co-evolve.

A Cognitive-Systemic Approach

The Concept of Autopoietic Systems

The *autopoiesis* concept is fundamental for understanding the systemic perspective (Maturana & Varela, 1987; Varela, Maturana, & Uribe, 1974). Autopoietic systems are not static entities that exist per se. Instead, they exist through their own dynamics. They create and recreate themselves in a dynamic process. This constitutes their autopoietic nature: They are only existent via their own operations. Luhmann (1986, 1995) differentiates among three kinds of systems:

- *Biological systems* operate by biological processes, that is, by living (see Maturana & Varela, 1987). It is an autopoietic and self-referential process in which, for instance, cells create new cells. New cells result from existing ones. In this process also external influences may play a role. For example, cells need an optimal temperature and an optimal breeding ground to reproduce themselves. Nevertheless, the reproduction of cells itself is a result of the cells' own activity. Temperature and breeding ground merely establish the environment where the cells exist.
- *Psychic systems* (which we in the following will refer to as *cognitive* systems) operate by cognitive processes such as thinking and making meaning. Cognitions are also self-referential and autopoietic, as each one is based on previous cogni-

tions. They may be triggered by stimuli (e.g., new pieces of information) that come from outside, but it is always the system itself that produces them.

- *Social systems* operate by communication. This is an autopoietic process as well: Communication can only be understood based on previous communication. Communication exists through an ongoing net of utterances, where one utterance builds on the others. People produce these utterances, and communication would not be possible without them. But for the communication itself, these people are not part of the system; they belong to its environment.[1]

All these processes reveal the autopoietic, reproductive, and self-referential nature of systems (Luhmann, 1990): Cells produce cells, cognitions produce further cognitions, and communication produces further communication. In order to further exist, the operations of a system must ensure connectivity to future operations. A biological system stops existing if it is not able to produce cells any more, a cognitive system stops existing when it cannot create thoughts any more, and a social system stops existing if it does not communicate any more. From the autopoietic nature of a system it follows that a system can exclusively function on its own operations—so it is *operationally closed*. This means, each system can only operate within its own border. Outside of its border it cannot operate. But that does not mean that systems cannot deal with influences from their external environments. A cell may be influenced by its environment, for instance, by the temperature or other linked cells, and a cognitive system may be influenced by information coming from outside the system. However, all these influencing factors remain part of the external environment for the systems. In the same way that oxygen is an environmental factor for a biological system (but is nevertheless essentially needed for the reproduction), a *cognitive* system is part of the environment for a *social* system. A cognitive system is indispensable to the autopoietic process of communication, but it remains outside the social system.

So, even if an autopoietic system is—by definition—operationally closed, it is still open to its external environment in view of the fact that its environment can stimulate a system and the system can then operate on this stimulation. A biological system, for example, can adapt to the outside temperature and can find an adequate niche to adapt and further exist. The temperature might modify the autopoietic process by stimulating an evolutionary process that may take many generations. Like biological systems, also cognitive and social systems can react to their environment, if they think or communicate about external stimuli. They are both *meaning-making systems*. They want to understand the world around them and be able to predict what will happen. They both use language as a tool for this process, and this use of language allows both systems to stimulate and couple with each other. In the following narrative, we describe the complex processes that lead to this coupling.

---

[1] The assumption of Luhmann that people are not part of a social system, but are part of this system's environment seems—at least at first glance—counterintuitive, and has often been criticized. However, we hope that our co-evolution model makes that assumption better understandable, as it describes individuals and communities as two systems that reciprocally provide a rich environment for each other.

First, we describe how a cognitive system develops; then, we explain why a cognitive system starts to socialize with others; subsequently, we describe how this leads to the constitution of social systems; and finally we show how social and cognitive systems may couple and co-evolve.

How Cognitive Systems Develop

We start our illustration with an arbitrary cognitive system. It exists in its environment, which includes everything that is outside the cognitive system, that is, outside its own cognitive operations. Accordingly, even the individual's own body is part of the system's external environment and not part of the cognitive system itself.[2] For a cognitive system, the brain, its neurons, and their synapses are necessary in order to perceive and think. Nevertheless, they remain external entities. A cognitive system constitutes itself exclusively through thinking and making meaning. From the perspective of a cognitive system, its environment is infinitely complex and contingent. It is a kind of undefined, random noise or "unmarked space" (a term that Luhmann borrowed from Spencer-Brown, 1969). Because of this, the cognitive system cannot perfectly predict what will happen in its environment. In order to adapt better to its environment, a cognitive system needs to make meaning of its environment. It needs to be able to forecast what could happen. In order to survive, for example, an individual needs food for its body. For this purpose, the corresponding cognitive system needs to know where it can find food. By constructing its own, subjective expectations and beliefs about its environment, the cognitive system reduces the external complexity and contingency of its environment and starts to build internal representations. So, the cognitive system starts to mark the previously unmarked space by observing its environment. But because the environment is so complex, a system can never observe and mark everything. Observation is a process of selection, and the possibilities of the system to observe are limited because it can only observe what it has sensitivity for. For example, a cognitive system may perceive that food is to be found in a nearby place. But it cannot construct cognition about far-away locations for food until it has experienced them cognitively. Very distant places necessarily remain unmarked space.

Through its operations, the cognitive system tries to make sense of its perceptions. For example, in one place the individual finds fruit in a tree in summer but not in winter. It may deduce that the fruit needs sun and warmth to grow. This assumption reduces the contingency of the environment. With the knowledge the cognitive system has developed, it can predict that it will find fruit in that place again the next

---

[2] At first glance, this assumption seems to contradict current psychological theories of embodied cognition, which state that cognition not only comprises abstract operations but is also influenced by situational and bodily factors. We emphasize, however, that the concept of operational closedness does not assume that cognition would be independent of bodily processes, rather that they can definitely be modulated by bodily experiences while at the same time being self-referential.

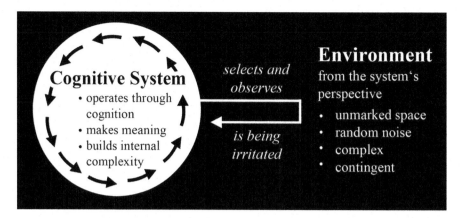

Fig. 7.3 Visualization of a cognitive system. A cognitive system is defined through its operations. It only operates within its borders (a circular process). The environment is unmarked space, that means, it is random noise, infinitely complex and contingent. The cognitive system can observe its environment and can be irritated by it. By operating on these irritations, it builds on its own complexity, which changes the system and defines how its individual knowledge is modified

summer but not the next winter. This process of making meaning out of what is perceived in the environment is an operation (cognition) that further operations (cognitions) can build on. But, of course, all mental concepts are subjective constructions. A cognitive system can never observe its environment objectively from an outside position. So, all kinds of observations and conclusions are results of an autopoietic process. In its observations and meaning-making processes, the system reproduces itself. Its cognitions create cognitions, its understanding shapes future understanding (see also von Foerster, 2002).

That does not mean, however, that a system cannot change its representations and develop in its understanding. Whenever a system observes and perceives something different than it had expected, it can operate on this difference and try to make new meaning out of it. These operations may change the internal representations. In the words of systems theory: operating on irritations enhances the system's own complexity and reduces external complexity. Through irritations, the cognitive system becomes more complex—we could say it becomes more intelligent. Figure 7.3 illustrates these processes.

Figure 7.3 implies that a cognitive system can never completely understand its environment and the world as it is with objectivity. A cognitive system is autopoietic, which means it is, inevitably, circular in its understanding and constantly referring back to itself. It is open to development, it can mark the space around it, it can react to the new experiences an observation allows, and it can adapt its making of meaning, but it can never perceive or represent the real word in a completely objective way.

The constructivist processes described here are in line with cognitive psychology's view of learning and knowledge acquisition. Most cognitive psychologists also assume that learning results from an interaction of a human being with its environment. Human beings understand their world based on their own mental structures, and learning takes place through equilibration processes (Derry, 1996; Limon, 2001; Piaget, 1977; Vosniadou, 1994): People aim to understand the world by assimilating their experiences and perceptions into their already existing internal mental structures. They also develop their mental concepts further by processes of accommodation when they adapt their internal structures to new experiences. In more recent theories, these processes have been described as bottom-up and top-down processes, where mental schemas influence ongoing perception and perception influences mental schemas (e.g., Connor, Egeth, & Yantis, 2004; Corbetta & Shulman, 2002). These two processes are not independent. In fact, they are strongly intertwined, and both processes often take place simultaneously (see, for example, the discussion on embodied cognition; Davis & Markman, 2012; Wilson, 2002).

Cognitive psychology also expects that conflicts trigger learning processes. When an individual's perceptions do not fit one's internal mental concepts, the individual may accommodate, that is, adapt her mental structures to fit. This change in mental structures describes the nature of learning (Derry, 1996; Posner, Strike, Hewson, & Gertzog, 1982; Rumelhart & Norman, 1981). So the cognitive psychological view of learning processes is largely in harmony with the systemic framework as introduced by Luhmann.

Why Cognitive Systems Socialize

As outlined above, a cognitive system wants to survive. It may have opportunities to exert influence and forces on its environment, but these are generally very limited. What the cognitive system can do is deepen its understanding of the environment and enrich and enlarge its internal representations of the world. But it needs to make sure that these representations and beliefs are valid (Festinger, 1954). The cognitive system has no direct access to the objective world, so it cannot simply compare its representations and beliefs with the objective world. But it can "socialize" with other cognitive systems, exchange information, learn from them, and compare its own perspective with the way the others express their view of the world. So, by socializing, the cognitive system has a chance to test its mental concepts and validate them through social interaction. It may also make use of others' experiences and learn from their knowledge.

Here, *communication* comes into play. According to Luhmann, communication has three components:

- An actor selects *information* (something that is new and relevant).
- The actor decides about the type of *message* he/she wants to use to utter this information.
- Another actor observes this utterance and *understands* that the utterer wanted to point out some information.

"Understanding" does not mean that this actor understands the message in exactly the way the first actor had in mind. It also does not necessarily mean that the understanding is shared. It just means that the receiver understands that the sender had something in mind he/she wanted to point out to others. "Understanding" only means that a recipient recognizes that a message points to information.

Applying the concept of autopoietic systems as an underlying theory, we have to be aware that mutual understanding between different cognitive systems is not at all a matter of course. The opposite is more the case. Understanding is highly unlikely because it is a process of *double contingency*: Understanding is contingent upon what a sender selects and how he/she puts it into words, and it is contingent upon the way in which a recipient observes and understands the message. Because communication is so unpredictable, a receiving cognitive system tries to ensure that its own interpretation of the other's message is approximately congruent with the information the sender initially wanted to express. The best way to achieve this is further communication. The recipient can ask back and may show agreement or disagreement. The sender then can specify or correct the message.

So the actors involved try to ensure understanding by continuous efforts to take the others' perspectives. When creating a message, the sender can take into account the receiver's perspective and expectations. Senders can design their messages with regard to their audience (see also Clark, 1985; Clark & Brennan, 1991; Fussell & Krauss, 1989). Likewise, the receiver of a message can consider the situation of the sender to be relevant when interpreting what a sender probably wanted to tell. As Grice (1975) has shown, communication works along some communication maxims that people expect others to follow. In Luhmann's systemic framework, however, communication does not necessarily aim to reach consensus with regard to content. Agreement or compliance do not make communication successful, only the opportunity for continuation with follow-up communication.

How Communication Creates a Social System

Continuity in mutual alignment of the communication partners is necessary in order to ensure communication. For example, if one person wants to show the other one where to find food, he/she has to take into account where the other person is located. He/she has to make sure that the other one can recognize the object as food, that the other person is aware that it is eatable and not toxic, etc. In most communication situations, however, people do not start from scratch. People are in situations where a previous history of communication has taken place that has already established regularities and shared expectations. If somebody tells other people "here is an apple," he/she would expect that the others know that "apple" is something to eat. He/she would also expect that the others are able to identify the apple as an object in their environment.

In families, communities, organizations, scientific disciplines, societies, etc. such terminologies and behavioral and social norms have been established over years and generations. So the communication partners have already formed stable expectancy patterns that reduce double contingency. These mutual expectations have in turn established a social system. This social system has established norms, for example, about what kind of information is seen as relevant, and what kinds of messages have to be used in order to enhance understanding and enable follow-up communication. In this sense, communication is always based on knowledge that has been previously constructed by other people.

When people visit a medical doctor, for example, who tells their patients that they need to take particular drugs, we can expect that the patients know that the pills are something different than food. They may also know that the pills are produced under highly controlled conditions, that they may have negative side effects but that their efficiency has probably been empirically tested with other patients. They may know that they have to buy it at a pharmacy. On the other hand, if they visit a homeopath, they may know that the pills given to them consist of natural elements with a very low dosage. Whether people visit a medical doctor or a homeopath, the communication is not based merely on the information exchange they are currently having with this specific consultant, but also on all the previous communication of countless people that were involved in shaping the knowledge and procedures that health systems in western countries rely on. So the communication of these particular people in a given situation builds on previous communications that have established standards and meanings regarding what health is, how it should be treated, who can treat it, or how the efficiency of treatments is evaluated.

Different social systems have different histories of communication and have developed different understandings with regard to the questions affecting the social system. Using again the example of different health systems, we find that the evidence-based, biomedically oriented scientific medical community has its specific concept of "health" (Bientzle, Cress, & Kimmerle, 2015). It has developed elaborated treatment methods, how to test their efficiency, and how to evaluate what characterizes a good doctor. Traditional Chinese medicine has developed quite different standards. They are also very elaborate but come to quite different appraisals about treatments and the quality of doctors. And if we think of shamanic cultures or extreme alternative medical communities, for instance, their concept of "health" also differs a lot from that of the others (Kimmerle, Bientzle, & Cress, 2016; Kimmerle et al., 2013).

This example makes clear that it is not absolute knowledge that a social system has developed. Analogous to the knowledge created by a cognitive system, the knowledge constructed in a social system is also relative. It is the result of the social system that operates in an autopoietic way through communication. It is based on previous communication. Its communication is operationally closed. Outside the system, the space is unmarked. Analogous to a cognitive system, a social system also perceives its environment as noisy and contingent, as unmarked space. The western health system may not know much about shamanic cults. But it is open to the influence of its environment (patients may tell their doctors stories about healing effects of nonscientific medicine), and the system can mark this space and can be irritated by it. The content that a social system marks depends upon its own communication and knowledge. So from its environment each social system is selective:

Evidence-based medicine is very sensitive to biochemical processes. Here, doctors may analyze an illness by observing irregularities within particular blood parameters, for instance. Traditional Chinese medicine is sensitive toward other regularities, toward symptoms, for example, that have to do with the body's vital energy ("qi") which is assumed to circulate through meridians and to influence organs and body functions. Thus, different social systems necessarily select different information. Each social system selects just those issues and pieces of information from its environment upon which it can operate. Any other issues remain noise.

So all communication within a system (no communication exists outside the social system) is necessarily based on previous communications. In order to stay "alive," a social system communicates and makes sure that further communication can be connected to it. A western doctor may get into difficulties if he talks to his patients like a shaman. This would not likely be accepted in evidence-based medicine, either from the patients, colleagues, hospitals, or health insurance companies. This communication would come to an end. It is possible that this doctor would even be suspended from official health services. However, as described above, there is a possibility that the social system may learn. It is open to its environment and can be irritated. Evidence-based medicine may be irritated by the information that homeopathic medicine would reduce particular symptoms, since homeopathic medicine has no ingredients that could cause this effect with the biochemical processes as they are understood by the evidence-based medical system. Subsequently, evidence-based medicine may start responding to this irritation by using its own operations. For example, it may conduct randomized controlled studies that would examine this effect. The biomedical system would then interpret the findings of these studies in its own terms. But, of course, this interpretation would again be the result of an autopoietic process different from that of the homeopathic health system.

These considerations illustrate that if we describe a social system and describe how it deals with its environment, we can draw an analogy to the cognitive systems. So Fig. 7.4 is designed analogously to Fig. 7.3.

Structural Coupling and the Co-evolution of Cognitive and Social Systems

As outlined above, cognitive systems as well as social systems develop and build internal complexity. However, each system remains an external environment for the respective other. The mental, intraindividual processes of the cognitive system remain a "black box" for the social system. People may communicate about their mental processes, but the cognitive system itself—its knowledge, its attitudes, its way of thinking—remains external to the communication. On the other hand, people may be involved in communication, but if and how this influences their individual thinking and appraisal is yet another thing. A medical doctor may act in clearly defined roles in a ward, but her private life, her personal attitudes, etc. remain

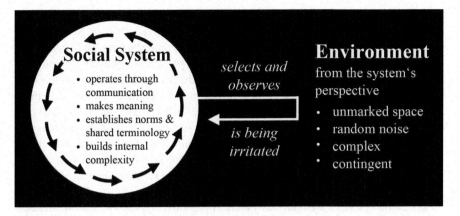

Fig. 7.4 Visualization of a social system: A social system is defined through communication as its mode of operation. Communication establishes norms and shared terminology. Communication can only take place within the border of the system. Everything that is not communication is outside the system, it remains unmarked space. The social system may observe its environment and may be irritated by it. By operating on these irritations, it may build on its own complexity, which changes the system and defines how its collective knowledge is modified

an external environment for this social system. Cognitive systems may reflect on the social system, on the relevance of information for others, on exchanged messages, and on the processes of understanding, but any actual communication itself remains outside all of these reflections, thus outside the cognitive system's border.

Cognition and communication may seem to be similar processes, but this impression only results from the fact that they both use language as a medium. In fact, cognition and communication are operations of distinct systems. These systems cannot merge because of their different modes of operation. Nonetheless, despite this strong operational separation, cognitive and social systems can establish a stable partnership and mutually influence each other. This happens when two systems continuously perceive each other and operate on these perceptions. In particular, they may provide mutual stimulation, when they irritate each other and contradict the other's expectations. Each system then can make use of the complexity of the other system to build its own complexity. If such a process happens continuously, this is referred to as "structural coupling."

As explained, the cognitive system with all its knowledge and beliefs is an external environment for the social system. However, a person may utter something based on this environment that irritates the social system. The social system then can start to operate on this information. A medical doctor in an evidence-based hospital, for example, who is interested in shamanism, may start to act like a shaman. In so doing, he may irritate the social system of evidence-based medicine. The social system could simply ignore or reject him, or it could also start to consider why this behavior might make sense in some cases. Thus, it may build internal complexity, that is, may construct new knowledge. Whether the social system ignores such an irritation or starts to operate on it largely depends on the incongruity of such an activity with what is expected within the system. If the doctor were to use hypnosis, it might be better accepted than when he dresses like a shaman. So it depends on a system's perception of incongruity with its existing norms and regulations whether or not the system is open for taking in particular input. The greater the incongruity, the greater the irritation is and, as a consequence, the more a system could potentially learn (i.e., the more complex it could become). At the same time, however, the greater the irritation, the smaller the chance is that the system will take this irritation into account and build on it. So *congruity* is a major predictor of whether a social system is open for new information and operates on it. A medium level of incongruity may thus be the best trigger for knowledge construction in a social system (Kimmerle, Moskaliuk, & Cress, 2011; Moskaliuk et al., 2009; Moskaliuk, Kimmerle, & Cress, 2012).

The same is true of a cognitive system. A cognitive system can also be irritated by the social system, and it may operate on some experiences it had with the social system by thinking about it. A person, for instance, who knows a lot about nutrition, may be irritated when she comes in contact with a community that has—from her viewpoint—strange beliefs about nutrition (see Kimmerle et al., 2013). She may or may not be open for the community's interpretations, and this could change her personal beliefs. A cognitive system that believes in the superiority of vegan food may be disgusted by a community that does not have this conviction and instead praises the value of eating meat. If both interact, over time, their opinions might even evolve in opposite directions. So they can influence each other and use each other's complexity to build on their own complexity, but this does not necessarily mean at all that greater agreement would follow.

Accordingly, co-evolution means that through stable processes of interaction, different systems continuously irritate each other and the systems become more sensitive to each other. In our advanced co-evolution model (Cress, Feinkohl, Jirschitzka, & Kimmerle, 2016), which is depicted in Fig. 7.5, we refer to these developments as "border-crossing processes." It is not a process in which knowledge content from one system is simply transferred to the other. Instead, it is an autopoietic and self-referential process. The systems become more sensitive to each other and continuously select information coming from the other system and operate on it. This changes both systems, giving them the opportunity to increase their internal complexities and leads to dynamic processes where internal knowledge increases, which we refer to as "drifting processes." The drift of the cognitive system is equivalent to what the psychological tradition views as individual learning; the drift of the social system is what we refer to as collective knowledge construction. As a result of this coupling, the systems may drift in a convergent or a divergent manner. But if border-crossing processes take place, the drifts of both systems will at least co-vary to some degree (Leydesdorff, 2003). Figure 7.5 illustrates these processes.

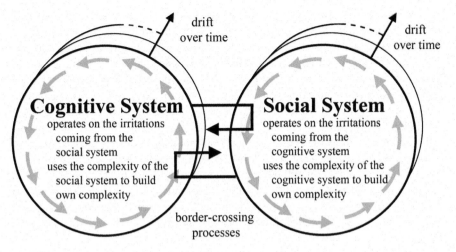

Fig. 7.5 Structural coupling of a cognitive and a social system. They observe each other and make use of the complexity of each other. This may result in drifting processes

Understanding Collaborative Learning in the Digital Age

Most research in educational psychology as well as research in CSCL is concerned with learning as it occurs in instructional settings, like school classes or universities. Some kind of curriculum usually exists in these formal educational settings, which more or less clearly defines what people are supposed to learn. There are teachers, lecturers, or mentors who guide the learners, trying to make sure that they are on the "right track." They try to ensure that learners do not develop misconceptions, or if they do, that they overcome them. In these situations, it is clear what people are intended to learn. The learners have more or less prior knowledge that is relevant for the learning goal, and the learning goal is defined as the delta between the knowledge they have before the learning process and the knowledge state that they should have according to this curriculum. So, in the end, learning in formal educational settings is considered to be a normatively coined process.

But large parts of everyday learning do not take place in such structured settings. In their everyday lives, people are often confronted with complex and ill-defined problems such as political questions, current societal developments, health issues, and the like. These are not clearly structured topics where people just have to find and acquire some universally accepted facts. Neither are these situations in which people can rely only on their own individual reflections. Instead, they talk to each other about these issues and go to multiple sources to search for information and advice. The Internet is an increasingly relevant source for most people. It offers fast and simple access to all kinds of information and allows people to easily participate in all kinds of knowledge communities. On the Internet, people can discuss various issues in political online portals, ask for advice in patient forums, comment on news or articles in blogs, contribute information to the Wikipedia, and engage in many other knowledge-related activities.

When people interact and search for information in these communities, their learning and attitude formation do not happen in a neutral space. Instead, all the information people come across and all the discussions they participate in are results of operations in autopoietic social systems as we have described them above. In many virtual communities, this systemic and self-referential aspect of knowledge exchange and communication is clearly visible. Wikipedia is a prototypical example of this self-reference. It is clear that it operates on norms that the community itself continuously negotiates and revises. There is a plethora of pages where these norms are evident and Wikipedians discuss them continuously. Articles are based on these self-generated and self-developed norms. Whether a contribution will persist in the encyclopedia or whether it will be deleted or revised depends on its compliance with these norms (Oeberst et al., 2014). Moreover, these norms and their application decide which topics are potentially relevant and how exactly Wikipedia is supposed to deal with them. So the norms determine to what stimuli the social system Wikipedia is sensitive.

It is the application of these rules that determine which information from outside the Wikipedia community will take in and operate on, and what the articles will look like. For example, Wikipedia has developed very explicit rules regarding the conditions under which a person can be given the honor of having his/her own Wikipedia article. In terms of our cognitive-systemic framework, we could derive from this fact that the majority of people in the world are unmarked space for Wikipedia. By operating on its own rules, Wikipedia observes what is going on in the world and reacts if it finds people that can be featured in an article of their own. For example, if a new president is elected in a country or if a new Nobel prize laureate is announced, there is a need for Wikipedia to have articles about those people. If there is no respective article so far, Wikipedia then starts to generate this article. This activity enhances the complexity of Wikipedia's offerings and leads to the construction of new knowledge.

In the case of Wikipedia, these norms have led to products of high quality—if we take the prevalent scientific criteria as indicators of quality. Our study involving the Wikipedia article on the Fukushima Daiichi Nuclear Power Plant yielded that any biased edit or any deviation from a neutral point of view tended to be deleted from the article within minutes (Oeberst et al., 2014). Added information only remained in an article when a valid reference was provided or when such a reference was found and added later on. In the talk page, a discussion was continually going on about which criteria a reference had to meet in order to be a valid source. For example, it was discussed whether a photo that was shown in the TV-news was an adequate source or not. All the different news that came in about the disaster that was going on in Fukushima irritated the system Wikipedia because it was unclear what had really happened and which news was delivering the "truth." The system tried to find out what was going on by applying its criteria for objectivity. In so doing, Wikipedia authors also refined the self-applied criteria and adapted them to this concrete situation. So the system operated through its self-given norms. In the end, in the eyes of independent content experts who we asked to evaluate the article, this led to a highly reliable source.

Other communities have established norms for quality that are quite different from those of Wikipedia. They lead to different discussions and results. For example, many alternative health communities do not agree that objectivity or a neutral point of view are the most relevant criteria for medical diagnoses, but favor instead subjective perception of health and feelings of well-being as more relevant. In order to study these attitudes, we observed the discussion going on in an Internet forum of an extreme nutrition community: the so-called Urkost community (Kimmerle et al., 2013). The protagonists in this Urkost forum proposed that people would live much longer (about 120 years) and could be totally healthy if they practiced the "right" nutrition, which means if they ate only raw fruits and vegetables. For them, it is not allowed to wash, peel, or cook the food. When people wanted to be accepted into this forum they had to comply with these ideas. Otherwise, they were heavily criticized or even thrown out of the forum. So through operating within these norms, people will internalize them more and more. Our studies showed that the longer people participated in the forum the more central they became as communication partners. They became more biased in favor of this special Urkost ideology. So also here we could see a drift in learning and knowledge construction. But in this community, the drift was not toward a higher level of objectivity as in Wikipedia, rather toward a more extreme and biased position.

In several experimental studies, we have analyzed these dynamic processes of individual learning and collective knowledge construction more in detail. In doing so, we used controversial topics such as whether playing video games makes children aggressive or whether schizophrenia has biological or social causes. We manipulated people's prior knowledge by providing them with arguments for one or the other position. We also varied the number and polarity of arguments that were provided in the wiki article. This enabled us to analyze whether learning and knowledge construction depended on the level of incongruity between individuals' prior knowledge and the information given in a wiki text (Kimmerle, Moskaliuk, & Cress, 2011; Moskaliuk et al., 2009, 2012). We found that people created the best wiki texts (with the most arguments and with the highest level of integration of opposing arguments) if the incongruity between prior knowledge and the information provided was at a medium level. With a medium-level incongruity, people also frequently remembered the most facts and they showed the highest conceptual change. This happened only through their participation in the wiki production—without any learning instruction and without any hint that a knowledge test would follow. Our manipulations were done in such a way that the participants in the different conditions had access to exactly the same information. We merely varied which parts of this information were provided as the preliminary basis of individual knowledge that people acquired before they collaborated (which means it became part of the cognitive system) or as part of a preliminary wiki text (which means it was part of the social system). When people worked on the wiki they had access to all of the arguments. But it was the distribution of arguments that influenced people's individual learning and the collective knowledge construction. With high and low levels of incongruity between people's knowledge and the wiki text, much less of the border-crossing processes took place. A medium level of incongruity, however, triggered system drifts.

In sum, the co-evolution model does not posit a normative but a descriptive point of view. It does not determine what people *should* learn, and its objective is not to recommend that people should continuously progress in their understanding in some ideal way or that they should acquire a more and more elaborate and exhaustive perspective on an issue over time. Quite the contrary, our approach describes individual learning and collective knowledge construction as observed activities that result from circular and self-referential processes of coupled cognitive and social systems. Our model considers learning "progress" and "knowledge construction" as a possible outcome of some border-crossing processes, where the systems involved select relevant information from the others and deal with possible irritations in order to make meaning (in terms of making order from noise). By highlighting these self-referential operations, our approach provides a sound theoretical basis for analyzing and understanding the frequently discussed phenomena involved in knowledge-related processes on the Internet. These may include the observation that people tend to search the Internet to confirm the attitudes they already have (confirmation bias; Nickerson, 1998) and that they tend to team up into homogeneous like-minded groups (Kobayashi & Ikeda, 2009; McPherson, Smith-Lovin, & Cook, 2001; van Alstyne & Brynjolfsson, 1996).

References

van Alstyne, M., & Brynjolfsson, E. (1996). Could the Internet balkanize science? *Science, 274*, 1479–1480.

Anderson, J. R., Reder, L. M., & Simon, H. A. (1996). Situated learning and education. *Educational Researcher, 25*, 5–11.

Bientzle, M., Cress, U., & Kimmerle, J. (2015). The role of tentative decisions and health concepts in assessing information about mammography screening. *Psychology, Health & Medicine, 20*, 670–679.

Bokhorst, F., Moskaliuk, J., & Cress, U. (2014). How patterns support computer-mediated exchange of knowledge-in-use. *Computers & Education, 71*, 153–164.

Buder, J. (2017). A conceptual framework of knowledge exchange. In S. Schwan & U. Cress (Eds.), *The psychology of digital learning: Constructing, exchanging, and acquiring knowledge with digital media*. New York: Springer.

Carey, S. (1985). *Conceptual change in childhood*. Cambridge, MA: MIT Press.

Clark, H. H. (1985). Language use and language users. In G. Lindzey & E. Aronson (Eds.), *Handbook of social psychology* (3rd ed., pp. 179–231). New York: Harper and Row.

Clark, H. H., & Brennan, S. A. (1991). Grounding in communication. In L. B. Resnick, J. M. Levine, & S. D. Teasley (Eds.), *Perspectives on socially shared cognition* (pp. 127–149). Washington, DC: APA Books.

Connor, C. E., Egeth, H. E., & Yantis, S. (2004). Visual attention: Bottom-up vs. top-down. *Current Biology, 14*, 850–852.

Corbetta, M., & Shulman, G. L. (2002). Controls of goal-directed and stimulus-driven attention in the brain. *Nature Neuroscience, 3*, 201–215.

Cress, U. (2008). The need for considering multi-level analysis in CSCL research. An appeal for the use of more advanced statistical methods. *International Journal of Computer-Supported Collaborative Learning, 3*, 69–84.

Cress, U., & Kimmerle, J. (2007). A theoretical framework of collaborative knowledge building with Wikis - a systemic and cognitive perspective. In C. Chinn, G. Erkens, & S. Puntambekar (Eds.), *Proceedings of the 7th Computer Supported Collaborative Learning Conference* (pp. 153–161). New Brunswick, NJ: International Society of the Learning Sciences.

Cress, U., & Kimmerle, J. (2008). A systemic and cognitive view on collaborative knowledge building with Wikis. *International Journal of Computer Supported Collaborative Learning, 3*, 105–122.

Cress, U., Feinkohl, I., Jirschitzka, J., & Kimmerle, J. (2016). Mass collaboration as co-evolution of cognitive and social systems. In U. Cress, J. Moskaliuk, & H. Jeong (Eds.), *Mass collaboration and education* (pp. 85–104). Cham: Springer International Publishing.

Cress, U., Held, C., & Kimmerle, J. (2013). The collective knowledge of social tags: Direct and indirect influences on navigation, learning, and information processing. *Computers & Education, 60*, 59–73.

Davis, J. I., & Markman, A. B. (2012). Embodied cognition as a practical paradigm: Introduction to the topic, the future of embodied cognition. *Topics in Cognitive Science, 4*, 685–691.

Derry, S. J. (1996). Cognitive schema theory in the constructivist debate. *Educational Psychologist, 31*, 163–174.

Engeström, Y. (2014). *Learning by expanding: An activity-theoretical approach to developmental research.* Cambridge, MA: Cambridge University Press.

Festinger, L. (1954). A theory of social comparison processes. *Human Relations, 7*, 117–140.

von Foerster, H. (2002). *Understanding understanding: Essays on cybernetics and cognition.* Berlin: Springer.

Fussell, S. R., & Krauss, R. M. (1989). The effects of intended audience on message production and comprehension: Reference in a common ground framework. *Journal of Experimental Social Psychology, 25*, 203–219.

Greeno, J. G. (1997). On claims that answer the wrong questions. *Educational Researcher, 26*, 5–17.

Grice, H. P. (1975). Logic and conversation. In P. Cole & J. Morgan (Eds.), *Studies in syntax and semantics III: Speech acts* (pp. 41–58). New York, NY: Academic Press.

Johnson, D. W., & Johnson, R. T. (1989). *Cooperation and competition: Theory and research.* Edina, MN: Interaction Book Company.

Kimmerle, J., Moskaliuk, J., & Cress, U. (2011). Using wikis for learning and knowledge building: Results of an experimental study. *Educational Technology & Society, 14*, 138–148.

Kimmerle, J., Moskaliuk, J., Cress, U., & Thiel, A. (2011). A systems theoretical approach to online knowledge building. *AI & Society: Journal of Knowledge, Culture and Communication, 26*, 49–60.

Kimmerle, J., Bientzle, M., & Cress, U. (2016). Learning communication skills for dealing with different perspectives: Technologies for health sciences education. In S. Bridges, L. K. Chan, & C. E. Hmelo-Silver (Eds.), *Educational technologies in medical and health sciences education* (pp. 139–157). London: Springer.

Kimmerle, J., Cress, U., & Held, C. (2010). The interplay between individual and collective knowledge: Technologies for organisational learning and knowledge building. *Knowledge Management Research & Practice, 8*, 33–44.

Kimmerle, J., Moskaliuk, J., Harrer, A., & Cress, U. (2010). Visualizing co-evolution of individual and collective knowledge. *Information, Communication and Society, 13*, 1099–1121.

Kimmerle, J., Moskaliuk, J., Oeberst, A., & Cress, U. (2015). Learning and collective knowledge construction with social media: A process-oriented perspective. *Educational Psychologist, 50*, 120–137.

Kimmerle, J., Thiel, A., Gerbing, K.-K., Bientzle, M., Halatchliyski, I., & Cress, U. (2013). Knowledge construction in an outsider community: Extending the communities of practice concept. *Computers in Human Behavior, 29*, 1078–1090.

King, A. (1989). Verbal interaction and problem-solving within computer-assisted cooperative learning groups. *Journal of Educational Computing Research, 5*, 1–15.

Kobayashi, T., & Ikeda, K. (2009). Selective exposure in political web browsing. Empirical verification of 'cyber-balcanization' in Japan and the USA. *Information, Communication & Society, 12*, 929–953.

Koschmann, T. (Ed.). (1996). *CSCL: Theory and practice of an emerging paradigm*. Mahwah, NJ: Lawrence Erlbaum.

Kump, B., Moskaliuk, J., Cress, U., & Kimmerle, J. (2015). Cognitive foundations of organizational learning: Re-introducing the distinction between declarative and non-declarative knowledge. *Frontiers in Psychology, 6*, 1489.

Leontiev, A. N. (1981). *Problems of the development of the mind*. Moscow: Progress.

Leydesdorff, L. (2003). *A soiological theory of communication. The self-organization of the knowledge-based society*. Parkland, FL: Universal Publishers.

Limon, M. (2001). On the cognitive conflict as an instructional strategy for conceptual change: A critical appraisal. *Learning and Instruction, 11*, 357–380.

Luhmann, N. (1986). The autopoiesis of social systems. In F. Geyer & J. van der Zouwen (Eds.), *Sociocybernetic paradoxes: Observation, control, and evolution of self-organization systems* (pp. 172–192). London: Sage.

Luhmann, N. (1990). *Essays on self-reference*. New York, NY: Columbia University Press.

Luhmann, N. (1995). *Social systems*. Stanford, CA: Stanford University Press.

Maturana, H. R., & Varela, F. J. (1987). *The tree of knowledge: The biological roots of human understanding*. Boston, MA: New Science Library/Shambhala Publications.

McPherson, M., Smith-Lovin, L., & Cook, J. M. (2001). Birds of a feather: Homophily in social networks. *Annual Review of Sociology, 27*, 415–444.

Moskaliuk, J., Bokhorst, F., & Cress, U. (2016). Learning from others' experiences: How patterns foster interpersonal transfer of knowledge-in-use. *Computers in Human Behavior, 55*, 69–75.

Moskaliuk, J., Kimmerle, J., & Cress, U. (2009). Wiki-supported learning and knowledge building: Effects of incongruity between knowledge and information. *Journal of Computer Assisted Learning, 25*, 549–561.

Moskaliuk, J., Kimmerle, J., & Cress, U. (2012). Collaborative knowledge building with Wikis: The impact of redundancy and polarity. *Computers & Education, 58*, 1049–1057.

Moskaliuk, J., Rath, A., Devaurs, D., Weber, N., Lindstaedt, S., Kimmerle, J., & Cress, U. (2011). Automatic detection of accommodation steps as an indicator of knowledge maturing. *Interacting with Computers, 23*, 247–255.

Nickerson, R. S. (1998). Confirmation bias: A ubiquitous phenomenon in many guises. *Review of General Psychology, 2*, 175–220.

Oeberst, A., Halatchliyski, I., Kimmerle, J., & Cress, U. (2014). Knowledge construction in Wikipedia: A systemic-constructivist analysis. *Journal of the Learning Sciences, 23*, 149–176.

Oeberst, A., Kimmerle, J., & Cress, U. (2016). What is knowledge? Who creates it? Who possesses it? The need for novel answers to old questions. In U. Cress, J. Moskaliuk, & H. Jeong (Eds.), *Mass collaboration and education* (pp. 105–124). Cham: Springer International Publishing.

Piaget, J. (1977). *The development of thought: Equilibration of cognitive structures*. New York, NY: The Viking Press.

Posner, G. J., Strike, K. A., Hewson, P. W., & Gertzog, W. A. (1982). Accommodation of a scientific conception: Toward a theory of conceptual change. *Science Education, 66*, 211–227.

Rumelhart, D. E., & Norman, D. A. (1981). Accretion, tuning, and restructuring: Three modes of learning. In J. W. Cotton & R. Klatzky (Eds.), *Semantic factors in cognition* (pp. 37–60). Hillsdale, NJ: Erlbaum.

Scheiter, K. (2017). Learning from multimedia: Cognitive processes and instructional support. In S. Schwan & U. Cress (Eds.), *The psychology of digital learning: Constructing, exchanging, and acquiring knowledge with digital media*. New York: Springer.

Schwan, S. (2017). Digital pictures, videos, and beyond: Knowledge acquisition with realistic images. In S. Schwan & U. Cress (Eds.), *The psychology of digital learning: Constructing, exchanging, and acquiring knowledge with digital media*. New York: Springer.

Schweiger, S., Oeberst, A., & Cress, U. (2014). Confirmation bias in web-based search: A randomized online study on the effects of expert information and social tags on information search and evaluation. *Journal of Medial Internet Research, 16*, e94.

Sharan, S. (Ed.). (1994). *Handbook of cooperative learning methods*. Westport: Greenwood Press.

Slavin, R. E. (1990). *Cooperative learning*. Englewood Cliffs, NJ: Prentice-Hall.

Spencer-Brown, G. (1969). *Laws of form*. London: Allen & Unwin.

Stahl, G. (2006). *Group cognition: Computer support for building collaborative knowledge*. Cambridge, MA: MIT Press.

Stahl, G. (2013). Learning across levels. *International Journal of Computer-Supported Collaborative Learning, 8*, 1–12.

Utz, S., & Levordashka, A. (2017). Knowledge networks in social media. In S. Schwan & U. Cress (Eds.), *The psychology of digital learning: Constructing, exchanging, and acquiring knowledge with digital media*. New York: Springer.

Varela, F. J., Maturana, H. R., & Uribe, R. (1974). Autopoiesis: The organization of living systems, its characterization and a model. *Biosystems, 5*, 187–196.

Vosniadou, S. (1994). Capturing and modeling the process of conceptual change. *Learning and Instruction, 4*, 45–69.

Vygotsky, L. S. (1978). *Mind in society: The development of higher psychological processes*. Cambridge, MA: Harvard University Press.

Webb, N. M. (1989). Peer interaction and learning in small groups. *International Journal of Educational Research, 13*, 21–39.

Wilson, M. (2002). Six views of embodied cognition. *Psychonomic Bulletin & Review, 9*, 625–636.

Chapter 8
Digital Design and Learning: Cognitive-Constructivist Perspectives

Carmen Zahn

Abstract In this chapter, "design" aspects of learning will be covered: Today, learners readily employ emerging digital tools for active participation in information design and knowledge communication—be it in schools, universities, vocational training, at workplaces, or simply "online". Not only do they acquire knowledge from digital information sources, but they also create their own knowledge artifacts (e.g., web pages, graphics, videos, hypertexts, social media, or computer programs)—both individually and in groups—to be shared with learning communities on intranets or official platforms. The present contribution explains from an integrative cognitive-constructivist perspective how design relates to complex problem solving and, hence, can foster knowledge-intensive group processes in learning-through-design. Five experimental studies will be summarized, investigating the specific example of learning through visual design with advanced video tools.

Keywords Digitalization • Knowledge processes • Problem solving • Collaborative information design • Learning-through-design • Digital video tools

Introduction

During the last decade, rapid changes in digital tools for connecting us with others have become a fundamental fact of everyday life. Average users can easily access complex information from anywhere at any time. Moreover, not only writing text messages with mobiles and smartphones, but also editing, commenting, designing, and sharing videos, photos, pictures, and spreadsheets has become common. In brief: Emerging digital media continuously create new rhetorical or "design" spaces where participation and sharing has defined a new culture that I call a *culture of*

C. Zahn (✉)
School of Applied Psychology, University of Applied Sciences and Arts Northwestern Switzerland (FHNW), Riggenbachstraße 16, 4600 Olten, Switzerland
e-mail: carmen.zahn@fhnw.ch

© Springer International Publishing AG 2017
S. Schwan, U. Cress (eds.), *The Psychology of Digital Learning*,
DOI 10.1007/978-3-319-49077-9_8

collaborative information design. In this culture, people create their own knowledge artifacts (often in groups) in order to exchange and share them with a worldwide audience.

At the same time, knowledge communication is becoming more *visual*—and particularly *video based*. The ways in which people send, share, like, and communicate with video today is very different from only a few years ago. As Zahn, Krauskopf, Hesse, and Pea argued in 2010: "Concurrently new specific skills grow important for people so that they can use the new (audio) visual media to participate in societal communication processes and to express themselves. Otherwise people will be limited in their opportunities to solve complex problems in the future" (p. 504). The New Media Consortium predicted in its 2008 edition of the Horizon Reports: "With video easily produced on all manner of inexpensive devices from phones to pocket cameras, faculty have more options than ever before to incorporate video into their curricula. Video papers and projects are increasingly common assignments … Increasingly, learning organizations, faculty, scholars, and students are using these tools as well, and … it is very likely that such practice will enter the mainstream of use in these institutions" (NMC, 2008, p. 11). Meanwhile, the NMC Horizon Project has explored and documented other emerging technology trends and their uptakes in K-12, museums, or in higher education from 2002 to 2015 in a series of reports (e.g., Johnson, Adams Becker, Estrada, & Freeman, 2015). Among them is a trend that we experience right now: video-based massive open online courses called MOOCs (Johnson et al., 2013) showing that the earlier 2008 NMC predictions were even outreached on a very large scale.

With emerging technologies, new educational challenges arise: On the one hand, changing media shape the key competencies and the skills that we need to be able to participate in societal processes and work (e.g., Jenkins, Purushotma, Weigel, Clinton, & Robison, 2009; Pea, 1985). They thus challenge existing educational goals. On the other hand, existing learning paradigms are being challenged because in the educational cultures themselves—be they formal school-based or university settings, training or informal learning settings—knowledge communication, teaching and learning, take different routes in times of digitalization" As already proposed by Pea as early as 1985, new technologies do not only amplify educational uses of digital media for learning purposes but also create *new* scopes with *new* options, which in turn can inspire *new* learning processes and *new* expectations, thus redefining educational cultures (Pea, 1985). It is important to grasp these new scopes in detail to make them fruitful for learning.

This chapter focuses on the new scope of *digital design for learning* and on using *advanced video collaboration tools* in this context (cf. Zahn, Pea, Hesse, & Rosen, 2010; Zahn et al., 2005). It consists of both theoretical and empirical approximations: First, in the theory section, I will summarize and integrate central well-established psychological and educational models that can explain the cognitive and collaborative processes involved in learning by designing one's own information structures. Second, in the empirical section, I will offer a contribution to the existing scientific work in the fields of design research and of research on collaborative learning. As a showcase, I will summarize a series of studies including both basic and applied experiments investigating collaborative design activities with digital video tools in real (and therefore complex) educational settings. Finally, I will explain how the research presented extends on larger and more informal learning contexts.

Theoretical Background

In this section, theory approaches will be presented that can explain how and under which conditions digital design leads to learning. As a starting point, let us first look at the topic more closely: What happens in learners' minds when they design their own digital information structures or knowledge artifacts? What kind of cognitive activity is digital design? And what kind of collaborative activity is digital design in a group or team?

On its most basic level, digital design consists of at least (a) *reading and producing* texts, speech, sound, pictures, videos, and visualizations, (b) *integrating* multiple visual, auditory, and text media, and (c) *structuring* information in nonlinear and interactive ways with advanced digital tools. In other words, at its core digital design combines generic aspects of both *writing* and *designing*. Writing and designing are central types of human cognitive activities. Respectively, the central models that provide for descriptions of the main knowledge processes involved in digital design are cognitive models of writing and design (e.g., Bereiter & Scardamalia, 1987; Goel & Pirolli, 1992; Hayes, 1996)—and (for groups) their extensions in terms of collaborative writing or collaborative design (e.g., Lahti, Seitamaa-Hakkarainen, & Hakkarainen, 2004; Stempfle & Badke-Schaub, 2002). These models are based on the generic problem-solving paradigm from cognitive psychology: Problem solving is generally defined as the cognitive processes of representing a problem as a "problem space," then planning actions and executing actions in a certain task environment to find a resolution to the problem (cf. Newell & Simon, 1972).

In the following paragraphs, I will briefly review the cognitive models and related theory developments. This review is necessarily highly selective for the purpose of this chapter. For comprehensive reviews over the huge body of research on writing and design, for more details and critical discussions, the interested reader may refer to the respective literature (e.g., Kellogg, 1994; Klein, 1999; MacArthur, Graham, & Fitzgerald, 2016).

Cognitive Processes in Writing and Design

Hayes and Flower (1980, 1986) defined *writing* as a special case of problem solving with the ill-structured rhetorical goal of creating a coherent text for a specific audience. Writing text according to Hayes (1996) includes activities such as creating visual–spatial representations, pictures, and graphs, too. The basic cognitive subprocesses of writing are specified as *text interpretation, reflection,* and *text pro-duction.* Text interpretation involves processes of reading texts, graphics, tables, etc.—be they external sources or one's own text—and constructing mental repre-sentations from it. Reflection includes activities of operating on one's mental repre-sentations to produce new or extended mental representations, for example, when phrases are combined to form a new sentence. Text production consists of external-izing mental representations, thereby producing concrete verbal or visual–spatial output in consideration of the concrete task (for details, see Hayes, 1996). Hayes explicitly emphasizes that writing is a social activity because it is directed towards an audience and because it occurs in a social context in many situations of collab-orative writing (such as at school, the workplace or in informal settings). Two major components influencing writing processes are specified: the task environment (i.e., all "factors influencing a writing task that lie outside the individual's skin," 1996, p. 3) and the writer (i.e., the writer's inner cognitive and memory processes). Concerning "task environment," this component is further divided into a *social envi-ronment* (e.g., the text for an audience, collaborators in writing) and a *physical environment* (e.g., the composing medium or tool). Concerning the "writer," it is important to note that there are further differences between cognitive processes of *writing text* and *producing visual media or multimedia* that refer to the writers' cognitive skills: School-based education that has long put much emphasis on stu-dents learning to write text and perform analyses and interpretations of written text as *cultural techniques,* while less emphasis has been put on similar activities con-cerning visual media and multimedia (e.g., video production, film analyses, and interpretations). Hence, we must expect differences in the writers' cognitive skills of writing *text* versus their skills of producing *videos* (i.e., verbal literacy vs. visual literacy) when they engage in writing as a social activity. This makes the model more complex, but also more realistic and leads to further interesting questions tackling the complexity of writing as a social or socio-cognitive task. Being a cogni-tive model, the Hayes and Flower model does not focus on such social aspects nor does it dig deeply into the role of different tools and technologies involved in writ-ing text versus producing visual information. This is a point to which I will return below.

Bereiter and Scardamalia (1987; Bereiter, Burtis, & Scardamalia, 1988) distin-guish two alternative modes of writing: one route that involves effortful problem-solving processes (and "knowledge-transforming") and an alternative route that does not (called "knowledge-telling"). In the latter case, the cognitive processes involved in writing only consist of memory search processes. Today, we would call it a "copy & paste strategy" where content is only tested for appropriateness in rela-tion to the writing assignment, whereas no deeper processing occurs and the product remains superficial at best. In our present context here, the formerly mentioned mode of writing is more interesting because it models writing as a knowledge-intensive rhetorical problem-solving process with writers creating and operating upon two problem spaces: *a rhetorical and a content problem space.* In attempting to attain the best fit between consciously pursued rhetorical goals (how to say some-thing for a certain audience) and the content to be presented (what to say), writers continuously translate problems from the rhetorical problem space to the content problem space and vice versa. It is thereby assumed that they elaborate on both the content-related problem space and the rhetorical problem space, and they deepen the related mental representations (i.e., content knowledge and rhetorical concepts). During such knowledge-transformation processes, the writer also can construct new ideas and knowledge. The contribution by Bereiter and Scardamalia is of major significance because they differentiate between different modes of writing with different cognitive processes involved, helping us to not be naïve when it comes to learning: Learners *may or may not* deeply process information in digital design. Another point to which I will return below.

Goel and Pirolli (1992) refer not to writing but to the design of usable visual or physical artifacts in their cognitive design model. Similar to the writing models, they assume a special case of complex problem solving—design as an ill-structured problem lacking any "right" or "wrong" answers. Design is defined as "…fundamentally mental, representational and a signature of human intelligence" (Goel & Pirolli, 1992, p. 396) and a distinction is made between two basic subprocesses in design: problem structuring and problem solving. In problem structuring, designers establish the design problem space based on the available information from the task environment (e.g., task assignment, brief, instructions, tools)—thereby adding missing information elements (e.g., from the designers' prior knowledge and experience from similar models). After problem structuring, designers develop their artifacts incrementally (being more likely to improve and refine their ideas than completely discarding initial solution states). Within this iterative problem-solving process, three phases are distinguishable: (1) preliminary design, with substantial consideration of people, purpose, goal, and resource aspects, as well as increased attention to the task assignment or brief, (2) refinement, and (3) detail design each with decreasing attention to the brief, but increasing detailed expression of concrete ideas. As the design ideas and the product evolve, the design problem space may be restructured continuously. Designers put substantial effort into structuring their design problem space, defining start and goal states before solving the design problem. Goel and Pirolli (1992) found that individuals devoted 25% of time to problem structuring when designing versus 0.3% when solving non-design problems.

Collaborative Processes in Writing and Design

As has become obvious in the previous paragraphs, writing or design are seldom individual processes, but often social or *group* processes of problem solving. Hence, models of collaborative writing and design extend the generic cognitive models by focusing on social dimensions and team-related processes as a further "problem" (e.g., Lahti et al., 2004; Lowry, Curtis, & Lowry, 2004; Stempfle & Badke-Schaub, 2002).

Lowry et al. (2004), for instance, relying on research into group perspectives (e.g., Galegher & Kraut, 1994 or Posner & Baecker, 1992) understand collaborative writing involving "…a team focused on a common objective that *negotiates, coordinates and communicates during creation of a common document*" (p. 72)—in other words, additional team formation and team planning (e.g., writers have to develop a joint writing strategy). In addition to individual cognitive activities, collaborative writing consists of group brainstorming, joint outlining, drafting, reviewing, mutual revision, and much communication among team members: Writers thereby develop new ideas, negotiate and make joint decisions on which ideas should be tracked further and which should not. Finally, they document and continuously reflect on their product and on their team process. The model describes the whole complexity of writing as group problem solving.

Lahti et al. (2004) investigated collaborative design as an iterative small group process "…of actively communicating and working together in order to jointly establish design goals, search through design problem spaces, determine design constraints and construct a design solution" (p. 351). They assume joint problem structuring and joint problem solving, along with decision-making and process organization to be the main processes in design teams. Two types of relations are considered important for the respective design solutions: the designer–object and the designer–designer relationship. These relationships influence how designers (re-)structure their problem according to the design brief, define the constraints of designing, and (de-)compose the problem, then generate design proposals, choose materials, consider capacities and tools, and discuss and test design solutions.

Stempfle and Badke-Schaub (2002) define collaborative design as activities directed towards both the content of a design problem and the organization of a group or team process. In their generic model of design as a team activity, they assume cognitive operations as applied to separate problem spaces: the goal space and the solution space of a given problem "…as well as to the organization of the collective process of teamwork…" (p. 473). The collaborators move back and forth between those problem spaces, thereby collaboratively considering the specific design or team constraints.

Computer-Supported Collaborative Writing and Design

Difference strands of research in the educational sciences have applied the problem-solving models of (collaborative) writing or design to the field of teaching and learning. These approaches are concerned with the educational value of (computer-supported) writing and design activities, for example, as *cognitive strategies for understanding lesson content* (e.g., in science, mathematics, or history lessons). The writing of compositions or reports, on the one hand, or visual design and *design* of physical artifacts (e.g., a model of a subway system or a miniature vehicle), on the other hand, are implemented as instructional methods in classrooms. The main concepts include "learning by design" (e.g., Hmelo, Holton, & Kolodner, 2000; Kolodner, Gray, & Fasse, 2003), "learning by hypermedia design" (e.g., Bromme & Stahl, 1999; Carver, Lehrer, Connell, & Erickson, 1992; Lehrer, Erickson, & Connell, 1994), and "learning through design" (e.g., Harel, 1990; Harel & Papert,

1991; Kafai & Ching, 2001; Kafai, Ching, & Marshall, 2004; Kafai & Resnick, 1996; Papert, 1993), and "writing to learn" (e.g., Klein, 1999; Newell, 2006). The rationale behind these applications is based on constructionism—Papert's (1993) variant of Piaget's constructivist developmental theory—meaning that (digital) media are used here as epistemic and expressive tools for children and juvenile students rather than as presentation tools. Design projects using the services of emerging digital technologies are considered recommendable due to their motivating and activating nature. They are also a fitting response to the prevailing claims for the necessity of integrating innovative computer technology into the classroom, not only as arbitrary and insular units but combined with authentic learning tasks, social interaction, and clear-cut educational goals.

Writing and Designing as Collective and Networked Processes

Bereiter (2002) and Scardamalia (2002) turned from their previous writing theory (described above) to collaborative knowledge-transformation processes and computer-supported collaborative learning (CSCL) in the classroom *and beyond*. They thereby suggested to implement a system of guidance into collaborative technology (CSILE = Computer Supported Intentional Learning Environments, Knowledge Forum ©, Scardamalia, 2002, 2004) that provides built-in procedural facilitation for reflective discussion, for example, on different perspectives. Their earlier approach has been extended by a view on knowledge transformation as *social by nature* and then the more radical notion of *knowledge building communities* in which knowledge transformation is seen as a community (not individual or small group) achievement and as an improvement of ideas rather than progress towards scientific "truths." In contrast to most cognitive and collaborative theories, it shifts the focus completely from individuals' activities towards collective processes of advancing and externalizing knowledge within a community system (be it fellow students or a large Internet platform). Accordingly, digital technologies are seen as expressive and flexible media for supporting collaborative discourse. Discourse within digital media workspaces or platforms is seen as basis for collaborative problem solving, moving towards emergent knowledge, and collective understanding (Scardamalia, 2002; Scardamalia & Bereiter, 2006). The crux of this approach is that its basic "ideal" is also an early emphasis on active participation for all, which we find quite normal in the social media today.

In sum, cognitive models sketch individual processes in writing and design, whereas collaborative models additionally include writer–writer or designer–designer interactions in small groups, which occur in many educational and training situations and in the workplace. Related educational and community approaches suggest that collaborative writing and design equals collaborative/collective problem-solving processes with negotiations among learners made possible by grounding (cf. Clark & Brennan, 1991), multiperspectivity, and process organization based on shared representations, tools, and activities that can be employed for learning purposes.

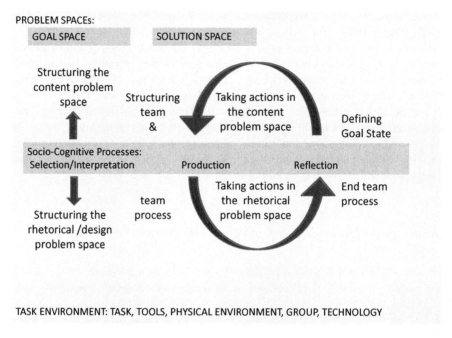

An integrative perspective on digital design which is based on earlier cognitive approaches (as referred to in the section "Theoretical Background")

An Integrative Perspective for Explaining Digital Design

The cognitive, collaborative, educational, and collective models of writing and design that were outlined in the previous paragraphs can be integrated: First, they all relate to the basic problem-solving paradigm from cognitive psychology, which reveals considerable overlaps in the models' assumptions about knowledge-intensive cognitive and socio-cognitive processes. Second, it has been argued before by some of the authors that writing and design can be understood as paradigmatic rather than specific (e.g., Goel & Pirolli, 1992). Third, it has been argued by other authors that writing is a type of design task (Dillon, 2002) and that models of writing include visual media (Hayes, 1996). Fourth, complex design—even when visual media are in the foreground—includes substantial amounts of text writing (Stahl, Zahn, Schwan, & Finke, 2006). Thus, considering the different models together jointly by means of an integrative perspective (and also considering their unique strengths) seems more suitable for explaining digital design than selecting one single model.

From an integrative perspective (summarized in Fig. 8.1), design with digital tools is best described as a collaborative and social practice where groups (e.g., student "design" teams) or participants in a web-community jointly structure a dual problem space (content and rhetorical problem space, see Fig. 8.1), and coordinate their social knowledge process within the reference frame of an activity system (i.e., a specific task environment and tools, see Fig. 8.1, bottom) to solve a design problem. In this social practice, learners engage in an iterative interplay between rhetorical/design goals (how to say or present something for a certain audience) and the content to be presented (what to say or present). During problem solving, they continuously translate problems from the rhetorical/design problem space to the content problem space and vice versa (see Fig. 8.1 arrows). It is assumed that they thereby cognitively elaborate on both the content-related problem space and the rhetorical/design problem space, deepening the related mental representations. The following socio-cognitive processes are assumed to be involved: Group or community members rely on or achieve common ground about design goals and design content when they make their design decisions or produce content, taking into consideration an anticipated audience, intended "message," and the constraints of their available technologies. They articulate and represent the reasons and the reasoning processes behind their design and negotiate meaning. This includes collaborative and cognitive processes (see Fig. 8.1, blue box) of reading, selecting, and interpreting texts, graphics, tables, and so forth—be they external sources, design briefs, task instructions, texts from other contributors, or one's own text produced so far—and constructing mental representations from it. It also includes production processes such as externalizing mental representations, thereby producing concrete verbal or visual–spatial output in consideration of the concrete task. Thus, learners operate upon their own mental representations, transform and (re-)structure knowledge, express and defend (or change) their own understanding of a topic, and concern themselves with how they represent that understanding. They reflect on their own and their collaborators' knowledge or opinions in design discussions and on their own design product. They therefore can deepen their knowledge, construct new knowledge and ideas, and develop thinking skills, and communication skills. In addition, learners also (re-)structure, document, and continuously reflect on their product and on their team process. Thereby, they can train their skills for teamwork.

The Educational Value of Digital Design Tasks: Potentials and Drawbacks

The potential educational value of students engaging in the socio-cognitive activities sketched in Fig. 8.1 seems obvious: They cannot but deeply understand the subject matter and develop a number of media-related skills on the level of both individual and group or community knowledge. The flip side of the coin is, however, the *demanding* nature of these activities that has been delineated by a number of authors (e.g., Bereiter, 2002; Bromme & Stahl, 1999; Lehrer et al., 1994; Stahl & Bromme, 2004; Stahl et al., 2006; Zahn, Schwan, & Barquero, 2002). There are clearly potential drawbacks to learning that lurk in real (as opposed to manipulated, or "ideal") collaborative design tasks with complex digital tools used in educational settings. One major drawback would be that learners are overwhelmed by the task of having to structure and monitor their own group process while also having to structure their dual design problem space. In the face of these challenges, students (especially those unfamiliar with the task or a new digital tool) may try hard at times but not achieve a satisfactory product—or they may avoid cognitive and team effort by switching to what Bereiter and Scardamalia (1987) described as the knowledge-telling mode of writing and a "copy and paste" strategy of designing information structures. Another drawback may be that they are not yet trained to solve team conflicts and decision-making. And still another drawback may be the use of unfamiliar digital tools. Design problems depend centrally on the organization of the learners' activity system in which the design takes place. In digital design, we expect technology not only to support design activities in the sense of assistive tools (MacArthur, 2008) but also in the sense of guiding collaboration—for better or for worse. Students may be either guided or *misguided* by the tools in their collaborative activities. Students may be cognitively overloaded by complex digital tools, not having enough cognitive resources left for group collaboration and learning activities. Research from the field of computer-supported collaborative learning (CSCL, see e.g., Roschelle & Teasley, 1995; Suthers, 2006; Suthers & Hundhausen, 2003, and many others) provides a long discussion about how technology affordances shape complex collaborative activities. Well-known small group approaches from social psychology such as, for example, the approach by McGrath, Arrow, Gruenfeld, Hollingshead, and O'Connor (1993) too have long considered group collaboration and outcome as dependent "on the degree of fit between the technology and the group, its tasks, and the context within which action is taking place" (McGrath et al., 1993, p. 407).

The question is now: How can we support this fit between technology, group, task, and activity context in digital design tasks? Proponents of the constructionist model provided cases with evidence of how students gain new knowledge and, therefore, how design can be a useful pedagogical strategy (e.g., Harel, 1990; Harel & Papert, 1991; Kafai & Ching, 2001; Kafai et al., 2004; Papert, 1993). Other empirical evidence supporting the educational value of design has been based on sound instructional programs derived from cognitive models. Such instructional programs build on the support of classroom processes or design subprocesses such as goal setting or understanding software functions and tools (Lehrer et al., 1994; Stahl & Bromme, 2004). Lehrer et al. (1994; see also Carver et al., 1992), for instance, investigated a program for middle-school students, designing complex hypertexts about American history topics (imperialism, immigration, World War I and 1870–1920) with a tool called "HyperAuthor" (and report a high quality of the hypermedia products and a substantial decrease of off-topic talk of the students from the beginning to the end of the project (from 30 to 3%). Further case studies (e.g., by Kafai & Ching, 2001) on learning science topics using Logo Microworlds™ provide hints for the effectiveness of having more experienced students shaping science talk in student teams of software design planning for science learning.

However, the results from case studies are only preliminary hints for several reasons: They are scattered over a large variety of very different design projects and different concepts applied for instructional guidance. They were sometimes part of large reform movements (e.g., the Headlight project) and confounded with additional instructional support systems (e.g., cognitive apprenticeship) in and outside the classroom, which makes it difficult to identify what actually caused learning. Too little attention has been paid to the possible obstacles for groups (e.g., process losses in groups as known from research in social psychology, see e.g., Stroebe & Diehl, 1994). Generally, MacArthur (2006) has described research on the effects on learning by writing or design with new technologies to be still "at an early stage." A major problem is a severe lack of systematic experimental research with only few exceptions (e.g., Braaksma, Riijlaarsdam, Couzijn, & van den Bergh, 2002)

While fully agreeing with the basic claims of constructionism that learners, by collaboratively constructing their own text or digital artifacts, also "construct" new knowledge, I also agree with some critical voices (e.g., Kirschner, Sweller, & Clark, 2006). It is valid to question the claim that collaborative design of digital artifacts is generally beneficial for learning without providing detailed empirical evidence from experimental studies.

The experiments that I will now turn to offer as a contribution to the research field address both sides of the coin—the upside and the downside. They are based on the integrative perspective explained above and very close attention is devoted to systematic investigations of possible task and technology effects when students engage in digital design for learning. The lab and field experiments presented were conducted with *advanced video tools as a particular showcase*. Why video tools? The example was not an arbitrary choice. It was purposefully chosen because it can be seen as paradigmatic for antedating how innovative technologies may redefine educational cultures. In the introduction to this chapter, I outlined how emerging web-based video tools (as provided, e.g., on YouTube or other video platforms) have changed the nature of participation in modern online communities and new educational uses. From observing this coevolution, we can learn a lot about other fundamental changes brought about by other advanced technologies for education.

Experiments on Digital Design and Learning with Advanced Video Tools

Research Goals and Research Questions

The overarching goal of the empirical research presented in this chapter was to systematically investigate digital design for learning using advanced video tools as a showcase (for *advanced video tools*, see Chambel, Zahn, & Finke, 2006; Pea, 2006; Zahn et al., 2005). The practical benefit from this goal lies in finding timely strategies for meaningful learning with digital videos in school-based or higher education (e.g., when students design a video-based web page). For this purpose, a series of experiments investigated how socio-cognitive processes involved in digital design tasks relate to the specific functions of advanced web-based video tools (to be described below). It was assumed that the functions of those video tools for socio-cognitive design processes define their potential to support learning in the sense of technology affordances (Suthers, 2006). The concrete research questions were: How do the technical properties (affordances) of digital video tools influence student collaboration, cognition, and learning? How do learners such as secondary school students approach collaborative visual design tasks (e.g., in a classroom setting)? Where, precisely, do students in class need instructional guidance? In order to provide answers to these questions, the empirical research reported here focuses purposely on both lab studies and field studies in real educational settings (e.g., a classroom).

Method

The research presented here combines interdisciplinary (technological, psychological, and educational) perspectives in the spirit of the "use-inspired basic research" paradigm (Hesse & Zahn, 2006). Substantial time and effort was put into the development of the experimental paradigm and into adapting the experimental setting to the specific needs of educational practice in school: Several research cycles involved tool and task developments for experimentation in addition to the usual tests and materials. In particular, instructional framing of the collaborative design task was developed not only according to the experimental rationale, but so that it was compatible with the respective curricula of the field sample (e.g., for German secondary school levels). This is not necessarily an easy way to go for a researcher in experimental cognitive psychology, nor is it common. It helps, however, to avoid oversimplification, which sometimes leads to detachment of psychological research from educational practice.

Tools and Technology. Two types of advanced video tools were used in our studies: Diver/WebDiver™ (Pea et al., 2004) and Hypervideo (Chambel et al., 2006; Zahn, Barquero, & Schwan, 2004; Zahn & Finke, 2003; Zahn, Oestermeier, & Finke, 2005). Both systems have repeatedly been described in detail before with a focus on their supportive socio-cognitive functions for learning (e.g., Zahn et al., 2005). Diver/WebDiver™ was developed at Stanford University (see Pea et al., 2004). It is a video collaboration tool that is based on the metaphor of a user "diving" into videos. Originally, its primary focus was for supporting video analyses in the learning sciences and in teacher education, but it was also discussed as a learning tool for students (Pea et al., 2004; Zahn et al., 2005). In Diver/WebDiver™ a user controls a virtual camera that can zoom and pan through space and time within an overview window of the source video. The virtual camera can take a snapshot of a still image clip, or dynamically record a video "path" through the video. The user thus may select visual information by virtually "pointing to it" in the much larger spatial–temporal data structure of the video for the purposes of collaborative reflection and analysis. The final product then is a collection of separate short video segments with annotations that represent the user's point of view on the video. These video segments can be shared over the Internet or in other scenarios and become the focus of knowledge building, argumentative, tutorial, assessment, or general communicative exchanges. The technology affordances of the system enable users to create new points of view onto a source video and comment on these by writing short text passages. Diving on video theoretically performs an important action for establishing common ground that is characterized as "guided noticing" (Pea, 2006).

Hypervideo (Zahn & Finke, 2003) is based on the notion of video-based hypermedia where video sequences form the backbone of the system and video is linked with different kinds of additional information (such as written or spoken texts, pictures, or further videos). It contains highlighted objects or persons within the video as sensitive regions for a predefined time frame. Users can mouse click on sensitive regions within the videos to access the additional information. Collaborative hypervideo integrates interactive videos, additional information, and a discussion area, thereby supporting web-based collaborative authoring of hypervideo systems, where groups or communities can share and discuss ideas. The system is informed by cognitive and collaborative theoretical perspectives and in this sense is defined as dynamic information space (*DIS*, cf. Zahn & Finke, 2003) that can be changed and extended by a group or community as a basis for sharing knowledge and communicating with each other. The technology affordances of collaborative hypervideo tools enable users to establish video-based nonlinear information structures and to focus their attention and discussion in collaborative learning on associated concepts or related external representations of knowledge (e.g., a visible object and a text, or visible object and a formula). Collaborative hypervideo was first explored as a support for learning through design for advanced university students in a psychology master's program taking courses on "e-learning" (Stahl, Zahn, & Finke, 2005; Stahl, Finke, & Zahn, 2006; Stahl et al., 2006).

Instructional Framing and Task. The field experiments took place in a German school (Gymnasium). The school subjects chosen for the studies were German language arts and German history. Language arts and history each represent domains in which constructive working with video is considered highly preferable while also providing a challenge for students and teachers. In history learning, factual knowledge is closely intertwined with specific thinking skills such as de-composing, evaluating, analyzing, and critically reflecting on historical film sources—along with (re-)constructing knowledge (Krammer, 2006; Smith & Blankinship, 2000). These are necessary skills for a full understanding of historical topics; however, they are difficult to teach in most traditional history lessons at schools. In line with these educational goals (which correspond to Jenkins et al.'s 2009 notions of social and cultural skills for community involvement), the experimental task involves the following components: critical analysis, judgment, collaborative problem solving, and appropriation. Prior to experimentation, the didactical value of the task was discussed in a workshop with experienced educational researchers. One major goal was to have a design task realizable within the constraints of an *average lesson*. The design task was thus restricted and adapted to the standard German time frame devoted to a subject in 1 day (two subsequent units of 45 min each), and the topic (historical contents described below) was chosen to satisfy curricular demands (according to the curricular standards of the cooperating schools at Gymnasium level). The prototypical task developed for the experiments involves collaborative visual design based on a video resource showing an historical newsreel about the 1948 Berlin Blockade. It also involves using digital video tools. Students are asked to act as a team of online editors who design a web page for a popular German virtual history museum. The explicated overall design goal is to comment on the video showing the historical newsreel for publication in the virtual history museum for future visitors. This product is to be based on the collaborative analysis of the source video by integrating additional information applying one of the digital video tools. Learners are explicitly made aware of the audience that they are designing for and the purpose the product should serve for this audience; that is, the future visitors of the virtual museum should be able to develop a good understanding of both the content and the filmic codes/style of the historical newsreel. Following the integrative perspective (see Fig. 8.1), the task initially includes an individual inquiry phase for planning in which learners first watch a digital video showing the historical Berlin Blockade newsreel from 1948. Then, they visit the virtual history museum LeMO (see https://www.dhm.de/lemo/), and finally they familiarize themselves with that specific period of German history. Students acquaint themselves with the contemporary use of newsreels as well as basic information on general filmic codes and style. They also explore the functions of the digital video tool with a thematically unrelated, instructional video clip. In the subsequent production phase, they pair up and collaboratively design elements for the web-museum, using one computer together. When working with the digital video tool, students are always free to evaluate and revise their evolving product. Thus, several generic aspects of the learning processes can be investigated that are assumed to take place during learning with collaborative visual design tasks. Among these are the elaboration of content and visual information, the transfer of visual literacy skills to the analysis of other video sources, and the collaborative negotiation of meaning during the design activities. Specifically, the students can learn to use modern digital video tools for critical analysis and discussion of archive video material; they can learn to de-compose and to evaluate the video source by using general film analysis methodology, thereby developing a critical stance and understanding of the diversity of ideas during their collaboration. Furthermore, they can learn to design a web page, a means of presenting their own ideas on the Berlin Blockade and working creatively with them.

General Procedure. For all experiments, the procedure was the same and contained four steps: First, students filled in questionnaires for their basic demographic data and for assessing prior knowledge, interest in history and in the topic, along with prior computer-related and visual literacy skills. Second, students were individually provided with background information and task instructions. Third, students worked collaboratively in dyads on the design task (described above) for about half an hour. Fourth, post-experimental questionnaires assessed the students' appraisal of the task, their group collaboration, and knowledge acquisition. The procedure lasted 90 min maximum.

Experiments 1–5

Experiment 1—Tool effects on collaborative design. The first study (for details see Zahn, Pea, Hesse, & Rosen, 2010) was a lab-experiment testing the general hypothesis that a video tool (here: WebDiver™ as a prototypical example) would provide specific technical affordances for support of collaborative activities and socio-cognitive efforts, while a simpler technology (video-player & text-editor) would not. This proof of the premise that was settled earlier in this chapter (that tools can influence design) was a basic prerequisite for the further use of advanced video tools as a learning technology in subsequent field studies. The study was also testing the design task itself and whether or not it would be appreciated by students and could lead to understanding and knowledge acquisition. The experimental setup compared two contrasting conditions (advanced video tool "WebDiver™" vs. simple "video-player & text-editor" tool) with a sample of 48 psychology students who performed the collaborative design task. This assumption was based on prior analyses of the socio-cognitive functions of video tools and the sub-hypotheses posited implicit impacts of the different tools on design products, dyads' conversations, and individual learning and skills acquisition as dependent variables. The results of this experiment revealed significant positive main effects of the video collaboration tool WebDiver™ on design, collaboration, and knowledge and visual skills acquisition (in our case—as explained on p. 10 on task framing—knowledge relates to *historical* knowledge about the Berlin Blockade in 1948 and the airlift established by the Western allied forces, and about newsreels as the primary information and propaganda media in those days; visual literacy skills relate to understanding filmic styles and features used to persuade film audiences in propaganda or advertisements). Moreover, the influence of the video tool extended to the quality of the socio-cognitive processes of focusing their interactions. Interaction patterns were observable in dyads working with WebDiver™ mirroring how dyads' elaborations on the source video are guided by the tool affordance ("guided noticing") when they create interpretive annotations. Certain example episodes illustrate the kinds of processes possibly lying behind the quantitative indicators. For example, when students created a new "dive" with WebDiver™ (as explained in the technology section, see p. 9) they created a new cut-out from the source video by marking it in the video and then name a dive for writing a new comment. During the activity of marking and creating or naming a new "dive," they usually ended up analyzing or discussing *contents* of the respective video sequence and discovered new details in the video content (both on the audio and on the video track). These episodes evidence learning and additionally give an impression of how learners' socio-cognitive processes are impacted by technology. They thus complement the quantitative findings. In sum, it can be concluded from the study that the task was effective for learning and that the affordances of the advanced video tool (WebDiver™) enhanced the quality of the participants' design activities, thus confirming the basic assumptions about the socio-cognitive functions of video tools. Also, the results revealed a generally high appraisal of the task. Hence, the effectiveness of the visual design task could be evidenced *before* subsequent use in a regular history lesson at school.

Experiment 2: Tool effects and task goals in real classroom settings. The second study was conducted in the classroom (for details, see Zahn, Krauskopf, & Hesse, 2009; Zahn, Krauskopf et al., 2010). The goals of this field experiment were to test the collaborative design task described above in a realistic setting with 10th grade students in a regular lesson and to replicate findings (impact of digital video tools on learning) found in Experiment 1. In addition, the topic of instructional guidance was initially explored. A 2 × 2 factorial experimental design was applied. Concerning the first factor of the impact of digital video tools, the same advanced video tool (WebDiver™) tested in Experiment 1 was again compared with a "video-player & text-editor" tool condition. The second factor was a moderate form of instructional guidance in the form of providing for different task goals ("creating dives" vs. "creating annotated movies"). The variation of this second factor was based on findings from studies on hypermedia design with secondary high school students (Bromme & Stahl, 1999), showing that different goals are differentially effective in hypertext writing of secondary school students. As dependent variables in the present study, again as in Experiment 1, the students' collaborative design activities, design products, dyads' conversations, motivation, and knowledge and visual skills acquisition were measured. The field data show that students' knowledge significantly increased during the collaborative visual design task. In all conditions, the task proved to be interesting for the students and applicable in regular classroom situations. Replicating findings from the prior lab study, the affordances of Diver™ significantly increased the quality of design products and influenced design processes positively by focusing the learners' interactions on task-relevant conversations. Students working with Diver™ considered design-related issues significantly more often than students in the control condition. They also displayed a tendency towards fewer help requests. Working with Diver™ influenced the collaborative interactions, indicating more autonomous design activities. Additional case analyses were conducted focusing on how the students used and integrated technology affordances during their design-related interactions. Qualitative findings from the lab study concerning processes of "guided noticing" were replicated here, too. Yet, the second factor of instructional guidance (two different metaphors epitomizing two different task goals) yielded no significant main or interaction effects. A closer analysis of the students' general problem-solving behavior revealed for all conditions that the students proceeded mostly action-oriented and lacked thoughtful planning and evaluation (less than 3% of the time on the task was devoted to planning and less than 1% on evaluation).

In sum, it can be concluded that the task is suitable for application to regular classroom settings and proved to be interesting and effective for 10th grade students. The technology affordances of an advanced video tool can enhance the quality of design activities as compared to those of a control condition, thus replicating the prior lab findings in the field. However, the missing effects of instructional guidance do need more attention. There are two possible explanations: First, the suboptimal problem-solving behavior of the students may be the reason. Instruction related to task goals is important during collaborative planning and evaluation phases in the design process, but our students did not invest time and effort in these activities and, consequently, instruction did not yield any effects. It could also be the case, however, that providing task goals is generally ineffective. This latter possibility was taken care of in a supplementary experimental study before the next major experiment with secondary school students.

Experiment 3: Tool effects and task goals in collaborative design. In this third experiment with 58 psychology students ($N = 29$ dyads), the question of providing task goals from Experiment 2 was reinvestigated under controlled experimental conditions. The goals of this experiment were to test whether setting task goals by providing metaphors was generally effective or not. Therefore, two different task goals were provided with the instructions. Metaphors were used that are familiar, and it was made sure that students invest time and effort in collaborative planning. They were asked to draw concepts of their design. The results of this experiment confirmed differential influences of different task goals on design products, collaboration, and skills acquisition in the research lab. This indicates that missing effects of instructional guidance in the classroom (Experiment 2) can be explained by the suboptimal problem-solving behavior of the students and their lack of planning and evaluation phases. In sum, it can be concluded from Experiments 2 and 3 that 10th graders in class need more or different explicit instructional guidance for collaborative visual design than just the task instructions and goals provided to them in Experiment 2. This conclusion was refined and tested in Experiment 4.

Experiment 4: Tool effects and instructional guidance in collaborative design. Participants in this fourth study (for details see Zahn, Krauskopf, Hesse, & Pea, 2012, 2013) were 176 students ($N = 88$ dyads) from four German secondary schools. There were two goals of this study: one was to compare the impact of two different types of advanced digital video tools, and the second one was to compare different types of explicit instructional guidance. A 2×2 factorial experimental design was applied. Concerning the first factor, a Hypervideo condition was compared with a WebDiver™ condition. Concerning the second factor, two different types of explicit instructional guidance were provided for the students (instruction to design vs. instruction to collaborate). The variation of the first factor was based on earlier analyses of the socio-cognitive functions of the different technology affordances. The variation in the second factor was based on the results from the field experiment (lack of collaborative planning and evaluation phases) and in accordance with the integrative perspective underlying this research. Two meaningful ways to improve the explicit instructional guidance for collaborative visual design were applied: one with a focus on optimizing the design workflow and one with a focus on optimizing group processes. Optimizing the design workflow means to guide the problem-solving process in designing, for example, by providing step-by-step instruction derived from "ideal" writing or design (Fig. 8.1). Optimizing group processes means to support group collaboration, for example, by explicit guidance on how to collaborate in a team (e.g., negotiate joint goals, coordinate workflow) provided with the instruction as described in Zahn et al. (2012). The study was explorative concerning the influences of the factors on the dependent variables (again: the students' collaborative design activities, design products, dyads' conversations, motivation, and knowledge and visual skills acquisition). The experiment was conducted as a naturalistic lab experiment: Classes of students came in with their teachers to participate in the study. The results of this experiment yielded no or only marginally significant main effects concerning the tool factor. The advanced tools did not differ significantly in their effectiveness for collaborative design activities or learning. However, significant main effects of the different types of instruction were found for the second factor: Instruction on how to collaborate did lead to better quality of the design products and to better visual skills acquisition.

Experiment 5: Tool effects and task in online learning. The purpose of this experimental study (for details, see Zahn, Krauskopf, Kiener, & Hesse, 2014) was to investigate the task in an online learning setting. In online learning, different task contexts framing the active use of video could make a big difference; hence, another goal was to investigate this possibility. Participants were 72 psychology students. For the experimental sessions, the participants were randomly combined into dyads for online collaboration and also randomly assigned to one of two experimental conditions (two different task instructions assigned within a video-based online history lesson: Students received either a discussion task or a collaborative design task). While both assignments were assumed to be meaningful ways of approaching the analysis and interpretation of historical materials, the interesting point here, however, was the fine-grained effects of the instruction to discuss versus the instruction to design with regard to online collaboration and learning outcomes. Two main results from this study are important: First, the discussion task stimulated significantly more collaborative activity on a surface level than the design task. Second, the design task stimulated for more knowledge-intensive elaboration on a deeper level than the discussion task, especially concerning visual information from the video such as paying more joint attention to visual details and integrating different aspects of video content and style. These differences occurred while overall content knowledge acquisition (measured by multiple choice questions in a post-test) did not differ significantly between conditions. In other words, under the surface of apparently similar learning outcomes obtained within the same overall lesson paradigm, fine-grained differences in group knowledge processes and specific aspects of online learning became explicit. Such fine-grained differences—as subtle as they may seem—are important because they can give first hints for designers of online-learning environments concerning how to meet the challenge of deciding what students may learn.

Discussion

In the introduction, the question of how emerging computer technologies and digital media may "redefine" educational cultures was posed in relation to the most recent tools that allow for digital design activities. To approach this topic, digital design was analyzed from an integrative perspective that sketches the basic details of the socio-cognitive processes in design tasks for learning. The empirical research studies presented in this chapter exemplify a specific case of recent digital video tools that may redefine classroom learning by allowing for collaborative design activities. Five studies were summarized. The experimental findings show overall that the digital design task investigated was effective for learning and applicable to diverse regular in-class, face-to-face, and online learning settings. It proved to be interesting and effective not only for German psychology student samples, but also the target group of German 10th grade students. The results of both, lab and field experiments reveal how students used the affordances of the advanced video tools to enhance their digital design process and collaborative learning. It was thereby evidenced by lab and field data that students' knowledge and skills significantly increased. Moreover, in Experiment 5 investigating digital design in an online-setting, the results revealed that a digital design task stimulated more knowledge-intensive elaboration on a deeper level than a discussion task, especially concerning visual information from the video such as paying more joint attention to visual details and integrating different aspects of video content and style. These differences did not affect content knowledge acquisition. Yet, the discussion task stimulated only more collaborative activity *on a surface level* than the design task, which stimulated *deep processing*.

Initial answers to the research questions posed above can be provided: *How do the technical properties (affordances) of digital video tools influence student collaboration, cognition and learning?* Results of Experiments 1 and 2 revealed significant positive effects of an advanced video tool (WebDiver™) in contrast to a control condition (simple video-player and text-editing tool) on digital design processes, content learning, and visual skills acquisition of students. Qualitative analyses further show how students used specific video tool functions for support of guided noticing and elaboration or grounding processes. This provides initial support for the assumption that implicit guidance by using specific tools can be effective for learning. Yet, a comparison of *two* advanced video tools with different technical properties (WebDiver™ and Hypervideo) revealed no or only marginally significant effects (Experiment 4). The advanced video tools did not differ significantly in their effectiveness for collaborative design activities or learning.

How do learners such as secondary school students approach collaborative visual design tasks (e.g., in a classroom setting)? In both Experiment 2 and 5, 10th grade students approached the task with much interest and a positive attitude. They also evaluated it positively afterwards. Results of Experiment 2 (field experiment) revealed suboptimal problem-solving behavior of the students, 10th graders in class. As opposed to an "ideal" model that can be derived from the integrative perspective on digital design (see above and Fig. 8.1), results indicated a lack of task and goal-related planning and reflective activities in design and in turn a need for explicit instructional guidance.

Where, precisely, do secondary school students in class need instructional guidance? Experiments 2 and 3 revealed that a moderate instruction strategy (setting instructional goals by metaphors epitomizing task goals) proved to be a useful strategy in the lab with a university student sample but obviously not in a classroom with

10th graders. In contrast, Experiment 4 showed with a sample of 10th graders how the explicit instructional guidance of collaborative processes could improve the qualities of both design and learning. Results thereby reveal that stimulating awareness of social rules is effective in contrast to instructional guidance of the design workflow: Instruction on how to collaborate in a social group did lead to a better quality of the design products and to better visual skills acquisition.

The studies do have limitations. They were limited to one exemplary learning scenario (history learning) and one showcase of digital tools (advanced digital video tools). The numbers of participants—especially participating school classes—were limited, too. Although such limitations are necessary for experimental rationales and internal validity, the external validity of the results is of course restricted. Hence, I would not yet generalize these experimental results to other subject areas or age groups (e.g., primary school). Nevertheless, results are in line with and extend earlier findings from related research on learning through design (see section "Theoretical Background").

Taken together the results provide initial supportive evidence for the integrative perspective as was offered in this chapter. The scientific merit of the results is their support of the assumptions derived from this perspective about the supportive socio-cognitive processes in digital design with digital video tools in school-based education (e.g., assumptions about functions of technology affordances and instructional guidance). This is a step towards improving our scientific understanding of digital design activities. The results imply, too, on the practical side, that the mediating functions of video tools can be used as support for constructionist and design-based learning in the classroom. However, in this larger context, further research needs to be developed. Open questions are, for example: Which educational goals should be addressed and how? What kinds of support and informative assessments do teachers need? What guidance can we offer educators for their design of activities that maximize the use of video tools for learning? In a still larger context of education, other topics need also to be addressed concerning how collaborative design with digital tools can be integrated into educational cultures removed from formal education in university courses or classrooms. For example, informal web-communities as complex educational settings create quite different educational situations than schools. We are likely to find quite new design activity patterns when we investigate free choice online-learning communities (e.g., MOOCs). Such results will be especially important, too, if we consider that new media and advanced video platforms are becoming widely available and are spreading as new important forms of social communication in the youth culture (e.g., Jenkins, 2009). Considering the new questions arising from such new scenarios, research on collaborative design activities with digital tools used in different educational cultures will remain an exciting and challenging field in psychology and the learning sciences.

Acknowledgements This research was funded by the Deutsche Forschungsgemeinschaft [German Science Foundation]—DFG and conducted at the Knowledge Media Research Center (KMRC) in Tübingen, Germany in cooperation with the Wildermuth Gymnasium, Tübingen.

References

Bereiter, C. (2002). Emergent versus presentational hypertext. In R. Bromme & E. Stahl (Eds.), *Writing hypertext and learning. Conceptual and empirical approaches. Advances in learning and instruction series* (pp. 73–78). Amsterdam: Pergamon.

Bereiter, C., Burtis, P. J., & Scardamalia, M. (1988). Cognitive operations in written composition. *Journal of Memory and Language, 27*, 261–278.

Bereiter, C., & Scardamalia, M. (1987). *The psychology of written composition.* Hillsdale, NJ: Lawrence Erlbaum Associates.

Braaksma, M., Riijlaarsdam, G., Couzijn, M., & van den Bergh, H. (2002). Learning to compose hypertext and linear text: Transfer or inference? In R. Bromme & E. Stahl (Eds.), *Writing hypertext and learning. Conceptual and empirical approaches. Advances in learning and instruction series* (pp. 73–78). Amsterdam: Pergamon.

Bromme, R., & Stahl, E. (1999). Spatial metaphors and writing hypertexts: Study within schools. *European Journal of Psychology of Education, 14*, 267–281.

Carver, S. M., Lehrer, R., Connell, T., & Erickson, J. (1992). Learning by hypermedia design: Issues of assessment and implementation. *Educational Psychologist, 27*, 385–404.

Chambel, T., Zahn, C., & Finke, M. (2006). Hypervideo and cognition: Designing video-based hypermedia for individual learning and collaborative knowledge building. In E. M. Alkhalifa (Ed.), *Cognitively informed systems: Utilizing practical approaches to enrich information presentation and transfer* (pp. 26–49). Hershey, PA: Idea Group.

Clark, H. H., & Brennan, S. E. (1991). Grounding in communication. In L. B. Resnick, J. Levine, & S. D. Teasley (Eds.), *Perspectives on socially shared cognition* (pp. 127–149). Washington, DC: American Psychological Association.

Dillon, A. (2002). Writing as design: Hypermedia and the shape of information space. In R. Bromme & E. Stahl (Eds.), *Writing hypertext and learning. Conceptual and empirical approaches. Advances in learning and instruction series* (pp. 63–72). Amsterdam: Pergamon.

Galegher, J., & Kraut, R. E. (1994). Computer-mediated communication for intellectual teamwork: An experiment in group writing. *Information Systems Research, 5*, 110–138.

Goel, V., & Pirolli, P. (1992). The structure of design problem spaces. *Cognitive Science, 16*, 395–429.

Harel, I. (1990). Children as software designers: A constructionist approach for learning mathematics. *Journal of Mathematical Behavior, 9*, 3–93.

Harel, I., & Papert, S. (Eds.). (1991). *Constructionism.* Norwood, NJ: Ablex.

Hayes, J. R. (1996). A new model of cognition and affect in writing. In M. Levy & S. Ransdell (Eds.), *The science of writing* (pp. 1–27). Hillsdale, NJ: Erlbaum.

Hayes, J. R., & Flower, L. S. (1980). Identifying the organization of writing processes. In L. W. Gregg & E. R. Steinberg (Eds.), *Cognitive processes in writing* (pp. 3–30). Hillsdale, NJ: Lawrence Erlbaum.

Hayes, J. R., & Flower, L. S. (1986). Writing research and the writer. *American Psychologist, 41*, 1106–1113.

Hesse, F. W., & Zahn, C. (2006). Verbindung von Erkenntnis- und Nutzeninteresse am Beispiel eines Forschungsprojektes aus der angewandten Kognitionspsychologie. In A. Brüggemann & R. Bromme (Eds.), *Entwicklung und Bewertung von anwendungsorientierter Grundlagenforschung in der Psychologie* (pp. 55–60). Berlin: Akademie-Verlag.

Hmelo, C. E., Holton, D. L., & Kolodner, J. L. (2000). Designing to learn about complex systems. *Journal of the Learning Sciences, 9*, 247–298.

Jenkins, H., Purushotma, R., Weigel, M., Clinton, K., & Robison, A. J. (2009). *Confronting the challenges of participatory culture: Media education for the 21st century.* Cambridge: MIT Press. Retrieved June 6, 2016, from https://mitpress.mit.edu/sites/default/files/titles/free_download/9780262513623_Confronting_the_Challenges.pdf

Jenkins, J. (2009). What happened before YouTube? In J. Burgess & J. Green (Eds.), *YouTube: Online video and participatory culture. Digital media and society series* (pp. 109–125). Malden, MA: Polity Press.

Johnson, L., Adams Becker, S., Cummins, M., Estrada, V., Freeman, A. and Ludgate, H. (2013). *NMC Horizon Report: 2013 Higher Education Edition*. Austin, TX: The New Media Consortium. Retrieved July 29, 2016, from http://cdn.nmc.org/media/2015-nmc-horizon-report-HE-EN.pdf

Johnson, L., Adams Becker, S., Estrada, V. & Freeman, A. (2015). *NMC Horizon Report: 2015 Higher Education Edition*. Austin, TX: The New Media Consortium. Retrieved July 29, 2016, from http://cdn.nmc.org/media/2015-nmc-horizon-report-HE-EN.pdf

Kafai, Y. B., & Ching, C. C. (2001). Affordances of collaborative software design planning for elementary students' science talk. *Journal of the Learning Sciences, 10*, 323–363.

Kafai, Y. B., Ching, C. C., & Marshall, S. (2004). Learning affordances of collaborative software design. In M. Rabinowitz, F. C. Blumberg, & H. Everson (Eds.), *The impact of media and technology on instruction* (pp. 77–100). Mahwah, NJ: Erlbaum Associates.

Kafai, Y. B., & Resnick, M. (Eds.). (1996). *Constructionism in practice: Designing, thinking, and learning in a digital world* (pp. XII, 339 S.). Mahwah, NJ: Lawrence Erlbaum Associates.

Kellogg, R. T. (1994). *The psychology of writing*. New York: Oxford University Press.

Kirschner, P. A., Sweller, J., & Clark, R. E. (2006). Why minimal guidance during instruction does not work: An analysis of the failure of constructivist, discovery, problem-based, experiential, and inquiry-based teaching. *Educational Psychologist, 46*, 75–86.

Klein, P. D. (1999). Reopening inquiry into cognitive processes in writing-to-learn. *Educational Research Review, 11*, 203–270.

Kolodner, J. L., Gray, J., & Fasse, B. B. (2003). Promoting transfer through case-based reasoning: Rituals and practices in learning by design classrooms. *Cognitive Science Quarterly, 3*, 183–232.

Krammer, R. (2006). Filme im Geschichtsunterricht: Analysieren, Interpretieren, Dekonstruieren. *Historische Sozialkunde, 3*, 26–33.

Lahti, H., Seitamaa-Hakkarainen, P., & Hakkarainen, K. (2004). Collaboration patterns in computer supported collaborative designing. *Design Studies, 25*, 351–371.

Lehrer, R., Erickson, J., & Connell, T. (1994). Learning by designing hypermedia documents. *Computers in the Schools, 10*, 227–254.

Lowry, P. B., Curtis, A., & Lowry, M. R. (2004). Building a taxonomy and nomenclature of collaborative writing to improve interdisciplinary research and practice. *Journal of Business Communication, 41*, 66–99.

MacArthur, C. A. (2008). The effects of new technologies on writing and writing processes. In C. A. MacArthur, S. Graham, & J. Fitzgerald (Eds.), *Handbook of writing research* (pp. 248–262). New York: Guilford Press.

MacArthur, C. A., Graham, S., & Fitzgerald, J. (2016). *Handbook of writing research*. Second Edition. New York: Guilford Press.

McGrath, J., Arrow, H., Gruenfeld, D. H., Hollingshead, A. B., & O'Connor, K. M. (1993). Groups, tasks, and technology. The effects of experience and change. *Small Group Research, 24*, 406–420.

Newell, A. (2006). Writing to learn: How alternative theories of school writing account for student performance. In C. A. MacArthur, S. Graham, & J. Fitzgerald (Eds.), *Handbook of writing research* (pp. 235–248). New York: Guilford Press.

Newell, A., & Simon, H. A. (1972). *Human problem solving*. Englewood Cliffs, NJ: Prentice Hall.

NMC—The New Media Consortium and EDUCAUSE Learning Initiative and EDUCAUSE Program. (2008). The Horizon Report. 2008 Edition. Retrieved June 8, 2016, from http://www.nmc.org/sites/default/files/pubs/1316816013/2008-Horizon-Report.pdf

Papert, S. (1993). *The children's machine: Rethinking school in the age of the computer*. New York: Basic Books.

Pea, R. D. (1985). Beyond amplification: Using the computer to reorganize mental functioning. *Educational Psychologist, 20*, 167–182.

Pea, R. D. (2006). Video-as-data and digital video manipulation techniques for transforming learning sciences research, education and other cultural practices. In J. Weiss, J. Nolan, J. Hunsinger, & P. Trifonas (Eds.), *International handbook of virtual learning environments* (pp. 1321–1393). Dordrecht: Kluwer Academic Publishing.

Pea, R., Mills, M., Rosen, J., Dauber, K., Effelsberg, W., & Hoffert, E. (2004). The DIVER™ Project: Interactive digital video repurposing. *IEEE Multimedia, 11*, 54–61.

Posner, I. R., & Baecker, R. M. (1992). *How people write together*. Paper presented at the Twenty-Fifth Hawaii International Conference on System Sciences, Kauai.

Roschelle, J., & Teasley, S. D. (1995). The construction of shared knowledge in collaborative problem solving. In C. O'Malley (Ed.), *Computer supported collaborative learning* (pp. 69–97). Germany: Springer-Verlag.

Scardamalia, M. (2002). Collective cognitive responsibility for the advancement of knowledge. In B. Smith (Ed.), *Liberal education in a knowledge society* (pp. 67–98). Chicago: Open Court.

Scardamalia, M. (2004). CSILE/Knowledge Forum. In: A. Kovalchick & K. Dawson (eds.) *Education and technology: An encyclopedia* (pp. 183–192). Santa Barbara, CA: ABC-CLIO.

Scardamalia, M., & Bereiter, C. (2006). Knowledge building: Theory, pedagogy, and technology. In R. K. Sawyer (Ed.), *The Cambridge handbook of the learning sciences* (pp. 97–117). New York: Cambridge University Press.

Smith, B., & Blankinship, E. (2000). Justifying imagery: Multimedia support for learning through explanation. *IBM Systems, 39*, 749–767.

Stahl, E., & Bromme, R. (2004). Learning by writing hypertext: A research based design of university courses in writing hypertext. In G. Rijlaarsdam (Series Ed.) and G. Rijlaarsdam, H. Van den Bergh, & M. Couzijn (Eds.), *Studies in writing*, vol. 14, Effective learning and teaching of writing (2nd ed., pp. 547–560). Dordrecht, The Netherlands: Kluwer.

Stahl, E., Finke, M. & Zahn, C. (2006). Knowledge acquisition by hypervideo design: An instructional program for university courses. *Journal of Educational Multimedia and Hypermedia, 15*, 285–302.

Stahl, E., Zahn, C., & Finke, M. (2005). How can we use hypervideo design projects to construct knowledge in university courses? In T. Koschmann, D. Suthers, & T.-W. Chan (Eds.), *Computer supported collaborative learning 2005: The next 10 years* (pp. 641–646). Mahwah, NJ: Lawrence Erlbaum.

Stahl, E., Zahn, C., Schwan, S., & Finke, M. (2006). Knowledge acquisition by designing hypervideos: Different roles of writing during courses of "new media production". In L. Van Waes, M. Leijten, & C. Neuwirth (Eds.), *Writing and digital media* (pp. 77–88). Oxford: Elsevier.

Stempfle, J., & Badke-Schaub, P. (2002). Thinking in design teams—An analysis of team communication. *Design Studies, 23*, 473–496.

Stroebe, W., & Diehl, M. (1994). Why groups are less effective than their members: On productivity losses in idea-generating groups. *European Review of Social Psychology, 5*, 271–303.

Suthers, D. D. (2006). Technology affordances for intersubjective meaning making: A research agenda for CSCL. *International Journal of Computer-Supported Collaborative Learning (IJCSCL), 1*, 315–337.

Suthers, D. D., & Hundhausen, C. D. (2003). An experimental study of the effects of representational guidance on collaborative learning. *Journal of the Learning Sciences, 12*, 183–218.

Zahn, C., Barquero, B., & Schwan, S. (2004). Learning with hyperlinked videos—Design criteria and efficient strategies of using audiovisual hypermedia. *Learning and Instruction, 14*, 275–291.

Zahn, C., & Finke, M. (2003). Collaborative knowledge building based on hyperlinked video. In B. Wasson, R. Baggetun, U. Hoppe, & S. Ludvigsen (Eds.), *Proceedings of the International Conference on Computer Support for Collaborative Learning—CSCL 2003, COMMUNITY EVENTS—Communication and Interaction* (pp. 173–175). Bergen, NO: InterMedia.

Zahn, C., Krauskopf, K., & Hesse, F. W. (2009). Video-Tools im Schulunterricht: Psychologisch-pädagogische Forschung zur Nutzung audiovisueller Medien. In M. Eibl, J. Kürsten, & M. Ritter (Eds.), *Workshop Audiovisuelle Medien 2009* (pp. 59–65). Chemnitz: Technische Universität.

Zahn, C., Krauskopf, K., Hesse, F.W., & Pea, R. (2010). Digital video tools in the classroom: How to support meaningful collaboration and critical thinking of students? In M. S. Khine & I.M. Saleh (Eds.), *New science of learning: Computers and collaboration in education*. New York: Springer.

Zahn, C., Krauskopf, K., Hesse, F. W., & Pea, R. (2012). How to improve collaborative learning with video tools in the classroom? Social vs. cognitive guidance for student teams. *International Journal of Computer-Supported Collaborative Learnin, 7*, 259–284.

Zahn, C., Krauskopf, K., Hesse, F. W., & Pea, R. (2013). Digital media in the classroom: A study on how to improve guidance for successful collaboration and learning in student teams. In Y. Crotty & M. Farren (Eds.), *Digital literacies in education: Creative, innovative and multimodal approaches* (pp. 37–52). New York, NY: Peter Lang.

Zahn, C., Krauskopf, K., Kiener, J., & Hesse, F. W. (2014). Designing video for massive open online-education: Conceptual challenges from a learner-centered perspective. In U. Cress & C. D. Kloos (Eds.), *EMOOCs 2014—European MOOCs Stakeholders Summit. Proceedings Research Track* (pp. 160–168). P.A.U. Education.

Zahn, C., Oestermeier, U., & Finke, M. (2005). Designs für audiovisuelle Hypermedien: Kognitive und kollaborative Perspektiven. In M. Eibl, H. Reiterer, P. F. Stephan, & F. Thissen (Eds.), *Knowledge media design: Theorie, methodik, praxis* (pp. 361–375). München: Oldenbourg.

Zahn, C., Pea, R., Hesse, F. W., Mills, M., Finke, M., & Rosen, J. (2005). Advanced digital video technologies to support collaborative learning in school education and beyond. In T. Koschmann, D. Suthers, & T.-W. Chan (Eds.), *Computer supported collaborative learning 2005: The next 10 years* (pp. 737–742). Mahwah, NJ: Lawrence Erlbaum.

Zahn, C., Pea, R., Hesse, F. W., & Rosen, J. (2010). Comparing simple and advanced video tools as supports for complex collaborative design processes. *Journal of the Learning Sciences, 19*, 403–440.

Zahn, C., Schwan, S., & Barquero, B. (2002). Authoring hypervideos: Design for learning and learning by design. In R. Bromme & E. Stahl (Eds.), *Writing hypertext and learning: Conceptual and empirical approaches*. Oxford: Elsevier Science.

Chapter 9
Knowledge Networks in Social Media

Sonja Utz and Ana Levordashka

Abstract Knowledge exchange no longer occurs only in private email conversations, but also takes place on (semi-)public social media such as Facebook, LinkedIn or Twitter. These media help people maintaining and extending their social networks. They also expose users to a constant stream of tiny bits of information (e.g., news feeds). In this chapter, we examine how social media users can derive professional informational benefits from their online networks. We integrate sociological literature on social capital, organizational psychological literature on networking and social psychological research on impression formation. Results from a large-scale study on actual informational benefits of social media users show that especially users of business networks derive informational benefits. The role of platform usage, networking behavior and network composition was examined. In the second part, we present empirical work on the deliberate (expert search, who-knows-what) and ambient processes fostering informational benefits.

Keywords Online networks • Social media • Social capital • Informational benefits • Ambient awareness • Knowledge exchange

Introduction

Knowledge exchange is also an important process in knowledge acquisition (see also chapters Buder, this volume and Sassenberg, this volume), even more so in professional contexts in which knowledge is quickly outdated and where it becomes more important to know who-knows-what than to remember every detail. This chapter focuses therefore on professional knowledge exchange. Professional knowledge exchange via media has mainly been studied under the heading of knowledge management from various disciplines ranging from information systems sciences to organization sciences. The focus has been on company-intern knowledge management tools (first databases; currently enterprise social media (ESM)) and knowledge management has often been studied at the level of organizations. Psychologists, on

S. Utz (✉) • A. Levordashka
Leibniz-Institut für Wissensmedien, Schleichstrasse 6, 72076, Tübingen, Germany
e-mail: s.utz@iwm-tuebingen.de; a.levordashka@iwm-tuebingen.de

© Springer International Publishing AG 2017
S. Schwan, U. Cress (eds.), *The Psychology of Digital Learning*,
DOI 10.1007/978-3-319-49077-9_9

the other hand, focus on individuals. Organizational psychologists, for example, have examined the antecedents and effects of networking, that is, building and maintaining informal contacts (Forret & Dougherty, 2001). Social psychologists have focused on the specific processes of knowledge exchange, for example, how knowledge seekers identify experts by judging the competence and trustworthiness of a potential expert (Andrews & Delahaye, 2000) or why knowledge holders are not willing to share all relevant information (Steinel, Utz, & Koning, 2010).

In addition to the company-intern ESM, there are also publicly available social media platforms such as LinkedIn or Xing that can be used for professional knowledge exchange. The present chapter focuses on these public social media and the informational benefits that people can retrieve when they use them to build and maintain their (knowledge) networks. The chapter sets up theoretical foundations by characterizing social media and giving an overview over the role of structure and content of networks for informational benefits. Next, the role that social media can play in maintaining knowledge networks and deriving informational benefits from them are described. The second part of the chapter presents the results of empirical studies conducted in the social media lab at Leibniz Institut für Wissensmedien. A strong focus is placed on findings from the ERC project "Redefining tie strength: How social media (can) help us to get non-redundant useful information and emotional support" (ReDefTie).

Theoretical Foundations

Social Media

Social media is an umbrella term for a large group of online tools. The most well-known are social network sites (SNS) such as Facebook. SNS are defined as "web-based services that allow individuals to (1) construct a public or semi-public profile within a bounded system, (2) articulate a list of other users with whom they share a connection, and (3) view and traverse their list of connections and those made by others within the system" (Boyd & Ellison, 2007). The market leader at the moment is Facebook with more than 1.79 billion monthly active users (September 2016). Some SNS are targeted at professionals (e.g., LinkedIn with more than 400 million users and Xing, which is more popular in German-speaking countries and has nine million German speaking users). In contrast to more leisure-oriented SNS, the profile fields on business closely resemble CVs and focus on education, professional experience and skill and do not offer the possibility to create photo albums. Another popular service is the microblogging-site Twitter. Users also have profiles, but they can only create short posts with a maximum of 140 characters, so-called tweets. Tweets are broadcasted to all people who follow the user. Networks on Twitter are asymmetric: User A can follow the updates of user B, but user B does not necessarily have to follow user A back. Weblogs, Wikipedia, YouTube and photo-sharing sites such as Instagram also fall under the header social media. All these social media are characterized by the fact that most of the content is user-generated: users write status updates, Wikipedia entrees, upload photos, share articles and so on. Moreover, social interaction is central, including light-weight forms of phatic communication such as pressing a button to indicate appreciation of a post (e.g., "Like"-button on Facebook, "favorite" on Twitter).

Social media platforms evolve rapidly and some of the early social media already disappeared or lost popularity (e.g., Hyves, MySpace). Therefore, researchers often focus on generic features that are shared by multiple platforms (Treem & Leonardi, 2012). Content on social media is usually created and edited by users. It is also highly visible (often public or semi-public by default) and persistent (posts can be traced back in time). These first three characteristics (editability, visibility, persistence) also apply to some older forms of computer-mediated communication, such as usenet-newsgroups. The public display of associations, however, is a new attribute. On social media, associations between people (friends, connections, followers) as well as between people and content (likes, shares) are displayed or can easily be associated with a user's profile.

The Effects of Knowledge Networks

The effects of (offline) knowledge networks have often been studied from a social capital perspective. Social capital refers to the benefits people can retrieve from their networks (Adler & Kwon, 2002). The source of social capital lies in the content and structure of the network, and its outcomes are the benefits people can get from their network. Social capital research distinguishes between emotional and informational benefits. Emotional benefits refer to emotional support, whereas informational benefits are based on three criteria: access to information, timeliness of this access and referrals, that is, being recommended to job opportunities (Burt, 1992). Social capital can be measured on the individual, organizational or even societal level (Adler & Kwon, 2002). This chapter focuses on informational benefits at the individual level.

The social network of a person consists of all people the person knows. The relationships with these people can be characterized according to tie strength. Relationships with people, to whom an individual feels emotionally close, such as family and friends, are called strong ties. Relationships with people, to whom an individual feels less emotionally close, such as acquaintances or former classmates, are called weak ties. The basic assumption of social network analysis is that strong ties provide people with emotional benefits, whereas weak ties provide informational benefits (see Adler & Kwon, 2002, for a review). The latter is the case because weak ties often have more non-redundant information than strong ties because they have access to different circles of people and can function as bridges between different circles.

In line with this assumption, sociological studies, weak ties turned out as more helpful when it comes to finding a new job (Granovetter, 1973). Studies on knowledge exchange in organizations, however, have revealed mixed results; some studies found that people retrieved more useful information from strong ties (Hansen, 1999; Reagans & McEvily, 2003). Levin and Cross (2004) pointed to the pivotal role of trust. Weak ties may indeed often have access to novel information, but people prefer to turn to their strong ties because they trust them more, talk to them more and feel less embarrassed when revealing a lack of knowledge by asking for advice. Levin and Cross (2004) found a positive relationship between tie strength and perceived usefulness of received knowledge that turned into a negative relationship when entering trust in the analysis; their data can thus explain the inconsistent earlier findings. Their results also show that a large number of weak ties alone are not sufficient; these weak ties have to be trusted to leverage their knowledge. This fits well to the ability and benevolence/integrity dimensions in trustworthiness judgments (Mayer, Davis, & Schoorman, 1995) that mirror the two fundamental dimensions of person perception, competence and morality (Wojciszke, Bazinska, & Jaworski, 1998).

Another relevant concept to explain the benefits from knowledge networks is networking. Networking is mainly studied by organizational psychologists and defined as "behaviors that are aimed at building, maintaining and using informal relationships that possess the (potential) benefit of facilitating work-related activities of individuals by voluntarily granting access to resources and maximizing common advantages" (Wolff & Moser, 2009, pp. 196–197). Networking is thus a behavior that can build social capital.

Literature on networking distinguishes between internal (colleagues within the same company) and external networking. Wolff and Moser (2009) differentiate further between maintaining, building and using informal relationships. Organizational psychologists have examined the relationship of (offline) networking with demographics and personality variables (Forret & Dougherty, 2001). Wolff and Moser (2009) found in a longitudinal study that networking had an effect on objective and subjective measures of career success assessed in three consecutive years. These studies did not pay attention to the medium used and focused (at least implicitly) on networking in face-to-face encounters.

(Enterprise) Social Media and Informational Benefits

The (potential) role of social media for retrieving professional informational benefits has frequently been discussed in communication and organization sciences. Most of this work is conceptual (Ellison, Gibbs, & Weber, 2015; Fulk & Yuan, 2013; Majchrzak, Faraj, Kane, & Azad, 2013; Treem & Leonardi, 2012) and refers to the social capital framework. The main argument for the effects of (enterprise) social media on knowledge sharing is that social media provide people with novel information because they (a) increase the number of weak ties and because they (b) can strengthen these weak ties and increase trust in them.

First, it is easy to add people as friends on Facebook or as contacts on a business network. It is even easier on Twitter, where relationships do not have to be confirmed by the other party. Accordingly, studies on business networks and Twitter found that it is more common to add weak ties and strangers on these platforms than on Facebook where the majority of friends are people known also face-to-face (Utz & Muscanell, 2014; Utz, 2016). Haythornthwaite (2005) introduced the term latent ties to refer to ties that are "technologically possible but not yet activated socially" (p. 137). A stranger followed on Twitter or LinkedIn might be considered as such a latent tie; after some time of regularly following the updates and online interactions, these ties might be turned into useful weak ties.

Moreover, one's entire network can be reached with a single update and social media provide light-weight and effective means of maintaining large networks, such as the like button (Hayes, Carr, & Wohn, 2016; Tong & Walther, 2011). Ellison, Steinfield and Lampe (2007), for example, found that Facebook use strengthened the bonds with stronger, but even more so, weaker ties.

Using social media, especially business networks, can be seen as online networking. Publicly available social media might be especially important for maintaining company-extern contacts. Whereas face-to-face networking is experienced as depleting (Wingender & Wolff, 2015), online networking costs less energy because a larger audience can be reached with just one update. Communication does not have to be synchronous; updates can be read whenever there is time. It is possible that for certain individuals (e.g., socially anxious people), contacting a stranger online is easier than it would be in a face-to-face interaction.

The focus on network size and structure represents the sociological tradition. The psychological perspective focuses more on the cognitive processes that help people to gain informational benefits from their online networks. Social media provide a continuous stream of information, some of which is potentially highly useful information (such as cues for who knows what in a network), but the majority is downright mundane. Whether and how people manage to pick up on important content amidst an information overload remains to be established. Therefore, it is important to consider underlying psychological processes. Psychological research has examined how people select the experts whom they approach for advice. Research on impression formation on social media has addressed how various cues in online profiles determine judgments of expertise and trustworthiness. In addition to the rather deliberate processes of expert/knowledge search, there are also other, less deliberate processes possible such as ambient awareness, that is, the "awareness of social others, arising from the frequent reception of fragmented personal information, such as status updates and various digital footprints on social media (for example, activity logs, location check-ins)" (Levordashka & Utz, 2016). Conceptual and empirical papers have recently claimed that ambient awareness can help people develop a cognitive map of "who knows what" and improve knowledge exchange by facilitating the relationship between a knowledge seeker and a knowledge source (Leonardi & Meyer, 2015; Leonardi, 2015). Before we explain these psychological processes in more detail, we would like to report some descriptive findings on (professional) social media use from our own work to put (professional) social media use in context. We further report the informational benefits of average social media users and people who use social media actively for professional purposes.

Empirical Results

(Professional) Social Media Use: Background on Datasets

Most findings in this chapter stem from the ERC project ReDefTie. Part of the project is a longitudinal study of Dutch online users. The sample is representative for the Dutch population with regard to sex, age, education level and urban/rural residence. In total, eight waves will be conducted. Twice a year, participants receive an online survey about their social media use and a number of social capital indicators. Data collection is still ongoing, and most analyses of the longitudinal effects will be carried out when the data collection is finished. Therefore, this chapter focuses on the cross-sectional results from wave 1 and reports some preliminary analyses of the first four waves.

The project concentrates on three types of social media: SNS used for private purposes, business networks and microblogging services. People who use one or more of these social media types, receive detailed questions on their use (e.g., frequence of reading, posting, self-disclosure). In wave 1, 3667 people participated. Among those, 72.1% were using SNS for private purposes (mainly Facebook), 23.2% were using business networks (mainly LinkedIn), and only 14.5% were active on Twitter. As can be expected, business network use was higher among the working participants (32%). These values remained remarkably stable across the first four waves. The data from this sample show which effects of social media use *actually* occur in society (reported in the next section).

To explore the *potential* of social media for knowledge exchange, we targeted more active social media users, namely, German professionals who used social media for professional purposes (Utz & Muscanell, 2014). Three hundred forty-five people started to participate in this study, and 175 completed all questions. In this sample, Xing was the most popular social medium, used by 58% of the respondents. These users read messages on Xing several times a week but wrote messages only occasionally. People who used Twitter for professional purposes were more active, reading almost daily and posting several times a week. The two platforms were also used for different reasons. The main reasons for using Xing were knowing who does what in the field, finding experts and work-related information. Twitter, in contrast, was mainly used for sharing work-related information, getting new ideas and finding work-related information. These findings make it clear that people perceive business social networking sites as useful for finding information. But do they actually benefit from using these sites?

Informational Benefits from Social Media Use

To measure informational benefits, we built on Burt's (1992) definition and used five items from Wickramasinghe and Weliwitigoda (2011) that cover the aspects of access, timeliness and referrals (e.g., "I can get access to knowledge that is helpful in mastering job tasks from my network members"). These questions were formulated in a general way (for example, referring to network and not to online network) so that all respondents, including the non-users of social media, could answer them. We then analyzed whether users of a specific type of social medium reported higher informational benefits than non-users.

In the longitudinal study with the representative sample of Dutch online users, users of business networks reported higher informational benefits than non-users. Twitter use had a smaller, but also positive effect. On average, Facebook users reported lower informational benefits than non-users (Utz, 2016).

In the sample of German professionals, on the other hand, we found significant effects for all types of social media. The effect was largest for Xing users who reported significantly higher informational benefits than non-users. Smaller, but also significant effects occurred for Twitter, with Twitter users reporting higher informational benefits than non-users. People who use Facebook for professional purposes also reported higher informational benefits than people who did not use Facebook professionally (Utz & Muscanell, 2014).

The discrepancy in the findings for Facebook can be explained with the different samples. In the Dutch representative sample general Facebook use but not Facebook use for professional purposes was measured, whereas Facebook use for professional purposes was assessed in the sample of German professionals. Facebook is mainly used for staying in touch with family and friends, so it is not surprising that there are no consistent effects on professional informational benefits. More important is the finding that users of business networks report higher informational benefits across both samples.

These cross-sectional data do not allow causal inferences. It could also be that people who have higher informational benefits have larger networks and are therefore also more prone to use business networks to help them maintaining those networks. To be sure that the use of social media pays off, one needs to demonstrate that using social media affects career outcomes even when controlling for the prior level of informational benefits (and thus also potential proxies such as a larger network).

The longitudinal-study data sheds some light on this question. In each wave, participants were asked whether they got promoted (defined as either a formal promotion or more responsibilities in their job) in the last 6 months. When using informational benefits and business network use one wave earlier as predictors of this indicator of career progress in a logistic regression, prior informational benefits consistently turned out as significant predictor. More important, the use of business networks increased the odds of getting promoted, even when controlling for informational benefits. This effect was only marginal for predicting promotion in wave 2 with business network use at wave 1, but significant for predicting of promotion at wave 3 with business network use at wave 2 and for prediction of promotion in wave 4 with business network use at wave 3. These results offer first evidence that using business networks pays off in objective measures of career success.

Predictors of Informational Benefits

After demonstrating that there are informational benefits, it makes sense to have a closer look at how exactly the use of business networks is related to informational benefits. Utz (2016) used the Dutch sample and examined three groups of variables: usage, network content and structure, along with control variables. Frequency of reading, posting and participating in groups were assessed to measure passive and active usage. The assumption was that active use is a necessary but not sufficient condition for retrieving informational benefits. Building on the social capital approach, we assumed that the content and the structure of the network play an important role (Adler & Kwon, 2002). Frequently posting what one had for lunch might strengthen interpersonal bonds in some cases, but for retrieving professional informational benefits, it should be more important that the content is work-related. The hypothesis was therefore that posting work-related content predicts informational benefits. With regard to the network, a higher number of weak ties should be helpful in retrieving information and thus predict informational benefits. Indeed, the comparison of the Facebook, LinkedIn and Twitter networks in the longitudinal study showed that there is a higher number of weak ties on LinkedIn than on Facebook or Twitter (Utz, 2016). This could be one reason why the users of business networks always reported higher informational benefits. However, considering the results of studies in organizational settings (Levin & Cross, 2004), an alternative hypothesis would be that a higher number of strong ties results in higher informational benefits. It is unclear yet whether latent ties, i.e., ties formed on social media but not yet activated, can be leveraged. They should have access to even more novel knowledge, but trust in them might also be lower. An open research question was therefore formulated for the role of latent ties. Additionally, the strategic networking behavior of participants was assessed. This scale contained items such as "I invite people who might sometimes be useful for me" and follows the tradition of behavioral networking as studied in organizational psychology (Wolff & Moser, 2009).

Stepwise regressions were used to examine the amount of variance that was uniquely explained by the groups of variables. The results showed that reading and even more so participating in group discussions were positively related to informational benefits. However, the effects of the frequency variables became smaller when work-related content was included in the analysis. With regard to the network variables, both the number of strong and weak ties turned out as significant positive predictors of informational benefits. Strategic online networking also had a significant impact. In general, the results are in line with the social capital framework that states that content and structure of networks are important. However, the finding on the importance of strong tie replicates prior findings from studies on organizational knowledge sharing. Additionally, they suggest that online networking has positive career outcomes. The strength of this study is the large representative sample. However, the findings are only correlational and no information on the underlying cognitive and affective processes is available. In the following section, we will describe conceptual and empirical work that has examined underlying processes, namely, how social media can help people learn "who knows what" and facilitate interaction with weak or latent ties. Again, the focus is on studies conducted in our own lab.

Potential Underlying Processes

Deliberate processes: choosing an expert. Finding an expert on social media is an important prerequisite for retrieving informational benefits. Social media can help locate expertise in several ways. One source of information regarding a person's expertise is personal profiles, which are relatively static. Especially on business networks and in enterprise social networks, the profile fields resemble CVs and provide information about the educational background, work experience and skills of a person. The updates posted by a person and presented in activity streams of his or her followers can also reveal expertise. Although the effect of various static cues on expertise and even more trustworthiness has been studied in the domain of online commerce, there are not many empirical studies that examine how people use static and more dynamic cues to infer the work-related expertise of a person. There are some case studies, often conducted in IT companies such as IBM or Microsoft, in which employees state locating expertise as one of the benefits stemming from social media use, but they usually do not specify which parts (profile, updates, likes) are most important (DiMicco et al., 2008; Zhao & Rosson, 2009).

The warranting principle can be used as theoretical framework for answering the question of cue use. It argues that cues that are more difficult to manipulate have a larger warranting value and consequently a higher weight in impression formation (Walther & Parks, 2002). On SNS, cues can be classified as self-generated, friends-generated and system-generated. Self-generated cues cover the profile picture and the information entered in the profile; friends-generated cues are for example the endorsements given on LinkedIn or ResearchGate. System-generated cues are indirectly also generated by others, but automatically displayed by the system such as the number of contacts, views or posts. According to the warranting principle, other-generated cues should have more impact in impression formation. Empirical support for this claim, however, has been mixed; clear warranting effects have been found for physical attractiveness, but self-generated information was frequently used as cue when judging the extraversion of a target (Utz, 2010; Walther, Van Der Heide, Kim, Westerman, & Tong, 2008).

When it comes to locating expertise, it is important to judge not only the expertise of a person but also his or her trustworthiness. Shami, Ehrlich, Gay and Hancock (2009) examined expertise location in an actual organization. Participants had the task to search for an AJAX (a web technology used in many web2.0 applications) expert in the ESM. Participants were asked to browse the profiles that showed up in the search and to report to which profile parts they paid attention and how helpful they were in making the decision whom to contact. Finally, they should indicate how likely they would be to contact the person. The profiles contained self-generated and system-generated information (e.g., job position; membership in mailing lists, use of social software or social connection information, i.e., information about the various alternative paths how the knowledge seeker and the expert are connected). Self-described expertise, social connection information and social software were the three factors that determined contact likelihood. The effect of self-described expertise is in contrast with the warranting principle, but the analysis of the interview data indicated that the self-described expertise was considered as more concrete and therefore valuable information than the (often identical) job titles generated from the system. Interestingly, the social software cues were mainly used to judge the sociability and helpfulness of a person and how likely it would be that the person responds quickly. Social connection information was used to judge the expertise. If an AJAX expert was related to several other AJAX experts, his self-described expertise claims were considered as more trustworthy. Moreover, the social connection information was also considered as useful conversation starter. These results demonstrate that competence and morality/sociability are both important in selecting an expert. These results indicate that the source and therefore the warranting value of a cue is not the only factor that plays a role; the informative value and the dimension (competence vs. morality) are also important.

Utz and Muscanell (2015) built on this work, but took an experimental approach to systematically control the various cues. The first goal was to contrast the impact of cues in the more static profiles with the impact of cues in updates. A second goal was to explore the role of personal information. Regarding the latter, there are two opposing lines of argumentation possible. On the one hand, personal information (e.g., hobbies, favorite books) could make a person more human and reduce the barrier to ask for advice. On the other hand, adding personal information to a professional profile might also lead to an unprofessional and inappropriate impression. The experiment had a 2 (expertise according to profile cues: low vs. high) × (expertise according to updates: low vs. high) × 2 (personal information in profile: yes vs. no) × 2 (personal information in updates: yes vs. no) − mixed design. The first two factors were varied within subjects whereas the latter two factors were varied between subjects. Participants ($n = 107$ students) should search an expert for touch technologies in teaching (e.g., iPad, multi-touch tables). They were asked to browse the eight profiles that allegedly showed up a search results in the ESM and indicate the likelihood with which they would contact the candidates. Additionally, the perceived competence in the area of multi-touch, availability, trustworthiness, sympathy and so on was assessed. For contact likelihood, a strong main effect of the expertise cues in the profiles emerged. Targets with profiles indicating high expertise were contacted with a higher likelihood than targets with profiles indicating low expertise. A weaker effect occurred for the expertise cues in the updates. Targets whose updates indicated high expertise were contacted with a higher likelihood than targets whose updates indicated low expertise. Interestingly, no main or interaction effect involving personal content in the profile or updates reached significance. A similar picture emerged for expertise in the domain of multitouch, although the main effect of expertise cues in the updates now was only marginally significant. For sympathy, trustworthiness and approachability, the main effects for both types of expertise cues were significant, but the effect sizes were much smaller and the dominance of expertise cues in the profiles was weakened. Again, personal information did not play a significant role. Perceived expertise was the main predictor of contact likelihood, indicating that judgments regarding the ability of the target were more important than judgments regarding his trustworthiness/sympathy.

These results indicate that expertise cues in social media matter, especially the ones provided in the profile. (Enterprise) social networks can thus help to identify experts. The relatively small effect of updates might seem surprising at first glance. However, the screenshots only displayed the four most recent updates and only two of them referred to the expertise of the target. The other two provided either personal information (e.g., "looking forward to the skiing trip this weekend") or neutral information (e.g., "going to the inaugural lecture of Peter Krems"). The expertise cues presented in the profile presented information on the educational background, research interests and current project and thus covered several years. Moreover, showing a small number of updates in a screenshot is not the same as following a person over weeks or months on social media. These results do thus not indicate that social media updates do not provide additional information. More important is the finding that personal information in profiles and updates did not have any effect. Companies sometimes wonder whether they should offer profile fields referring to personal information and worry that internal social media would be used for too much private conversation. According to the current results, personal information does not prevent people from extracting the relevant expertise cues. Although we did not find effects on contact likelihood, it could be that information on personal interests is used as a facilitator when actually contacting a person. Future research should therefore use additional measures (e.g., emails to the expert) and more dynamic and realistic manipulations of updates.

Ambient processes: ambient awareness and ambient intimacy. In addition to deliberately searching for information, social media users often browse content with no particular intention. Browsing can also contribute to knowledge exchange processes. Thompson (2008) proposed that by regularly browsing updates, users develop ambient awareness of what the members of their social media network are doing. He calls this process ambient because the awareness is rather a by-product of browsing updates than the result of a deliberate impression formation process. The concept of ambient awareness has been picked up to argue how social media can foster knowledge exchange.

One possibility is that following the conversations on social media helps people to identify who-knows-what in their network (Fulk & Yuan, 2013). This cognitive process has been studied primarily in the context of ESM. Data from qualitative interviews suggests that following the conversations of colleagues, especially from other departments, enhanced understanding of their daily activities (Leonardi, 2014).

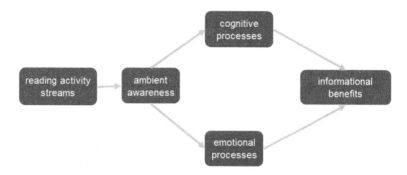

Fig. 9.1 Theoretical model of the effects of ambient awareness on informational benefits

Interestingly, employees trusted their own inferences made from the updates on the daily activities sometimes more than the explicitly declared expertise of the colleagues. Leonardi (2014) elaborates on how the visibility of conversations in a company can create meta-knowledge of "who knows what" by increasing message transparency and network translucence and how this in turn increases innovation and reduced knowledge duplication. In a recent test of this idea, Leonardi (2015) showed that using enterprise social media enhanced employees awareness of "who knows what" and "who knows whom" within the organization. Interestingly, it was awareness ("frequently notice"), rather than active monitoring ("carefully reading"), that was associated with enhanced meta-knowledge.

Another proposed function of ambient awareness is related to emotional processes. It is assumed that regularly reading the updates of a person can also strengthen the relationship with this person and foster trust (Ellison et al., 2015). Leonardi and Meyer (2015) claim that ambient awareness functions as a social lubricant and can increase satisfaction with knowledge exchange, especially when it comes to sticky knowledge that is difficult to explain and share (Fig. 9.1).

Although the authors provide evidence for this effect, several aspects of the study prevent from drawing firm conclusions regarding ambient awareness. Ambient awareness was not measured directly. Instead, media use served as a proxy. The authors compared employees who asked a colleague for advice immediately after a problem occurred with colleagues who delayed asking for advice. For the group who did not ask immediately, the use of an ESM platform predicted satisfaction with the retrieved knowledge. This is only indirect evidence for the claim that these people used social media to get to know more about the potential expert and that they used the information gathered as social lubricant for the conversation. Furthermore, people were aware of an upcoming knowledge transfer, which would suggest a deliberate information search strategy and somewhat contradict the idea of *ambient* awareness, which is gained in a non-intentional way.

Overall, the empirical evidence for ambient awareness and its effects is somewhat weak. In our own work, we wanted to first explore whether social media users indeed experience ambient awareness for their online networks ("who does what") before turning to the underlying processes and the question whether these processes can also be extended to ambient awareness for "who knows what". In an exploratory study (Levordashka & Utz, 2016), we recruited active Twitter users and assessed ambient awareness towards the network in general, as well as awareness for specific members of a person's network. This allowed us to explore whether ambient awareness is just a vague feeling or whether people do indeed know something about their online network. We chose Twitter because the percentage of strangers in the network is higher and communication takes place primarily in the form of brief updates. On Facebook where many friends are also known in real life and extensive communication in the form of personal messages is common, it would have been difficult to claim that awareness of others is due to skimming updates, rather than prior knowledge or extensive communication.

To assess general ambient awareness, a definition based on the description by Thompson (2008) was given and participants were asked to what extent and for how many people in their network they experienced ambient awareness. The majority of active Twitter users experienced ambient awareness, but this was true in most cases only for a few or several people in the network and not for everyone in the network. In addition to general awareness, we assessed awareness of individual contacts. Participants were first asked to browse through their list of contacts and identify people they know primarily through Twitter. Next, we presented them with a random selection of their Twitter-only contacts and examined what particular knowledge they had about the people they recognized. The fact that participants were able to recognize and report knowledge of individuals they knew only through Twitter suggests that ambient awareness is not merely a vague sense of knowing, but is instead based on actual knowledge. Most often they had formed an impression regarding the personality/humor of the person and knew the profession or hobbies. Awareness of a particular individual was positively associated with how often people saw posts from the person, even when the frequency of direct contact was controlled for. This research offers first evidence that ambient awareness occurs and that it is an ambient process, occurring without a deliberative goal and effort.

In a series of experimental studies, we examined spontaneous trait inferences as a potential cognitive process underlying ambient awareness. Psychological research on spontaneous trait inferences has consistently demonstrated that people automatically form personality impressions when reading behavioral statements about strangers. A typical procedure is to present people with a photo of a person and a behavioral description, such as "She threw a chair at her classmate". Various implicit measures have demonstrated that people form an impression of the person that is consistent with the description (e.g., a person who "threw a chair at her classmate" is aggressive). In terms of format, the behavioral descriptions used in psychological studies can resemble social media posts, and it is likely that similar spontaneous inferences occur as people browse social media. But there are also important differences that prevent from drawing this conclusion. Content on social media is often shared by the person to whom it refers. As such, it can be seen as ambiguous (e.g., "I am the best in my class!" implies that a person is clever, but the act of posting it can be interpreted as arrogance) and less reliable (Utz, 2010; Walther et al., 2008). Online posts also tend to be mild and appropriate, especially by people who use social media professionally. Moreover, updates are usually not presented one by one, but in a continuous stream. Thus, there are several reasons why spontaneous trait inferences might not occur or be weaker on social media. We therefore examined in a series of experiments (a) whether spontaneous trait inferences also occur for mild, self-generated statements and (b) when several targets are presented at the same time (Levordashka & Utz, 2017). First studies showed that spontaneous inferences occur under these circumstances. The evidence for spontaneous trait inferences on social media offers conceptual support for the idea that ambient awareness is a cognitively efficient process.

Together, the exploratory surveys and experimental studies offer support for ambient awareness on social media. This research complements existing work on ESM by offering a closer look into the processes underlying ambient awareness and extends the phenomenon to public social media and personal networks. It also sets the stage for future research on the role of ambient awareness in knowledge exchange. Trait inferences are the basis of interpersonal impressions and thus relevant to the proposed mechanism of ambient awareness as social lubricant (Leonardi & Meyer, 2015). Another relevant process, which needs to be addressed in future research, is that of mere exposure: According to the principle of mere exposure, awareness itself can increase feelings of familiarity, liking and trust, thus facilitating social interactions. This mechanism remains to be tested. With regard to role of ambient awareness in developing a cognitive map of who knows what, a next step would be to examine whether similar inferences are made regarding a person's expertise.

Conclusion

The present chapter focused on the role of social media in knowledge exchange. It shows that users of business networks do indeed report higher informational benefits, and that this is partly due to their larger number of strong and weak ties that can be maintained with the help of social media. The role of weak ties is in line with sociological work on social capital, whereas the role of strong ties point to the important role of trust and confirms findings from studies on knowledge exchange in organizations. Not only the structure but also the content of the network matters. Informational benefits were higher for users of business networks that concentrate on work-related content. Additionally, posting work-related content and strategic networking, i.e., adding potentially important contacts on social media, were related to higher informational benefits. Moreover, we have shown that deliberate and ambient processes can contribute to these informational benefits. More research is needed to integrate the findings on deliberate and ambient processes and to determine the relative importance of cognitive (expertise location) and affective (developing trust) processes.

Acknowledgements Parts of the research leading to these results has received funding from the European Research Council under the European Union's Seventh Framework Programme (FP7/2007-2013)/ERC grant agreement no. 312420.

References

Adler, P. S., & Kwon, S.-W. (2002). Social capital: Prospects for a new concept. *Academy of Management Review, 27*, 17–40.

Andrews, K. M., & Delahaye, B. L. (2000). Influences on knowledge processes in organizational learning: The psychosocial filter. *Journal of Management Studies, 37*, 797–810.

Boyd, D., & Ellison, N. B. (2007). Social network sites: Definition, history, and scholarship. *Journal of Computer-Mediated Communication, 13*, 210–230.

Buder, J. (this volume). A conceptual framework of knowledge exchange.

Burt, R. S. (1992). *Structural holes: The social structure of competition*. Cambridge, MA: Harvard University Press.

DiMicco, J., Millen, D. R., Geyer, W., Dugan, C., Brownholtz, B., & Muller, M. (2008). Motivations for social networking at work. In *Proceedings of the 2008 ACM Conference on Computer Supported Cooperative Work* (pp. 711–720). New York, NY: ACM.

Ellison, N. B., Gibbs, J. L., & Weber, M. S. (2015). The use of enterprise social network sites for knowledge sharing in distributed organizations: The role of organizational affordances. *American Behavioral Scientist, 59*, 103–123.

Ellison, N. B., Steinfield, C., & Lampe, C. (2007). The benefits of Facebook "friends:" Social capital and college students' use of online social network sites. *Journal of Computer-Mediated Communication, 12*, 1143–1168.

Forret, M. L., & Dougherty, T. W. (2001). Correlates of networking behavior for managerial and professional employees. *Group & Organization Management, 26*, 283–311.

Fulk, J., & Yuan, Y. C. (2013). Location, motivation, and social capitalization via enterprise social networking. *Journal of Computer-Mediated Communication, 19*, 20–37.

Granovetter, M. S. (1973). The strength of weak ties. *American Journal of Sociology, 78*, 1360–1380.

Hansen, M. T. (1999). The search-transfer problem: The role of weak ties in sharing knowledge across organization subunits. *Administrative Science Quarterly, 44*, 82–111.

Hayes, R. A., Carr, C. T., & Wohn, D. Y. (2016). One click, many meanings: Interpreting paralinguistic digital affordances in social media. *Journal of Broadcasting & Electronic Media, 60*, 171–187.

Haythornthwaite, C. (2005). Social networks and Internet connectivity effects. *Information, Communication & Society, 8*, 125–147.

Leonardi, P. M. (2014). Social media, knowledge sharing, and innovation: Toward a theory of communication visibility. *Information Systems Research, 25*, 796–816.

Leonardi, P. M. (2015). Ambient awareness and knowledge acquisition: Using social media to learn "who knows what" and "who knows whom". *MIS Quarterly, 39*, 747–762.

Leonardi, P. M., & Meyer, S. R. (2015). Social media as social lubricant: How ambient awareness eases knowledge transfer. *American Behavioral Scientist, 59*, 10–34.

Levin, D. Z., & Cross, R. (2004). The strength of weak ties you can trust: The mediating role of trust in effective knowledge transfer. *Management Science, 50*, 1477–1490.

Levordashka & Utz (2017). Spontaneous trait inferences on social media. *Social Psychological and Personality Science, 8*(1), 93–101.

Levordashka, A., & Utz, S. (2016). Ambient awareness: From random noise to digital closeness in online social networks. *Computers in Human Behavior, 60*, 147–154.

Majchrzak, A., Faraj, S., Kane, G. C., & Azad, B. (2013). The contradictory influence of social media affordances on online communal knowledge sharing. *Journal of Computer-Mediated Communication, 19*, 38–55.

Mayer, R. C., Davis, J. H., & Schoorman, F. D. (1995). An integrative model of organizational trust. *Academy of Management Review, 20*, 709–734.

Reagans, R., & McEvily, B. (2003). Network structure and knowledge transfer: The effects of cohesion and range. *Administrative Science Quarterly, 48*, 240–267.

Sassenberg, K. (this volume). Knowledge exchange as a motivated social process.

Shami, N. S., Ehrlich, K., Gay, G., & Hancock, J. T. (2009). Making sense of strangers' expertise from signals in digital artifacts. In *Proceedings of the SIGCHI Conference on Human Factors in Computing Systems* (pp. 69–78). New York, NY: ACM.

Steinel, W., Utz, S., & Koning, L. (2010). The good, the bad and the ugly thing to do when sharing information: Revealing, concealing and lying depend on social motivation, distribution and importance of information. *Organizational Behavior and Human Decision Processes, 113*(2), 85–96.

Thompson, C. (2008, September 5). Brave new world of digital intimacy. *New York Times.* Retrieved from http://www.nytimes.com/2008/09/07/magazine/07awareness-t.html?_r=0

Tong, S., & Walther, J. B. (2011). Relational maintenance and CMC. In K. B. Wright & L. M. Webb (Eds.), *Computer-mediated communication in personal relationships* (pp. 98–118). New York, NY: Peter Lang.

Treem, J., & Leonardi, P. (2012). Social media use in organizations: Exploring the affordances of visibility, editability, persistence, and association. *Communication Yearbook, 36*, 143–189.

Utz, S. (2010). Show me your friends and I will tell you what type of person you are: How one's profile, number of friends, and type of friends influence impression formation on social network sites. *Journal of Computer Mediated Communication, 15*, 314–335.

Utz, S. (2016). Is LinkedIn making you more successful? The informational benefits derived from public social media. *New Media & Society, 18*(11), 2685–2702.

Utz, S., & Muscanell, N. (2014). Beruflicher Wissensaustausch auf sozialen Medien. Vortrag auf den 10. *Stuttgarter Wissensmanagement-Tagen*, Stuttgart.

Utz, S., & Muscanell, N. (2015). Der Einfluss von Profilinformationen und Status Updates auf die Identifizierung von Experten [The influence of profile information and status updates on location of expertise]. In *Menschen, Medien, Möglichkeiten [People, media, possibilities] 9. Fachgruppentagung Arbeits-, Organisations- und Wirtschaftspsychologie der DGPs in Mainz*, p. 61.

Walther, J. B., & Parks, M. R. (2002). Cues filtered out, cues filtered in: Computer-mediated communication and relationships. In M. L. Knapp & J. A. Daly (Eds.), *Handbook of interpersonal communication* (3rd ed., pp. 529–563). Thousand Oaks, CA: Sage.

Walther, J. B., Van Der Heide, B., Kim, S.-Y., Westerman, D., & Tong, S. T. (2008). The role of friends' appearance and behavior on evaluations of individuals on Facebook: Are we known by the company we keep? *Human Communication Research, 34*, 28–49.

Wickramasinghe, V., & Weliwitigoda, P. (2011). Benefits gained from dimensions of social capital: A study of software developers in Sri Lanka. *Information Technology & People, 24*, 393–413.

Wingender, L.-M., & Wolff, H.-G. (2015). Führt Networking zu Ressourcenerschöpfung? [Does networking lead to ego depletion?]. In T. Rigotti, V. C. Haun, & C. Dormann (Eds.), *Menschen, Medien, Möglichkeiten [People, media, possibilities] 9. Fachgruppentagung Arbeits-, Organisations- und Wirtschaftspsychologie der DGPs in Mainz* (p. 134). Lengerich: Pabst Science Publishers.

Wojciszke, B., Bazinska, R., & Jaworski, M. (1998). On the dominance of moral categories in impression formation. *Personality and Social Psychology Bulletin, 24*, 1251–1263.

Wolff, H.-G., & Moser, K. (2009). Effects of networking on career success: A longitudinal study. *Journal of Applied Psychology, 94*, 196–206.

Zhao, D., & Rosson, M. B. (2009). How and why people twitter: The role that micro-blogging plays in informal communication at work. In *Proceedings of the ACM 2009 International Conference on Supporting Group Work* (pp. 243–252). New York, NY: ACM.

Afterword

Hans Spada

The Leibniz-Institut für Wissensmedien (IWM): A Success Story of Friedrich Hesse

The beginning was marked by an ending: The closing of the German Institute of Research for Distance Education (Deutsches Institut für Fernstudienforschung) in the year 2000. For many years, this institute had successfully developed and distributed distance learning materials. However, with the advent of the Internet and digital learning, the significance of classical study materials soon decreased. Research at the institute stagnated. A group of consultants of the German Council of Science and Humanities (Wissenschaftsrat) very critically voiced their concerns regarding the institute. Consequently in 1998, the committee in charge of the so-called "Blaue Liste" (blue list)—in the framework of which the German Institute of Research for Distance Education was financed—advised to end financial support. A few months later, the German Council of Science and Humanities followed this advice. In 1999, the Bund-Länder Commission (BLK) set the seal on the resolution to discontinue common funding of the institute.

A final seal? No! One department of the institute—which constituted only a small part of the financial and human resources—had absolutely convinced in the evaluation. Friedrich Hesse, director of this Department of Applied Cognitive Science, was entrusted to develop and implement a concept for a new institute. Klaus von Trotha of the Ministry of Science, Research and the Arts of the State of Baden-Württemberg as well as the former Secretary General of the Bund-Länder Commission Jürgen Schlegel advocated immediate establishment of a research

H. Spada
Universität Freiburg, Engelberger Strasse 41/3, 79085,
Freiburg im Breisgau, Germany
email: spada@psychologie.uni-freiburg.de

© Springer International Publishing AG 2017
S. Schwan, U. Cress (eds.), *The Psychology of Digital Learning*,
DOI 10.1007/978-3-319-49077-9

institute specializing in learning and knowledge processes in the context of new media, i.e., digital learning.

Already in the first quarter of 1999, Hesse and colleagues presented a concept draft for a Leibniz-Institut für Wissensmedien (IWM). The draft was assessed by a BLK's committee. Having passed additional assessment by the German Council of Science and Humanities and the Bund-Länder Commission, the IWM was awarded financial support in the framework of the "Blaue Liste" starting on January 1st, 2001. In 1995, the research institutions of this list had founded the "Scientific Association Blaue Liste" which was later renamed Gottfried Wilhelm Leibniz Association, for short Leibniz Association (Leibniz-Gemeinschaft). Thus, the new institute became a member of the Leibniz Association and had to prove itself in regular rigorous evaluations.

But who is this Friedrich Hesse, who had saved his department from the demise of the German Institute of Research for Distance Education and had conceived a pioneering new institute for digital learning? Hesse had studied psychology at the Universities of Marburg and Düsseldorf. He earned his doctorate at the RWTH Aachen and his qualification to be a professor (Habilitation) at the University of Göttingen. A research stay at the Learning Research and Development Center (LRDC) and Carnegie Mellon University (CMU) in Pittsburgh, USA, in the early 1980s proved vital for his future activities. Here, he received important impulses for use-inspired basic research (Pasteur's Quadrant, Stokes, 1997). Here, he realized the potential of Cognitive Science (cf. Anderson, 2000)—the interdisciplinary science of the nature of the human mind—which quickly gained importance for the understanding of any kind of human learning processes. Hesse began to implement these ideas, when appointed director of the Department of Applied Cognitive Science at the German Institute of Research for Distance Education in 1993. They have truly effected research since the establishment of the IWM under his direction in 2001.

In its beginnings in 2001, the IWM had about 40 employees. A Supervisory Board commenced its duties. A Scientific Advisory Board was implemented, a cooperation agreement with the University of Tübingen made, a virtual library established, and the technological prerequisites for research and development in the area of net-based, multimedia knowledge acquisition were created. In 2006, as many as about 60 individuals, including two additional professors, worked at the IWM. This was the year of the first external assessment conducted by the Senate Evaluation Committee and the Senate of the Leibniz Association. The results were exceptionally positive. Among other things, the senate (Leibniz Gemeinschaft, Senat, 2006, p. 2) reported that "since its establishment in 2001, the IWM has developed into an internationally renowned research institution in the field of media-related teaching and learning research." The research projects were attested top level quality in several areas concerning individual and cooperative knowledge acquisition in net-based multimedia learning environments.

But what had enabled such quick success? I would like to explore this question. It is of more general interest than the mere description of the quantitative and qualitative rise of an institute. I suppose, the success was not based on unusually high levels of financial resources or on employees with entirely unusual competencies.

It was the result of Hesse's deliberate, strategic course of action, supported by a range of allies within and outside of the IWM.

In order to develop the IWM into an "internationally renowned research institution," Hesse initially strove to root the institute in the Deutsche Forschungsgemeinschaft (DFG) with a profile that gave direction to all future endeavors of the institute.

In 1999, already, Hesse had been one of the initiators of the DFG's Virtual Ph.D. Program: "Knowledge Acquisition and Knowledge Exchange with New Media" (Virtuelles Graduiertenkolleg, VGK). He remained the Ph.D. program's spokesperson until its completion in 2008. In 2001, the DFG's Special Priority Program (SPP) "Net-Based Knowledge Communication in Groups" was launched, likewise initiated by Hesse and colleagues, and he remained spokesperson of this SPP until it ended in 2006.

In addition to the Tübingen's IWM, the Virtual Ph.D. Program VGK comprised institutions located in Freiburg, Greifswald, Heidelberg, München, Münster, and Saarbrücken; aside from Tübingen the SPP comprised institutions from Darmstadt, Duisburg, Freiburg, Hagen, Köln, Lüneburg, München, and Münster. These research networks resulted in a wide emanation of the new ideas in Germany. Dozens of doctoral students worked on their theses concerning issues in digital learning. Tübingen's IWM thus became optimally interconnected in Germany's research community. As international contacts were also established through these research networks, it was likewise a first step towards global interconnectedness. But more on that later.

Just as important as establishing connections was setting the agenda by initiating these two joint endeavors, the SPP and the VGK. New research contents were defined and manifold concepts and methods to investigate them were put to the test. This resulted in a line of research closely associated with the IWM and well known within and beyond Germany: Empirical-experimental research investigating individual and cooperative learning in net-based multimedia contexts. This may well be illustrated in terms of the VGK as well as the SPP.

Commonly, the DFG's Ph.D. programs, the "Graduiertenkollegs," have always been located at one particular university. The VGK was different (Hesse, 2008; Kollar et al., 2004). As a pilot project for digital learning, the VGK was distributed across several universities in different parts of Germany. A special feature of the VGK was that digital learning was both content and method at the same time. Digital learning was the way the doctoral students learned and worked on their theses. Likewise, the object of research was individual and cooperative digital learning—or more precisely, individual information processing with external representations and multimedia and information processing in groups interacting with new media. It may not come as surprise that these two subject areas match the two main research areas of the IWM at that time: individual knowledge acquisition with multimedia-based learning environments and cooperative knowledge acquisition in net-based learning environments.

In the lifespan of the VGK, it comprised a faculty of 12 scientists with backgrounds in cognitive science and/or psychology and about 50 doctoral students. In the following years quite a few of these (former) students were employed by the IWM or by departments with a similar research agenda.

A central aim of the VGK was to account for technological and societal progress related to learning with new media. This affected the chosen communication media and the way the doctoral students were supervised. A typical example was a virtual doctoral seminar. The students reported on the current state of their Ph.D. projects using a learning platform for asynchronous exchange of documents. Each project was discussed over the course of three weeks. In the first week, a student uploaded materials reflecting the current state of her/his work, which she/he already had discussed with their supervisor from her/his home institution. The materials also included descriptions of problems and open questions. In the second week, written feedback was provided by (a) a second supervisor from another institution, (b) the faculty member in charge of organizing this virtual doctoral seminar, and (c and d) last but not least two fellow doctoral students. In the third week, the doctoral student who had presented her/his work in the first week reflected on the received feedback and outlined the consequences for her/his work. This format proved very successful and provided the doctoral students with constructive and detailed advice in a manner transparent for all faculty and students.

The Special Priority Program (SPP) "Net-Based Knowledge Communication in Groups" was the second joint research initiative commenced by Friedrich Hesse (Buder & Hesse, 2004) and was funded by the DFG from 2000 until 2006. Its aim was "to understand the generic qualities of computer-mediated knowledge communication by performing research of both a social and technical nature (p. 9). Researchers from various psychological research areas, education researchers, and computer scientists worked together in this program. Subject areas primarily comprised net-based communication between experts and laypersons and between experts of different fields, collaboration scripts for facilitating learning in groups, other forms of instructional support for collaborative learning, social presence in virtual teams, and knowledge exchange with shared databases and workspaces.

Research on digital learning, characterized as experimental, use-inspired, and theoretically well grounded in psychology and cognitive science, was a hallmark of VGK, SPP, and IWM during that time.

As part of the SPP's activities a partnership with junior and senior researchers working on projects funded by the American National Science Foundation was established. This partnership was implemented by a series of joint workshops in Germany and the USA. Junior scientists were supported by a mentor-mentee approach. Starting in 2004, the European-funded Network of Excellence "Kaleidoscope" opened an additional perspective for cooperation.

These networks were only one of several measures of an internationalization strategy in which Hesse played a strong role to make the SPP, the VGK and above all the IWM visible on a global scale.

Presentations at international conferences were another concern, particularly at the alternating biannual Computer-Supported Collaborative Learning (CSCL) Conferences and the biannual International Conferences of the Learning Sciences (ICLS). At both conferences, scientists of the SPP and the VGK played a major role as presenters and reviewers. The cognitive, experimental, and quantitative approach of the German scientists provided a counterpart to the increasingly design oriented, case-based research orientation of the American scientists.

Publications in renowned international journals with substantial impact were of course another goal of the projects of both programs. To provide an additional platform for research on CSCL and the top papers of the corresponding CSCL conference series, a new journal was founded, the *International Journal of Computer-Supported Collaborative Learning* (ijCSCL). Gerry Stahl and Friedrich Hesse were appointed as executive co-editors.

The book *Barriers and Biases in Computer-Mediated Knowledge Communication—And How They May Be Overcome* (Bromme, Hesse, & Spada, 2005), a joint publication by scientists of the SPP and scientists from the Netherlands, the USA, and Switzerland working in the same field, was a further approach to making current work known.

The present volume covers research on digital learning conducted by scientists of the IWM over the period of ten years following the above outlined founding phase. Before reflecting and commenting this work I will sketch the further development of the IWM shortly to provide context to this work.

To strengthen its relationship with the University of Tübingen, the IWM initiated the DFG research group "Analysis and support of effective learning and instruction processes," a joint effort by scientists of the center and of the university's Department of Education. In 2010, Hesse was also the initiator of the ScienceCampus "Informational Environments" (Bildung in Informationsumwelten) and has been its spokesperson since then. ScienceCampi provide opportunities for joint research of scientists from Leibniz institutes and universities. The Tübingen one was the first ScienceCampus, a pilot project, one of Hesse's numerous efforts to successfully overcome traditional barriers, in this case, severing lines between centers of the Leibniz Association and universities. The Leibniz-Graduate School for Knowledge Media Research launched in 2008 should be mentioned here, too. The year 2012 marked a major success when the Graduate School "Learning, Educational Achievement, and Life Course Development" (LEAD)'s application for the German Excellence Initiative was successful. In the light of these developments, the second review of the IWM by the Senate Evaluation Committee and the Senate of the Leibniz Association in 2013 resulted in a very positive grading. The work by the IWM was judged to be "very good," partially even "excellent." It was outlined in the report that "the IWM's exceptional development is largely owed to its acting director..." (Leibniz Gemeinschaft, Senat, 2013, p. 3).

At the time of writing this text the staff of the IWM comprises about 120 individuals. About 40 doctoral students are working at the center. Six senior fellows and two junior fellows carry main responsibility for different research themes. Research at the IWM, as far as it is addressed in this book, is mainly organized in two research areas: "Individual Learning with Hypermedia, Cybermedia, and Multimedia" and "Collaborative Learning Scenarios and Internet-based Communication." Within each research area, three multidisciplinary labs and one junior research group focus on specific aspects of these research areas.

The present volume shows the wide range of high quality research conducted at the IWM during the last ten years. The story, thus far delineated as a success story under the leadership of one man, Friedrich Hesse, has to be complemented by emphasizing the research of the many outstanding scientists at the center. Of course, the institute's scientific success has many mothers and fathers and Friedrich Hesse himself is likely amazed by the diversity of ideas, projects, and results. Commenting on the chapters concerning work conducted in the various labs will allow me to illustrate general developments at the IWM with concrete examples.

I will start with "Learning and problem solving with hypermedia in the 21st century: From hypertext to multiple web sources and multimodal adaptivity," the paper by Gerjets (this volume). It provides an example for the readiness and competence of the researchers of the IWM to adapt their work to the dynamic technical developments in the field of computer-based learning environments and information retrieval systems. At the same time, the chapter demonstrates the importance of contributions coming from psychology for answering the question which technology in combination with which instructional support might be promising for a given type of learner and learning task.

The chapter starts with a brief overview of the historical development of hypermedia environments. Next, early research on hypertext is reflected showing the complexity of the issue and the need for improving the theoretical foundations of hypertext design (Gerjets & Scheiter, 2003; Scheiter & Gerjets, 2007). Particularly research on hypermedia (learners interacting with multiple external representations) pointed to the fact that corresponding multimedia design principles must be reconsidered given the high learner control in this case (Gerjets, Scheiter, Opfermann, Hesse, & Eysink, 2009). One of the findings was that design recommendations for animations in hypermedia environments need to be very sophisticated for promoting learning successfully.

Despite the fact that the World Wide Web is one of the most important sources for learning and problem solving, it is a multiple information source not designed for this purpose. Gerjets coined the expression "hypermedia learning in the wild." He and his group focused on the important question of the evaluation of information sources by Web users. They identified factors influencing learner's evaluation and developed support measures for critical source evaluation (Kammerer & Gerjets, 2012).

Stimulated by the new ways of navigating hypermedia environments, like touching and swiping using mobile devices, such as smartphones or tablets, multimodal adaptivity is a recent field of research of Gerjets and his group. First results indicate that this multitouch navigation facilitates orientation in these environments and might have several cognitive and emotional advantages.

In the first part of "Learning from Multimedia: Cognitive Processes and Instructional Support," the chapter by Scheiter, Schüler, and Eitel (this volume), a short but nevertheless comprehensive overview is provided of the multimedia effect (Mayer, 2009; Schüler, Scheiter, & Gerjets, 2013), the superiority of text and pictures for learning over text alone, and preconditions for this effect (Eitel, 2016; Renkl & Scheiter, 2015).

The focus is then shifted from preconditions to processes. In line with the paradigm of cognitive science (remember the research philosophy of Hesse), underlying cognitive processes when learning with multimedia are studied to move from a trial and error approach of supporting multimedia learning to a theoretically based one. Current theories, both the Cognitive Theory of Multimedia Learning (CTML, Mayer, 2009) and the Integrated Model of Text and Pictures (Schnotz, 2005), rest on the assumption that linking text and pictures is the most relevant step in integrating the information. Open questions concern at which stage of multimedia learning integration takes place, early or late, and whether integration yields a single mental model or two interconnected models. Experimental studies in Katharina Scheiter's Multimedia Lab have indicated that the gist of the spatial structure of a picture is extracted very early (Eitel, Scheiter, & Schüler, 2012), and that integration while learning is likely to yield a single mental model (Schüler, Arndt, & Scheiter, 2015).

But how to support learning from multimedia? One approach taken was a methodological one. In their meta-analysis, Richter, Scheiter, and Eitel (2016) found that signaling, i.e., highlighting the correspondences in text and pictures, has a positive effect on comprehension. An innovative idea was the concept of Eye Movement Modeling Examples (EMME; Jarodzka, van Gog, Dorr, Scheiter, & Gerjets, 2013). To improve their competence in integrating information from both sources, students are shown eye movements of a skilled learner analyzing text and pictures.

In many ways, research at the Multimedia Lab headed by Scheiter reflects best practice and may be considered a model of use-inspired basic research: Questions driven by the demand of promoting multimedia learning are framed in a way to be tackled by basic research, and excellent results are published in the field's leading international journals and applied to answer these questions.

"Digital Pictures, Videos, and Beyond: Knowledge Acquisition with Realistic Images" by Schwan (this volume) is not on contrasting pictures with text or on integrating the information of pictures and text. Instead, Schwan proposes to analyze differences and communalities between realistic visual depictions and the depicted reality itself. With his colleagues he looks at perception, knowledge acquisition, and memory to better understand the instructional strengths and weaknesses of pictures, films, and fancier forms of visual representational media compared to real world objects and events. Results are based on experiments in his so-called Cybermedia Lab or on field experiments, particularly in museums. Both formal and informal learning are in the focus. The results indicate that there is no easy answer to the question, what form of visual depiction is most appropriate to promote knowledge acquisition. But the results allow for designing modes of presenting information with predictable effects on learning in given situations.

Schwan, Bauer, Kampschulte, and Hampp (2016) in the context of a museum showed that a photograph of an object did not get the same amount of attention compared to the real object resulting in less memorized details. Schwan and Ildirar (2010) provided evidence that insightfully following a film with adjacent shots presupposes experience, i.e., learning. The naïve hope that enhancing realism will automatically improve learning was challenged by several experiments conducted by Schwan and his colleagues and other researchers of the KMRC. Schwan and

Papenmeier (in press) showed this with stereoscopic presentations, and Scheiter, Gerjets, Huk, Imhof, and Kammerer (2009) by comparing simple line drawings with photorealistic depictions in dynamic visualizations. On the contrary, perceptually and cognitively advantageous deviations from reality may promote understanding and learning. Years ago, Schwan, Garsoffky, and Hesse (2000) showed that placing film cuts at event boundaries increased recall. The importance of the visual perspective was highlighted by results obtained by Garsoffky, Schwan, and Huff (2009). And it was shown that by changing the speed of the presentation comprehension of an event's temporal characteristics can be facilitated (Fischer, Lowe, & Schwan, 2008).

The work of Schwan and his colleagues demonstrates that valid theories of perception and cognition may be very helpful for precisely designing pictures and films to support comprehension and learning. The expertise acquired in the Cyber Lab is thus of great importance for improving digital learning in a target-oriented way.

The perspective of social psychology gives distinction to the Social Processes Lab chaired by Sassenberg and the chapter "Knowledge Exchange as a Motivated Social Process" by Scholl, Landkammer, and Sassenberg (this volume). Compared to the mainstream of research at the KMRC this is quite another approach. Scanning the references of this chapter also indicates that there are only a few papers jointly published by members of the Social Processes Lab and other KMRC labs. Nevertheless, their research is very well published and receives substantial attention in the field of social psychology.

Computer-mediated-communication, the catchword in this lab, has been analyzed concerning preconditions of successful information exchange. In this chapter, such an exchange refers to sharing all relevant information with others and integrating relevant information provided by others in decision-making. In controlled laboratory studies and experiments in real-life contexts Sassenberg and colleagues focused on social relations as preconditions of these processes.

Woltin and Sassenberg (2015) proved the impact of social identification with the group on actively sharing information provided that the information helped to solve the task at hand. Social comparisons played a major role in experiments by Ray, Neugebauer, Sassenberg, Buder, and Hesse (2013); this is a joint publication by members of different labs! and they demonstrated that an awareness tool can be detrimental for sharing information with group members of comparatively lower knowledge. Scholl and Sassenberg (2014a) provided evidence that higher ranked individuals took not much time and reflection in communicating via e-mail with persons in a lower role. The picture changed in the case of a task demanding great effort (Scholl & Sassenberg, 2015) and if the person had failed at the task before (Scholl & Sassenberg, 2014b).

The so-called confirmation bias plays a negative role in decision-making. Particularly information which supports one's initial opinion is processed. Personality characteristics associated with defensive or positive information processing strategies were investigated by Sassenberg, Landkammer, and Jacoby (2014). The results were in accordance with the expectations. The confirmation bias was stronger in case of defensive strategies.

The work conducted in Friedrich Hesse's Knowledge Exchange Lab is introduced by Jürgen Buder (this volume), titled "A Conceptual Framework of Knowledge Exchange," and by Carmen Zahn, a former staff member, titled "Digital Design and Learning: Cognitive-Constructivist Perspectives on Individual and Group Knowledge Processes in Design Problem Solving."

The "Conceptual Framework of Knowledge Exchange" is a very general model with input, process, and output variables on both the individual and the group level. Context variables are included, too. Buder speaks of the Context-Input-Process-Output-Model (C-I-P-O-Model). He sees its role in describing, comparing, and integrating scientific studies on knowledge exchange and expects that it can be developed further to infer assumptions on knowledge exchange. As of now, the framework allows for categorizing and ordering scientific research on knowledge exchange.

The empirical research at the Knowledge Exchange Lab was primarily concerned with effects of technological tools structuring and supporting knowledge exchange, like group awareness tools, digital concept maps, and advanced collaborative video design tools, and of cognitive and social factors characterizing collaborating individuals. Group awareness tools were developed by Buder and Bodemer (2008) and Dehler-Zufferey, Bodemer, Buder, and Hesse (2011). Results proved that these tools have a positive effect on elaboration, make cognitive conflicts between collaborating learners salient, and help to script knowledge exchange in an implicit way. Awareness of individual content representations supported by tools, like digital concept maps, was relevant for solving problems collaboratively and for pointing out unshared information (Engelmann & Hesse, 2010, 2011). Confirmation bias and approaches for reducing it were investigated by Schwind and Buder (2012) and Schwind, Buder, Cress, and Hesse (2012). Certainly the research on awareness tools at the Knowledge Exchange Lab provided new insights into the importance of fostering metacognition regarding the knowledge of collaborating partners in knowledge building and learning.

The chapter by Zahn (this volume) summarizes a research program on learning through designing videos with advanced video tools. The tools used were Diver/WebDiver (Pea et al., 2004) and Hypervideo (Chambel, Zahn, & Finke, 2006). In designing a video with Diver/WebDiver learners can implement their point of view in a very flexible way by selecting visual information through highlighting details of a video. This design process and the resulting sequence of video segments with annotations were shown to be very conducive to collaborative communicative reflection and, finally, knowledge building (Zahn, Krauskopf, Hesse & Pea 2010; Zahn, Pea, Hesse & Rosen 2010). Hypervideo allows for linking video sequences with various kinds of additional information. Students may click on sensitive regions within the videos to access texts, pictures, or other videos. Designing these videos and studying and discussing them proved advantageous for learning (Zahn, Krauskopf, Hesse, & Pea, 2012; Zahn, Krauskopf, Hesse, & Pea, 2013). A comparison of the effects did not show substantial differences between designing videos via Diver/WebDiver versus Hypervideo. Both tools promoted digital design skills and collaborative learning. The innovative feature of this research program run in collaboration with international partners was its focus on active design for learners.

In developing learning materials, the students engaged in activities which in and by themselves promoted effective learning. Collaborative creativity was the key to knowledge exchange and acquisition.

The Knowledge Construction Lab, headed by Cress & Kimmerle (this volume), is represented by a chapter on "The Interrelations of Individual Learning and Collective Knowledge Construction: A Cognitive-Systemic Framework." What an undertaking: The authors, Cress and Kimmerle, strive to reconcile the perspective of cognitive psychology on individual knowledge acquisition (cf. Anderson, 2000; Slavin, 1990) with social-cultural theories (cf. Engeström, 2014), the latter viewing knowledge as being embedded in people's joint activities and cultural practices. The object of their research is collaborative digital learning, particularly when people participate in technology-supported knowledge communities like Wikipedia. Luhmann's (1995) "General Autopoietic Systems Theory" provides the framework for their "co-evolution" approach integrating cognitive individual learning with collective knowledge construction.

Most of the research conducted at the IWM follows the tradition of cognitive science focusing on information processing activities to explain the effects of digital learning environments on knowledge exchange and acquisition. Emphasis is placed on controlled experiments and field studies. Introducing the spirit of social-cultural approaches in CSCL-studies, ethnographic methods and single case studies also gain importance to analyze collaborative processes in complex situations. In the last decade, Cress, Kimmerle, and their colleagues published several papers on their co-evolution theory (Cress & Kimmerle, 2008; Kimmerle, Moskaliuk, Oeberst, & Cress, 2015; Oeberst, Halatchliyski, Kimmerle, & Cress, 2014). It will be very interesting to see whether this integrated approach will be successful to better understand some of the effects of collaborative learning in the digital age in the years to come.

Reflecting on the research conducted in the IWM six laboratories, the Hypermedia Lab, the Cybermedia Lab, the Multimedia Lab, the Social Processes Lab, the Knowledge Exchange Lab, and the Knowledge Construction Lab, has helped to demonstrate the amazing development of the IWM since 2001. In no more than 15 years the IWM has become a central player in the global network of digital learning. This was achieved by Friedrich Hesse heading the center, supported by Ulrike Cress, Peter Gerjets, Kai Sassenberg, Katharina Scheiter, Stephan Schwan, and many others. The research of the IWM is rooted in cognitive, educational, and social psychology but today embraces a comprehensive variety of questions tackled and methods used. Central aspects of the research philosophy of the center, particularly use-inspired basic research and theory-based measures for fostering learning, have kept their role in guiding work conducted at the IWM.

References

Anderson, J. (2000). *Cognitive psychology and its implications*. New York: Freeman and Company.

Bromme, R., Hesse, F. W., & Spada, H. (Eds.). (2005). *Barriers and biases in computer-mediated knowledge communication—and how they may be overcome*. New York: Springer.

Buder, J., & Bodemer, D. (2008). Supporting controversial CSCL discussions with augmented group awareness tools. *International Journal of Computer-Supported Collaborative Learning, 3*, 123–139.

Buder, J., & Hesse, F. (2004). *2nd documentation on the special priority program (SPP) "Net-based knowledge communication in groups"*. Tübingen: Knowledge Media Research Center.

Chambel, T., Zahn, C., & Finke, M. (2006). Hypervideo and cognition: Designing video-based hypermedia for individual learning and collaborative knowledge building. In E. M. Alkhalifa (Ed.), *Cognitively informed systems: Utilizing practical approaches to enrich information presentation and transfer* (pp. 26–49). Hershey, PA: Idea Group.

Cress, U., & Kimmerle, J. (2008). A systemic and cognitive view on collaborative knowledge building with Wikis. *International Journal of Computer-Supported Collaborative Learning, 3*, 105–122.

Cress, U., & Kimmerle, J. (this volume). The interrelations of individual learning and collective knowledge construction: A cognitive-systemic framework.

Dehler-Zufferey, J., Bodemer, D., Buder, J., & Hesse, F. W. (2011). Partner knowledge awareness in knowledge communication: Learning by adapting to the partner. *The Journal of Experimental Education, 79*, 102–125.

Eitel, A. (2016). How repeated studying and testing affects multimedia learning: Evidence for adaptation to task demands. *Learning and Instruction, 41*, 70–84.

Eitel, A., Scheiter, K., & Schüler, A. (2012). The time course of information extraction from instructional diagrams. *Perceptual and Motor Skills, 115*, 677–701.

Engelmann, T., & Hesse, F. W. (2010). How digital concept maps about the collaborators' knowledge and information influence computer-supported collaborative problem-solving. *International Journal of Computer-Supported Collaborative Learning, 5*, 299–320.

Engelmann, T., & Hesse, F. W. (2011). Fostering sharing of unshared knowledge by having access to the collaborators' meta-knowledge structures. *Computers in Human Behavior, 27*, 2078–2087.

Engeström, Y. (2014). *Learning by expanding: An activity-theoretical approach to developmental research*. Cambridge, MA: Cambridge University Press.

Fischer, S., Lowe, R. K., & Schwan, S. (2008). Effects of presentation speed of a dynamic visualization on the understanding of a mechanical system. *Applied Cognitive Psychology, 22*, 1126–1141.

© Springer International Publishing AG 2017

S. Schwan, U. Cress (eds.), *The Psychology of Digital Learning*,

DOI 10.1007/978-3-319-49077-9

Garsoffky, B., Schwan, S., & Huff, M. (2009). Canonical views of dynamic scenes. *Journal of Experimental Psychology: Human Perception and Performance, 35*, 17–27.

Gerjets, P. (this volume). Learning and problem solving with hypermedia in the 21st century: From hypertext to multiple web sources and multimodal adaptivity.

Gerjets, P., & Scheiter, K. (2003). Goal configurations and processing strategies as moderators between instructional design and cognitive load: Evidence from hypertext-based instruction. *Educational Psychologist, 38*, 33–41.

Gerjets, P., Scheiter, K., Opfermann, M., Hesse, F. W., & Eysink, T. H. S. (2009). Learning with hypermedia: The influence of representational formats and different levels of learner control on performance and learning behavior. *Computers in Human Behavior, 25*(2), 360–370.

Hesse, F. (2008). *Abschlussbericht des Virtuellen Graduiertenkollegs, GRK 443/4 "Wissenserwerb und Wissensaustausch mit neuen Medien"*. Tübingen. Manuscript unpublished.

Jürgen Buder. (this volume). A conceptual framework of knowledge exchange.

Jarodzka, H., van Gog, T., Dorr, M., Scheiter, K., & Gerjets, P. (2013). Learning to see: Guiding students' attention via a model's eye movements fosters learning. *Learning and Instruction, 25*, 62–70.

Kammerer, Y., & Gerjets, P. (2012). Effects of search interface and internet-specific epistemic beliefs on source evaluations during web search for medical information: An eye-tracking study. *Behaviour & Information Technology, 31*, 83–97.

Kimmerle, J., Moskaliuk, J., Oeberst, A., & Cress, U. (2015). Learning and collective knowledge construction with social media: A process-oriented perspective. *Educational Psychologist, 50*, 120–137.

Kollar, I., Keller, T., Ründal, E., Scheuermann, M., Spada, H., & Hesse, F. (2004). *The virtual Ph.D. program "VGK": "Knowledge acquisition and knowledge exchange with new media"*. Tübingen. Manuscript unpublished.

Leibniz Gemeinschaft, Senat. (2006). Stellungnahme zum Institut für Wissensmedien (IWM). Retrieved from http://www.leibniz-gemeinschaft.de/fileadmin/user_upload/downloads/Evaluierung/Senatsstellungnahmen/Senatsstellungnahme-IWM-2006.pdf.

Leibniz Gemeinschaft, Senat. (2013). Stellungnahme zum Leibniz-Institut für Wissensmedien (IWM) Tübingen. Retrieved from http://www.leibniz-gemeinschaft.de/fileadmin/user_upload/downloads/Evaluierung/Senatsstellungnahmen/IWM_-_Senatsstellungnahme_mit_Anlagen_28-11-2013.pdf.

Luhmann, N. (1995). *Social systems*. Stanford, CA: Stanford University Press.

Mayer, R. E. (2009). *Multimedia learning* (2nd ed.). New York, NY: Cambridge University Press.

Oeberst, A., Halatchliyski, I., Kimmerle, J., & Cress, U. (2014). Knowledge construction in Wikipedia: A systemic-constructivist analysis. *The Journal of the Learning Sciences, 23*, 149–176.

Pea, R., Mills, M., Rosen, J., Dauber, K., Effelsberg, W., & Hoffert, E. (2004). The DIVER™ project: Interactive digital video repurposing. *IEEE Multimedia, 11*, 54–61.

Ray, D. G., Neugebauer, J., Sassenberg, K., Buder, J., & Hesse, F. W. (2013). Motivated shortcomings in explanation: The role of comparative self-evaluation and awareness of explanation recipient's knowledge. *Journal of Experimental Psychology: General, 142*, 445–457.

Renkl, A., & Scheiter, K. (2015). Studying visual displays: How to instructionally support learning. *Educational Psychology Review*. doi:10.1007/s10648-015-9340-4.

Richter, J., Scheiter, K., & Eitel, A. (2016). Signaling text-picture relations in multimedia learning: A comprehensive meta-analysis. *Educational Research Review, 17*, 19–36.

Sassenberg, K., Landkammer, F., & Jacoby, J. (2014). The influence of regulatory focus and group vs. individual goals on the evaluation bias in the context of group decision making. *Journal of Experimental Social Psychology, 54*, 153–164.

Scheiter, K., & Gerjets, P. (2007). Learner control in hypermedia environments. *Educational Psychology Review, 19*(3), 285–307.

Scheiter, K., Gerjets, P., Huk, T., Imhof, B., & Kammerer, Y. (2009). The effects of realism in learning with dynamic visualizations. *Learning and Instruction, 19*, 481–494.

Scheiter, K., Schüler, A., & Eitel, A. (this volume). Learning from multimedia: Cognitive processes and instructional support.

Schnotz, W. (2005). An integrated model of text and picture comprehension. In R. E. Mayer (Ed.), *The Cambridge handbook of multimedia learning* (pp. 49–69). New York, NY: Cambridge University Press.

Scholl, A., & Sassenberg, K. (2014a). While you still think, I already type: Experienced social power reduces deliberation during e-mail communication. *Cyberpsychology, Behavior and Social Networking, 17*, 692–696.

Scholl, A., & Sassenberg, K. (2014b). Where could we stand if I had...? How social power impacts counterfactual thinking after failure. *Journal of Experimental Social Psychology, 53*, 51–61.

Scholl, A., & Sassenberg, K. (2015). Better know when (not) to think twice: How social power impacts prefactual thought. *Personality and Social Psychology Bulletin, 41*, 159–170.

Scholl, A., Landkammer, F., & Sassenberg, K. (this volume). Knowledge exchange as a motivated social process.

Schüler, A., Arndt, J., & Scheiter, K. (2015). Processing multimedia material: Does integration of text and pictures result in a single or two interconnected mental representations? *Learning and Instruction, 35*, 62–72.

Schüler, A., Scheiter, K., & Gerjets, P. (2013). Is spoken text always better? Investigating the modality and redundancy effect with longer text presentation. *Computers in Human Behavior, 29*, 1590–1601.

Schwan, S. (this volume). Digital pictures, videos, and beyond: Knowledge acquisition with realistic images.

Schwan, S., & Ildirar, S. (2010). Watching film for the first time: How adult viewers interpret perceptual discontinuities in film. *Psychological Science, 21*, 970–976.

Schwan, S., & Papenmeier, F. (in press). Learning from animations: From 2D to 3D? In R. Lowe & R. Ploetzner (Eds.), *Learning from dynamic visualizations – Innovations in research and application*. Berlin: Springer.

Schwan, S., Bauer, D., Kampschulte, L., & Hampp, C. (2016). Presentation equals representation? Photographs of objects received less attention and are less well remembered than real objects. *Journal of Media Psychology*. doi:10.1027/1864-1105/a000166.

Schwan, S., Garsoffky, B., & Hesse, F. W. (2000). Do film cuts facilitate the perceptual and cognitive organization of activity sequences? *Memory & Cognition, 28*, 214–223.

Schwind, C., & Buder, J. (2012). Reducing confirmation bias and evaluation bias: When are reference-inconsistent recommendations effective—And when not? *Computers in Human Behavior, 28*, 2280–2290.

Schwind, C., Buder, J., Cress, U., & Hesse, F. W. (2012). Preference-inconsistent recommendations: An effective approach for reducing confirmation bias and stimulating divergent thinking? *Computers & Education, 58*, 787–796.

Slavin, R. E. (1990). *Cooperative learning*. Upper Saddle River, NJ: Prentice-Hall.

Stokes, D. (1997). *Pasteur's quadrant—Basic science and technological innovation*. Washington: Brookings Institution Press.

Woltin, K., & Sassenberg, K. (2015). Showing engagement or not: The influence of social identification and group deadlines on individual control strategies. *Group Processes & Intergroup Relations, 18*, 24–44.

Zahn, C. (this volume). Digital design and learning: Cognitive-Constructivist Perspectives on Individual and Group Knowledge Processes in Design Problem Solving.

Zahn, C., Krauskopf, K., Hesse, F. W., & Pea, R. Digital video tools in the classroom: How to support meaningful collaboration and critical thinking of students? In M. S. Khine & I. M. Saleh (Eds.), *New science of learning: Computers and collaboration in education*. New York: Springer.

Zahn, C., Krauskopf, K., Hesse, F. W., & Pea, R. (2012). How to improve collaborative learning with video tools in the classroom? Social vs. cognitive guidance for student teams. *International Journal of Computer-Supported Collaborative Learning, 7*, 259–284.

Zahn, C., Krauskopf, K., Hesse, F. W., & Pea, R. (2013). Digital media in the classroom. A study on how to improve guidance for successful collaboration and learning in student teams. In Y. Crotty & M. Farren (Eds.), *Digital literacies in education: Creative, innovative and multimodal approaches* (pp. 37–52). Oxford: Peter Lang.

Zahn, C., Pea, R., Hesse, F. W., & Rosen, J. (2010). Comparing simple and advanced video tools as supports for collaborative design processes. *The Journal of the Learning Sciences, 19,* 403–440.

Index

© Springer International Publishing AG 2017
S. Schwan, U. Cress (eds.), *The Psychology of Digital Learning*,
DOI 10.1007/978-3-319-49077-9

Printed by Printforce, the Netherlands